An utterly remarkable book, in which the words themselves emanate the energies of Moldavite!

> —Robert Sardello, Ph.D., director of The Fort Worth Center for Consciousness Studies and author of *Steps on the Stone Path*

Robert Simmons has a highly developed ability to connect with the energies of stones and to perceive their effects on one's chakras, subtle body, and awareness. He is then able to combine these energies with meditations, assisting his readers and students in accessing multiple nuances of Consciousness. This is especially true regarding Moldavite—in its synergistic interactions with other stones and with one's bioenergetic system, as this book reveals.

> —Lee Nelson, meditation teacher and author of *Happiness for No Apparent Reason*

Moldavite tektite sent out a beam and attracted to it two special caretakers, Robert Simmons and Kathy Warner. Their devotion, sensitivity, love, and attunement to Moldavite's frequency are among the guiding forces in the unfoldment of this special stone's destiny and its powerful effects on our own evolution process.

> —Katrina Raphael, author of *Crystal Enlightenment*

Is the present mysticism of space affecting the consciousness of those who hold so beautiful a piece of visitation from outer space? Is there something in the symbol or substance of Moldavite that inhibits the brain's inhibitors, like certain psychedelic drugs were thought to do? Can it be that Moldavite just might contain the frequency of a larger domain of being, and so engender in us the pulse and music of times to come?

> —Jean Houston Ph.D., cofounder of The Foundation for Mind Research

For me, Moldavite is as magical as its reputation.

> —Marilyn Ferguson, author of *The Aquarian Conspiracy*

THE BOOK OF
MOLDAVITE

OTHER BOOKS

by Robert Simmons

The Book of Stones

The Pocket Book of Stones

Stones of the New Consciousness

The Alchemy of Stones

Earthfire

THE BOOK OF MOLDAVITE

STARBORN STONE OF TRANSFORMATION

A Sacred Planet Book

ROBERT SIMMONS

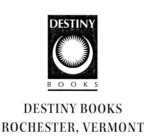

DESTINY BOOKS

ROCHESTER, VERMONT

Destiny Books
One Park Street
Rochester, Vermont 05767
www.DestinyBooks.com

Destiny Books is a division of Inner Traditions International

Sacred Planet Books are curated by Richard Grossinger, Inner Traditions editorial board member and co-founder and former publisher of North Atlantic Books. The Sacred Planet collection, published under the umbrella of the Inner Traditions family of imprints, includes works on the themes of consciousness, cosmology, alternative medicine, dreams, climate, permaculture, alchemy, shamanic studies, oracles, astrology, crystals, hyperobjects, locutions, and subtle bodies.

Cataloging-in-Publication Data for this title is available from the Library of Congress

ISBN 978-1-64411-912-9 (print)
ISBN 978-1-64411-913-6 (ebook)

Printed and bound in Canada by Transcontinental Printing

10 9 8 7 6 5 4 3 2 1

Text design and layout by Margery Cantor
Cover design by Robert Simmons and Patrick Gaudreault
This book was typeset in Kepler

To send correspondence to the author of this book, mail a first-class letter to the author c/o Inner Traditions •
Bear & Company, One Park Street, Rochester, VT 05767, and we will forward the communication, or contact the author directly at **http://heavenandearthjewelry.com.**

CONTENTS

ACKNOWLEDGMENTS

First and most, I offer my deepest love and gratitude to my wife, Kathy Helen Warner, who has shared life's journey with me for more than thirty-six years. Her amazing perceptiveness, spiritual awareness, love, and wisdom have aided and guided me in innumerable ways.

Next I want to thank Patrick Gaudreault, manager of Heaven and Earth, our company in Vermont, USA. Because of Patrick's diligent work and creative talent, we continue to offer thousands of beautiful and powerful stones (including Moldavite) to people all over the world. Much appreciation also goes out to the Heaven and Earth staffs, in both New Zealand and the USA. You all make us proud.

To Ehud Sperling and Richard Grossinger of Inner Traditions, much gratitude for your interest in publishing my work, and for the generosity of spirit you have always shown. Thanks also to all the staff of Inner Traditions, for your high standards, friendliness, and willingness to help.

To our dear friend and book designer, Margery Cantor, kudos and thanks for another job well done. You're the biggest reason that my books are beautiful!

A big wave of love and gratitude goes out to Lee Nelson, dear friend and guide. You showed me Shiva and Shakti—how they live within all of us, and in all worlds.

Keryn and Amber, thank you for letting me experiment on you with Photonic stone layouts, and for allowing me to share your photos. I'm glad the results have been good!

I offer special thanks to all those who shared their Moldavite stories. It's been a joy to connect with you and to recognize the common threads of our experiences.

And, of course, I most definitely thank the the amazing energy and intelligence that I call the Being of Moldavite. It woke me up three and a half decades ago, and it has been doing the same for thousands of others ever since then. It's a blessing and a trickster and an ally of human evolution. I don't know where we'd be without it!

INTRODUCTION

If a union is to take place between opposites like spirit and matter, conscious and unconscious, bright and dark, and so on, it will happen in a third thing, which represents, not a compromise, but something new.

—Carl Jung

The Stone symbolised something permanent that can never be lost or dissolved—something eternal that men have compared to the mystical experience of God within one's soul.

—Carl Jung

This book is about a stone that is not a stone. It is about a substance that is neither heavenly nor earthly, but is something new that emerged from their union. It seems somehow to be alive, and its presence can revise the plot of one's life story. By some reports, it is capable of capriciously disappearing and reappearing. Like the Philosophers' Stone Jung wrote of, it can trigger "the mystical experience of God within one's soul." I know that, because it happened to me.

Moldavite is a treasure born of a cataclysm—a meteor crash far more powerful than the sum of all the atom bombs in the world. Its shock wave circled the planet. The explosion ejected a vapor of meteoric substance and earthly rock into the stratosphere. And in that high oven of instantaneous alchemy, the gas condensed as a third thing—a new substance that fell again to Earth in a molten green rain. It landed more than a dozen million years before human beings existed, yet when our ancient ancestors found it, they felt the numinous presence that it carried. We still feel that presence when we pick up a Moldavite today.

The world—which is not separate from our consciousness—is full of mysterious symbols, and our lives play out like stories. It is in the perceiving, or creating, of our stories that we discover, or create, meaning. We are all in the middle of a mystery, or an infinitude of mysteries, and our paths are strewn with symbols. In this book, I have tried to follow the thread of Moldavite's mystery—a mystery rich in symbols—which has bestowed much meaning upon my life.

My first book about Moldavite was published in 1988, near the time when the most recent chapter of Moldavite's tale began. Now we are thirty-four years deeper into the story, and I felt it was time for a new book. Much has happened to validate the early intuitions my wife Kathy had about Moldavite's purpose and destiny. And Moldavite's fame has now reached around the world, just as thoroughly as the shock wave of its explosive genesis. Many thousands of people, from Shanghai to Chicago, have acquired their own Moldavites, and their experiences today echo those of myself and others several decades ago, in odd but unmistakable ways.

The reported energies and effects of Moldavite are not rational, nor measurable with instruments, but people perceive them anyway. Upon the first encounter, there is most frequently a sensation of warmth or heat, sometimes light-headedness, or even temporary nausea. Occasionally, dramatic phenomena such as chakra activations or visions occur in the initial experience. Upon closer acquaintance, dreams change, meditations become profound, and the rhythm and directions of one's life can shift dramatically, ready or not. But thirty-six years of experience have shown me that I can trust the magic of Moldavite. I believe we all can.

In trying to tell Moldavite's story in a way that will give some glimpses into the mystery and what it means, I have looked from multiple perspectives. Readers will first encounter the personal story of myself and my wife, and the remarkable things that occurred when Moldavite entered our lives. Through our anecdotes of synchronicity, opportunity, disappointment, and regeneration, I believe you will see the signature pattern of Moldavite's dynamic quickening of one's spiritual evolution. Our own story weaves through much of this book, because we have been living in the Moldavite mystery, experimenting within it, and encouraging others to dive in with us.

Everyone whose interest is piqued by Moldavite wants to know where it came from, and some want to know its history. In the chapter entitled Scientific & Historical Perspectives, we'll go into those questions. To me, it's important to know Moldavite's physical history, in part because the science of its origin seems to symbolically resonate with the mystic tales with which it is connected—the legend of the Holy Grail and the alchemical Emerald Tablet. We'll explore both of these after digesting the science and history. Then, for a deeper spiritual perspective, you'll get a chance to check out the original Moldavite channelings. In Chapter Eleven, you'll read Kathy's musings on Moldavite's meaning and purpose, and how we can align with it.

What would a book about Moldavite be without eye candy? Near the middle of the book, you'll find a Moldavite Gallery of beautiful raw pieces, carvings, jewelry, and gems. The best of our own pieces are shown there, as well as an array of amazing specimens from two of the world's premier collections. And, to be fair, this is more than eye candy. You can attune to Moldavite's energy from the photographs alone!

Now let's say you've gotten sufficiently intrigued to get yourself a piece of Moldavite, and perhaps you've felt its unique warmth and energy. You may even have begun to notice some changes in your life that just might have something to do with Moldavite's arrival. What's next? If you're anything like me, you'll want to experiment. There are chapters ahead that describe a menagerie of Moldavite templates, wands, pendulums, waters and essences, body layouts, grids, and other Moldavite-enhanced energy tools that you can create and work with.

At the end of Chapter Fifteen, there's a section I want to recommend. It discusses using Moldavite in Photonic Layouts via which one can transmit energy to people, places, landscapes, and bodies of water, in order to heal and revitalize them. There is also a chapter with some powerful Moldavite meditations you can try, and another one devoted to combining Moldavite with an extensive list of crystals, minerals, and stones.

Along the way, we'll check out the vibes of crop circles and the energy vortexes of Sedona, Arizona. We'll visit Stonehenge, and we'll go on an adventure in Moldavite country. Here and there, we'll encounter some celebrities who are into Moldavite, as well as one flying saucer, a handful of ETs, and a pair of Men in Black.

I've organized the book to be read straight through, with the chapters arranged in a kind of progression that leads you through the kaleidoscopic world of Moldavite. But you can also dip in wherever you like. Each chapter is more or less self-contained.

Whatever you do, don't miss the last and longest chapter, The Moldavite Stories. There we have gathered a trove of fascinating letters we received from people who wanted to share their Moldavite experiences. I find it amazing to read the widely vary-ing details, while still perceiving the underlying, unmistakable influence of Moldavite.

After all this, I hope you'll have your own inner answer to the question, "What is Moldavite?" Better than that, if you are having experiences with your own Moldavite, this book may help you see more clearly the invisible presence behind Moldavite—the mystery behind these weird green stones that are not stones. And by then you'll be within the mystery tale yourself, and within the mystery of yourself. For me, those are inextricably, enigmatically, and serendipitously woven together.

Moldavite's formation emerged from a physical catastrophe—a horrendous colli-sion of Heaven and Earth. Yet the substance born of that event has been an astonishing blessing to me—a talisman of rebirth and transformation. And it has played a similar role for countless people all over the world.

When opposites come together, it can feel like a disaster, but such collisions offer the opportunity for transcendence. As Jung wrote, the union of opposites will be "not a compromise, but something new." In this book, we shine a light upon the ancient "new thing" that unites spirit and matter—the rare and wonderful celestial gem, Moldavite.

May your path be full of love, joy, and wonder.

CHAPTER 1
A TALE OF TRANSFORMATION

One morning in 1987, I sat down in the living room with my piece of Moldavite, having turned on meditation music. I did this every morning, and I'll admit that I was rather bored with the routine, even though I always felt calm and refreshed afterwards. On this day, I thought, "I'm tired of waiting for an out-of-body experience or some other cool thing to happen, so I'm just going to imagine one." I wrapped my fingers around my Moldavite and closed my eyes, letting myself listen to the music, while at the same time imagining that I was rising out of the top of my own head, looking down at my body.

As I continued to visualize, I could see a mental image of myself as if I were looking down from the ceiling. Then I decided to try to go higher, so I envisioned floating upwards through the ceiling and the roof, looking down on the house and surrounding neighborhood. I kept going in my imagined flight, rising higher and higher, seeing the town and the seacoast landscape, and my house as a tiny dot below me. I began to feel exhilarated as I rose higher and faster. The flight seemed to take on a life of its own. Soon I could see the curvature of the Earth, and then the whole globe, as I flew off into space.

I felt no fear, and no disconnection from my body. I remained, on some level, aware of the music and my own breathing. Yet I became completely captivated by the visionary experience that was unfolding. Soon I had left the Earth behind and was far out among the stars. It seemed that I could move in whatever direction I chose simply by willing it.

At one point, I saw a golden star far away, and I knew that I wanted to go to it, so I willed myself there. In a short time, the golden star had become an immense golden sun, and it emanated a light that felt holy. Then I noticed that there were thousands, or perhaps millions, of golden orbs circling the golden sun, each with a thin gold thread linking the orb to the Sun. The orbs seemed to be alive, like a procession of souls, circling in adoration around the golden Sun. I was deeply moved by this vision, and I wondered if the golden orbs might be souls. At that point, I also wondered what my own 'body' might look like in this place. I turned my attention downward, toward where my chest would have been, and was surprised to see another golden orb about twelve inches in diameter, encompassing the space around my heart. And there was a golden thread that linked my own orb to the great golden Sun.

I was filled with awe and wonder, and my thoughts became silent. Then I suddenly heard a deep, resonant voice—perhaps like the voice of an angel—saying clearly, "The Light you seek without is identical to the Light within."

In the next moment, several things happened. I suddenly realized that the golden orbs were souls, and that I was one of them, and this knowledge hit me with a rush of emotion. At the same time, back in the living room, the Moldavite in my right hand sizzled with an energy that moved quickly up my arm and went straight into my heart. There was an instant sensation of something opening, like a big flower inside my chest, and the flower was made out of spiritual Light. Then the energy moved upwards and downward along my spine, causing more flowerings of Light at each of my chakras.

In just a few seconds, all seven energy centers from the base of my spine to the top of my head were filled with Light and a curving, flowing energy. And my entire being was flooded with an ecstatic joy. I opened my eyes and saw the whole room was glowing, just like the Light that moved inside me.

My wife Kathy had been upstairs getting ready to open our shop for the day when all of this occurred. Her intuition suddenly told her that something important was happening with me, so she hurried to the living room. When she opened the door, she looked at me and said, "Robert, you're full of Light!"

I was nearly speechless, still bathed in ecstasy. All I could say was, "I know."

Kathy sat with me for nearly an hour, as the experience of the inner Light moved through me. Eventually, the intensity began to soften, and I was able to tell her what had happened. After a while, we decided to go and open our shop, but there was one more surprise ahead of me.

When I entered Heaven and Earth, our crystal and jewelry store in Gloucester, Massachusetts, I could, for the first time, sense the energy of the stones on the shelves and tables. It filled the room. And when I picked up a stone, I could instantly feel the vibrational currents of "crystal energy" that our customers and friends had described to me. In fact, I could, on that morning, feel every single stone in the store, and could sense the similarities and differences among them. I spent almost the entire day in a state of calm, wonderful rapture, picking up stone after stone, feeling them all. And while that exquisite sensitivity has ebbed and flowed through the years, it has never left me, and I have learned how to focus and work with it.

As I write these words, it is thirty-six years later, and much has happened since my dramatic awakening. You might say that my destiny opened up on that morning in my quiet living room, and I have been walking its path ever since.

I give Moldavite the credit for stimulating and awakening my latent capacity to sense and interpret the energies and spiritual qualities of crystals, stones, and minerals. This initiation began my career in the world of stones and their energies, includ-

ing writing six books about stones and developing a worldwide mail order business. More importantly, it transformed me into a spiritual seeker, guided me to a wonderful marriage, and led me into innumerable adventures with the crystals, minerals, and gemstones, and with the people who love them.

Through the years, I have learned that my Moldavite experience and its results were not as unique as I might have first imagined. I have spoken to literally thousands of people who say that the power of Moldavite catalyzed rapid and profound spiritual transformations in their lives. I have received letters from hundreds of

The Moldavite that took me to the Golden Sun

others who voluntarily shared their Moldavite experiences with me. (You'll find some of them in Chapter Eighteen of this book.)

So, what is going on here? What is Moldavite and what are its spiritual qualities? Where does it come from, and what is its history? Where is it found and how is it unearthed? What does science have to say about Moldavite? What myths and legends are connected to this stone of celestial origins? How can we work with Moldavite for spiritual healing and awakening? Are there tools we can make, or elixirs we can partake of that carry the currents of Moldavite? Now that Moldavite has emerged from obscurity and become world famous, what are people saying about it? And how can we connect with Moldavite to experience it for ourselves?

These are the questions that this book endeavors to answer. I encourage you to read on and learn all about the story of these unique starborn stones. Moldavite is a transformational talisman that can move us forward on the path of our highest destiny. We are already on that journey.

The Venus of Willendorf is an 11.1-centimeter-tall (4.4 in) figurine estimated to have been made around 25,000-30,000 years ago. It represents one of the earliest known Goddess statues. This figurine was discovered in an archaeological excavation, along with several Moldavite amulets. It has been suggested that the presence of Moldavite amulets with this ancient depiction of the Great Goddess implies that Moldavite was viewed as a sacred stone among neolithic peoples of that region.

CHAPTER 2
HOW IT ALL STARTED

About 14.7 million years ago, a huge meteorite, estimated as being up to one kilometer in diameter, struck the Earth at the unthinkable speed of about 22 kilometers per second (49,000 miles per hour), causing a huge explosion. Just before the impact, the incoming shock wave of the cosmic projectile blasted away sand and surface rock from the impact site, vaporizing it and throwing it tens (or even hundreds) of kilometers into the sky. The vapor cooled into droplets of hot liquid glass, which landed 250 to 400 kilometers away from its point of origin. There it cooled and solidified, and there it sat for millions of years, as the Earth shifted and the land changed.

One day in August of 1984, I was driving from Amesbury, Massachusetts, on my way to Hyannis, on Cape Cod. I was making one of my frequent trips there to sell my jewelry line to the stores. As I often did, I was free-associating, designing jewelry in my mind. This time, the thought came up, "what about setting meteorites in jewelry?" The thought captivated me for several miles, as I imagined rings, pendants, and the like, studded with the dark metallic gray of the nickel-iron meteorites.

Then an unexpected idea popped in. Suddenly, I was struck with the image of a comet, with a real meteorite at the head and a golden tail flecked with diamonds. Of course! In about fifteen months, Halley's Comet would be visible in the sky. Comet fever would grip the nation and the world! Everyone would want my pendants. I would be rich!

As visions of golden comets danced in my head, I became so absorbed in my thoughts that I missed my turn for Hyannis and ended up twenty miles further down the road, near the town of Orleans. When I realized where I was, I decided to abandon my plans for the day and visit a friend and fellow jewelry designer I knew in nearby Eastham. I was eager to tell him my idea. When I arrived at his door, I was bubbling with enthusiasm for my new concept of extraterrestrial jewelry.

My friend also liked the idea, but he kept trying to remember the name of a special type of meteorite about which he had read. After a fair amount of head-scratching, he shouted, "Tektites! That's what they're called." Then he set about searching through his papers, looking for an article he had read about them some years back.

After about ten minutes, he found it. The article, from the 1958 *Lapidary Journal,* was titled "Agni Mani: The Celestial Gem," and was written by George Bruce. Looking back, it seems remarkable to me that this article, which put me on the track of Moldavite, should have fallen spontaneously into my hands. After all, it had been written twenty-six years earlier, and it didn't come out of a stack of old *Lapidary Journals.* It was in fact the only old copy of the magazine that my friend had.

I read the article with interest and mounting excitement. In it I learned that *agni mani* was a Sanskrit term meaning "fire pearl" and that it referred to the whole class of mysterious glassy objects known as tektites. I read that they had been found in Asia, Africa, Australia, and in North America, and that these stones were almost all an almost opaque brownish black color. Only the rare Czech Republic tektites, called Moldavites, are a rich translucent green. Thus, only they are fit for cutting into gems.

The article discussed both the physical attributes and the mystical powers attributed to these stones. According to Bruce, the *agni mani* stones were revered and worshiped in Indonesia, India, China, and Tibet for 2500 years of recorded history. He recounted an anecdote in which Professor Nicholas Roerich, "went so far as to draw a close analogy between the Stone of Shambala and the *agni mani,* further asserting that it was the same stone contained in the Holy Grail." Bruce went on to state that such notables as Queen Elizabeth II and Winston Churchill owned and prized *agni manis,* and that the magical properties attributed to the stones included wealth, prescience, victory, long life, health, and success.

After reading the article, I knew I had found the stones I wanted to work with. I was drawn immediately to the Moldavites, at first because they lent themselves most readily to being cut into gems. Beyond that, I was excited because of the apparently mystical aspects of the stones. (What a strange place to run into stories about magical gems from space—a rockhound magazine from 1958!) I felt the urge to try to contact Mr. Bruce. The article had listed an address for him from 1958. I called Information (which still used live operators in those days) and they gave me a number. I dialed it and it rang. Then, twenty-six years after the article that prompted the call, to my surprise and delight, Mr. Bruce answered the phone.

In my enthusiasm, I plunged into the call: "Hello, my name is Robert Simmons and I've just read your article about *agni mani* stones and Moldavites."

There was a long pause. Then Mr. Bruce answered, somewhat incredulously, "You've *just* read my article?" It had, after all, been published twenty-six years earlier.

After I explained the unusual circumstances of my call, including my daydream inspiration, Mr. Bruce and I talked for four hours. I don't know which one of us was more excited. I was elated to find out about the existence of tektites, and Mr. Bruce was equally thrilled to speak to someone who wanted to learn about them. In his earlier life, Mr. Bruce had been both a gemologist and a student of esoteric ideas. Although he had all kinds of tektites, his real love was Moldavite. He had tried very hard to interest the gem and jewelry community in these celestial gemstones, but to no avail. My showing up on the telephone that day felt as significant to him as it did to me.

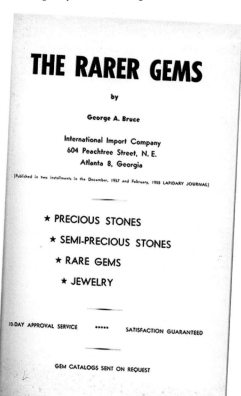

I recall that there was a point in the conversation where I got prickles down my neck and I had a strange feeling that destiny was unfolding in that moment. Something about the purpose and path of my life was beginning. I didn't understand that feeling, but its power stayed with me.

During the call, I learned a great deal from Mr. Bruce about the various theories of the possible origin of the *agni*

Booklet by George Bruce published in two installments in *Lapidary Journal,* 1957-1958 *mani*/Moldavite stones. He also told me a number of stories about their purported magical properties. I was intrigued by our conversation, although I did not know what to make of the stories about the stones' powers. My scientific training in college told me that such things were impossible.

Nonetheless, when samples arrived from Mr. Bruce, I was excited to see and touch them myself. The package included a dozen of the more common black tektites and a few of the rare green Moldavites. There were also several cut and faceted Moldavite stones.

Over the next six to eight weeks, as I began putting together my project for the Halley's comet jewelry, I showed the tektite and Moldavite collection to friends and jewelry designers. I had decided, because of the price and rarity of Moldavites, to use the black tektites in my jewelry. Nonetheless, practically all of my friends and fellow jewelers were drawn to the translucent green Moldavites. I even found myself touching and looking at them more often. Still, I pressed on with my plans to use the other tektites.

My friend from Cape Cod had helped me make contact with a buyer from a large mail order company. She and her superiors were interested in marketing my Halley's comet jewelry. On my first trip to New York with my designs, the buyer took one look at the black stone and said, "That's the ugliest thing I've ever seen!" Taken aback, I hurriedly mentioned that it might be possible to procure enough of the green Moldavite for the project. I showed her a sample piece and got a much more positive response. Hoping to make everything work, I went home to create new comets using Moldavite.

During this period, in April of 1985, I met Kathy Helen Warner. We were introduced by a mutual friend who thought we might benefit through a business relationship. Kathy was a practicing clairvoyant and spiritual healer who had recently left the field of engineering to start a small crystal business. As we talked, she mentioned the "energies" of various stones.

I was quite skeptical of these ideas but was also strongly drawn to this obviously intelligent, peaceful, and clear-eyed person. The second time we met, I impulsively handed a Moldavite to her. "Here," I said. "You're supposed to be able to feel all these

stone energies. What do you get from this?" She took the stone and held it, with her eyes closed. She stood still, not speaking for several minutes. When she opened her eyes, I was surprised by the story she told. She later wrote it down for our first Moldavite book:

"I looked at the small green stone in my palm and then closed my hand and my eyes. Immediately I felt my consciousness expand beyond my body, beyond

The first Moldavite I handed to Kathy

the Earth, and out into the endlessness of starry space. A feeling of peace, deep nurturing, and protection filled my being, as I experienced great joy. I continued expanding and felt totally at one with all of the Infinite. I knew intuitively that this was an important stone for connecting and communing with the oneness of life. I stayed in the blissful consciousness for some time, and, when I finally decided to come back to my normal state, I opened my eyes. 'What is this stone!?' I asked Robert, telling him of the profound experience I had just had.

"We talked for hours about stones and their use as tools in our spiritual questing. I told Robert of the spiritual focus that had always been central in my life and of my desire to serve in the world. I shared a lot about who I was and why, with this gentle and curious man."

I was moved, even taken aback somewhat, by the quiet certainty with which Kathy spoke. The confidence she felt in her intuition seemed stronger than the opinions I could muster with my intellect. Her spiritual focus and desire to be of service in the world seemed like ideals I had long ago left behind. And yet, the ideals drew me. I felt a buried part of myself trying to emerge. Kathy and I spent more time together, and we began to join forces in our businesses. I made trips to New York, focusing the comet jewelry project on the deal with the mail order company.

The jewelry project seemed to be going well. By late May, we had settled on a design for the comet necklace and earrings, with beautiful faceted Moldavites at the heads and glittering diamonds in the golden tails. I had spent all of my cash reserves, plus much more that I borrowed from the bank, friends, and family, on twenty kilos

Front of Comet Brochure

OPPOSITE

Inside of Comet Brochure

Cosmogems
presents •
THE STAR GEM COLLECTION
in commemoration of a celestial event

The 1985 - 1986 return of
HALLEY'S COMET

of raw Moldavite, hoping it was enough for the whole project. Then, in June, while we were finalizing postage and handling fees, Kathy got a call from the buyer. One of her superiors had vetoed the project. Goodbye comets.

I was devastated, and very worried. I had invested all of my own money, plus all I could borrow, into buying Moldavite—a stone almost no one had ever heard of—for a project that now would not happen. But Kathy simply said, "This just means something better is going to happen. Even if we try to do the comet project on our own, Moldavite's purpose is much bigger than that."

I wasn't ready to completely give up on my Halley's Comet Moldavite project, and I eventually convinced Kathy that we should try to do it ourselves, without the help of the big marketing company. We invented the name Cosmogems for our comet jewelry enterprise. We made several sets of the comet necklace and earrings, in 14k gold with faceted Moldavites and diamonds. We created our own brochures, with Kathy modeling the pieces. I sent copies to all the jewelry stores on my customer list, and to the media outlets around New England. I was proud of what we had created, and I really believed that "Moldavite, the Gem from Space," was just about the coolest thing ever.

Kathy was right about Moldavite's greater purpose. Halley's Comet would come and go, but Moldavite was just getting started. Still, perhaps our efforts were worthwhile. One of our press releases got someone's attention at a major newspaper. And, although it didn't lead to many comet jewelry sales (just one set, to be exact), it did serve to launch Moldavite into greater public awareness.

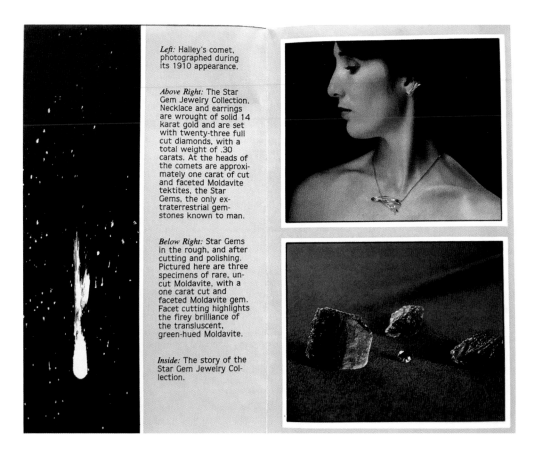

Left: Halley's comet, photographed during its 1910 appearance.

Above Right: The Star Gem Jewelry Collection. Necklace and earrings are wrought of solid 14 karat gold and are set with twenty-three full cut diamonds, with a total weight of .30 carats. At the heads of the comets are approximately one carat of cut and faceted Moldavite tektites, the Star Gems, the only extraterrestrial gemstones known to man.

Below Right: Star Gems in the rough, and after cutting and polishing. Pictured here are three specimens of rare, uncut Moldavite, with a one carat cut and faceted Moldavite gem. Facet cutting highlights the firey brilliance of the translucent, green-hued Moldavite.

Inside: The story of the Star Gem Jewelry Collection.

Heaven & Earth storefront, 1986

CHAPTER 3

MOLDAVITE TALES FROM THE EARLY YEARS

The Robbery and Nothing but Moldavite Left

After Kathy and I fell in love, we didn't want to have separate employment, so we decided to work together in my jewelry business. Before meeting her, I had designed and sold traditional gold and silver jewelry, with well-known stones like Ruby, Emerald, Sapphire, and Diamond, as well as semi-precious stones like Turquoise and Amethyst. But as soon as possible, I had some gems cut from the raw Moldavites I had purchased for the Halley's Comet Project, and I set them in my various rings, pendants, and earrings.

Kathy was very much in tune with crystals and their energies, as well as with the burgeoning subculture of people who appreciated their spiritual qualities. She told me from the beginning that Moldavite's destiny was much bigger than my comet project, and she encouraged me to try marketing Moldavite jewelry to the stores that were my customers.

At first it was difficult to make many sales, because conventional jewelers had never heard of Moldavite, and they weren't eager to take a chance on it.

When the Christmas season rolled in, I asked a friend who had a jewelry shop if we could use one of his empty showcases to display my jewelry. Kathy and I agreed to work behind that counter to make the sales, and we would split the sales with the shop owner. We planned to start on Black Friday, the day after Thanksgiving. What happened next gave the phrase Black Friday a new meaning for me!

Two days earlier, we had taken all my precious-stone jewelry to the shop's back room, planning to set up our display on Friday. We had forgotten to bring the Moldavite jewelry, but we planned to have it with us when the shop opened. On Thanksgiving, Kathy and I had a lovely day off together, and felt much promise for the future.

The next day, when Kathy was in her morning meditation, her spirit guides said to her, "Be empty so that you may be filled." She was puzzled by the message, and mentioned it to me at breakfast. After that, we put on our coats and drove to the jewelry store.

When we arrived, we both felt an immediate sense of concern. The door of the shop was ajar, and there was a police car in the parking lot.

When we went inside, it was obvious what had happened. There was a man-size hole in the flimsy back wall of the building, and the store owner was talking with two policemen. All of the jewelry we had left in the shop's back room was gone.

As it happened, only my jewelry was stolen. The store owner had put his own stock into a safe, which the burglars had not been able to open, although the marks of sledge hammers on the door made it clear that they had tried.

I wondered why the alarm had not gone off and brought the police when the break-in occurred. I later learned, to my astonished dismay, that the owner of the local security company, who monitored the alarms from his home, had died from a heart attack two or three nights earlier. The policed discovered his body when they went to ask about the alarm on the night of the robbery.

I spent the day in a state of shock and disbelief. Not only had almost my entire inventory of gold and precious gems been stolen, but I also owed my gem suppliers for much of what was lost. My sense of optimism from the day before vanished.

In my anguish, Kathy reminded me of the words of her guides, "Be empty so that you may be filled." And, true to her nature, she accepted what had happened and went calmly about setting up a display of the only inventory we had left—Moldavite jewelry.

I also remember that I tried several times to use my tarot card deck, which I had brought with me, to try to make sense of what happened. Three times I laid out the cards. Each time, various images depicted the calamity and my grief at our loss. But each time, the outcome card was the same—Strength.

At the time, I would gladly have given up the promise of Strength to get my jewelry back!

Looking back on the story now, some thirty-six years later, I can say that both the cards and Kathy's guides were right. Struggling through the loss and having to start our life together from a financially impoverished position did bring Kathy and I closer together. And we gained strength through the process of persevering in our plans, being very frugal, and sharing our adversities and the little victories that slowly came to us.

Also, I find it rather amazing that I lost *everything except my Moldavites.* I see now that the apparent "disaster" actually needed to happen. From the start, Kathy knew that Moldavite was going to be important, and that it would take center stage in our personal and business lives. But I was unsure, and preferred to hang onto the security of what I knew. I could make a living with the precious gems and gold, even though I was not as excited about them as I was about Moldavite.

But the spirit guides were right. I needed to have that illusion of security taken away ("be emptied"), so that I would have no choice but to commit myself totally to Moldavite and its mission. Slowly we began to connect with more and more people who resonated with Moldavite, and we managed to eke out a living while preparing, as we gradually whittled down my debts, to start our own shop together. And from the day we opened it, the promise that we would "be filled" has come abundantly true.

Moldavite's Debut

During the several weeks between the Thanksgiving robbery and Christmas, things began looking a little better for Kathy and me. We had managed to sell some Moldavite jewelry, as well as a number of rings, earrings, and pendants with conventional gemstones—pieces I had hastily put together after we came home each evening. We were making payments for the lost gems, and we had accumulated, to us, impressive sum of almost $2000 in our bank account.

Then one day while I was away, Kathy took a phone call from a promoter for the Whole Life Expo—a New Age show to be held in a Boston exhibit hall in February. The promoter explained that his main crystal vendor had just cancelled his reservation for a double-size corner booth in a prime location, and he wondered if we would like to take it. The price would be discounted to $1500.

When I came back Kathy happily told me that she had agreed to take the booth. I was not so happy: "You just spent three quarters of our money! And we don't have any crystals to sell. All we have is Moldavite. How are we going to fill up a double booth?"

"We'll have crystals," she replied serenely. "This is going to be great." It still amazes me to remember how many times she was right about things like this.

We got our crystal inventory for the show in a surprising way. I happened to call up one of my customers who owned a jewelry store on Cape Cod, and I was lamenting to him that Kathy had committed to a big exhibit booth when we had so little merchandise to sell.

"You can borrow a bunch of my stock," he suggested. "I'm closed for the winter, so you might as well try to sell some of my things. I have a lot of crystals, geodes, and polished agates. If you'll pick them up and bring back what you don't sell, we can split the profits."

I soon made the long drive from Gloucester to Provincetown, coming back with a station wagon load of merchandise that was exactly what we needed, along with our Moldavite, to fill the booth. In the ensuing weeks, we added an additional few hundred dollars worth of Quartz and Amethyst points that we bought from a local wholesaler. We built some glass cases, bought clamp-on lights and table cloths, and we managed to create an attractive, abundant display.

The Boston Globe Writes about Moldavite

We were very lucky (or was it Moldavite's destiny at work again?) to receive a call from a reporter at the Boston Globe. We had sent out press releases about the Halley's Comet pendant project in the Fall, but had received no replies. Now that the approach comet itself was beginning to make news, she wanted to do an article about our comet jewelry and Moldavite.

The piece was done, and it made the front page of the Living section of the Sunday Globe, just weeks before the Whole Life Expo. (We got almost a whole page!)

Moldavite Is a Big Hit

When the weekend of the show arrived, we were pleasantly surprised by the quantity of sales we made. (A couple who had read the Globe article even came to our booth and purchased a 14k gold set of the comet pendant and earrings for $1000.) But what amazed me more was the people's response to Moldavite.

The attendees at the Expo were mostly familiar with crystals, and many of them could feel their energies. I watched as they held their hands above different stones to see which ones resonated for them. Having never felt stone energies myself, I didn't know quite what to make of this. But, again and again, when one of them reached the Moldavite display, there was a powerful reaction. Holding their hands over the display case, people would often exclaim out loud or take a step back. And dozens of times, when someone asked to hold one of the raw pieces, the person would comment, "This stuff is really making me feel hot! This has a lot of energy!" Our sales of Moldavite alone were more than the total for the entire rest of the booth.

And Kathy, true to her trusting nature, announced to numerous people that we would be opening a shop in Gloucester in April, just two months away. This was despite the fact that we had not yet found a location, and we still owned very little inventory, except for Moldavite.

But once again we received help we had not expected. The Cape Cod shop owner, pleased with our success, told us we could keep his inventory on consignment through

LIVING/ARTS

FASHION | JULIE HATFIELD

Out of this world

*Using ancient stones from the heavens,
Robert Simmons of Gloucester
designs jewels fit for a comet's return*

Halley's comet, which is supposed to be most easily seen by Bostonians during the next few weeks, has inspired the sale of all sorts of memorabilia from T-shirts with "I Saw Halley's Comet" printed on them to telescopes. But how much more classy to wear, in honor of the comet, a piece of jewelry made from the only extraterrestrial gemstone known to man – very possibly a stone that actually was once a piece of a comet?

Robert Simmons, a jeweler in Gloucester, has designed a small collection of gold earrings, necklaces and pendants with moldavite tektite stones in them.

The most spectacular piece, a pendant, features a moldavite tektite stone with a gold spray of tiny diamonds in a comet tail shape spreading out behind. Tektites (from the Greek word "tektos," meaning molten), are black/brown stones, spheroid-shaped, or cylindrical, button-shaped, teardrop and dumbbell-shaped, that are said to be as old as 35 million years. The stones have been found in Indonesia, Indochina, the Philippines, Australia, Tasmania, Texas, Georgia and the Ivory Coast of West Africa. Although scientists have proven that tektite is not an earth substance – or at least was first formed when an object from space crashed into the Earth – they have a variety of theories as to its origin. These include the belief that tektites are meteorites or pieces of comets or asteroids.

The average tektite, looking like a little black rock, is not very pretty, but the rarer moldavite tektite is a glassy green. It is the moldavite, found in Eastern Europe, that Simmons purchased in its rough form – all 12 pounds of what he could find – and cut and polished to make up his "Star Gem" collection.

"It's a soft, fairly fragile stone, comparable to emerald," Simmons explained. It is a lighter, glassier green than emerald; the larger moldavite stones are murky, the smaller the stone, the lighter and prettier is the shade. While it is much rarer than diamonds, it sells at this point for about $100 to $250 per carat.

"I can cut about 20,000 stones, and then it will be gone," Simmons said, noting that since tektite is an outer space material, he cannot find an unlimited supply. He is selling his earrings of one-half carat of Moldavite tektite encased in 14-karat gold for $50, a one-carat necklace for $500, a 1-carat necklace encased in a 14-karat gold chain and 1 carat pendant for $650, a pair of earrings, necklace, and a piece of the raw stone for $1,000, and $550 for a brooch or pendant.

FASHION, Page 71

Designer Robert Simmons says this earring made of tektite was inspired by Halley's comet.

Boston Globe article, January 9, 1986

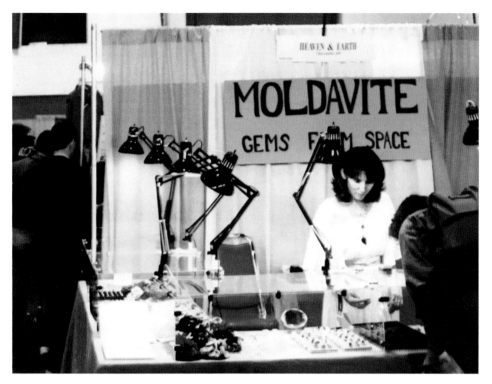

Kathy shows Moldavite to a buyer at the Whole Life Expo

the summer. With our newly earned funds and Kathy's knowing confidence, we proceeded to carefully allocate resources toward additional inventory, and we started thinking more and more about the store we hoped to open.

Building the Shop

We knew that our shop would combine crystals, gems, minerals, and jewelry with Moldavite, which was to become our signature stone. Since we had almost no cash, we worked on trust, doing whatever we could each day to move our dream forward.

And we still meditated in the mornings. Kathy was always getting guidance and having spiritual experiences, while I mostly sat distractedly in the dark. But it did make me calmer.

Then one day, something different happened. We had been discussing what to name our store, but had not come up with anything that felt right. However, during that morning's meditation, a loud, authoritative voice spoke inside my head: "The name of the store is Heaven and Earth." That was all it said.

But I liked the name a lot, and so did Kathy when I told her. So, now that we knew the name, we thought we would look for a location.

We had been living in Gloucester, Massachusetts, sharing a single bed in a small apartment made from the former servant's quarters of the massive Birdseye Mansion. We went out one morning, cruising the streets of the town, looking for vacant buildings.

In less than an hour, we found our place—the first floor of a two-story house with the landlady living upstairs. Rent was $125 a month. It had once been a little fishing tackle and bait store, and the back half was taken up by a huge walk-in cooler that would need to be removed. But I looked at the cooler as a possible source of free lumber to build our showcases. I volunteered to take it apart if the landlady would let me use the wood, and she agreed.

Kathy and I spent many days together, ripping apart the cooler, cleaning, painting, building tables, shelves, and cases for our inventory. My unskilled carpentry and second-hand building materials gave our furnishings a decidedly rustic look.

We had consulted an astrologer to choose our wedding day and the store's first day of business. As it turned out, our beginnings, both matrimonial and business, were ordained by the stars to take place on consecutive days—April 11 and April 12, 1986. We knew what we were committed to doing, but getting there was another story.

The Woman from Block Island

We kept on working hard to finish building, painting, and lighting the inside of the store before our astrological deadline. We designed our sign and commissioned a sign painter. We had a telephone installed. We were making progress, but it looked like we would have to work long hours seven days a week to get ready in time for the opening date. Then we ran out of money.

I had continued going out and selling my jewelry pieces to stores, as a way to make ends meet, but I stopped at some point during the store construction. There was just not enough time to do both. Now we had reached a place where we needed money to complete the renovations, and to put food on the table. But if I went on a selling trip, we would miss our deadline.

We sat in the sawdust on the shop floor and talked it over. I feared that there was no choice but to take the selling trip. But Kathy said we needed to stick with our schedule and to trust that we would be taken care of. My heart already agreed with her, so I gave in. We got up and went back to work.

About an hour later, the phone rang. I was shocked, because it was a brand-new phone line, and I thought nobody had our number.

A woman's voice spoke to me, "Hello, I'm looking for some Moldavite pieces. And I really need to get them right away. I live on Block Island, in Rhode Island, and I'm ready to drive up to Gloucester right now, if you have Moldavite."

I told the woman that, yes, we had Moldavite, and we would be working on the renovations all day, so she was welcome to come. She arrived three hours later, and she purchased $800 worth of raw Moldavites from us. When we asked how she knew we were there, since we had not done any advertising, she showed us a single photocopied page we had given out to a few people at the Whole Life Expo. Sure enough, our phone number was on it, even though the phone itself had not yet been installed at the time.

When she left, I looked at Kathy and said, "You were right again. If I hadn't agreed to trust and we had taken off on a selling trip, we would have missed her. And if we hadn't had Moldavite, she wouldn't have come. Now we have enough money to finish the shop and get it open."

I began to understand that there were some higher forces at work, and that Moldavite's destiny was being nudged along. Our job was to trust and cooperate.

Kathy's penchant for following her intuition and trusting the universe continued to stretch the limits of my comfort level, and our bank account. A few weeks before we opened, we got a call from Earthstar Magazine, the biggest New Age/Health and Wellness magazine in New England. Their back page was unexpectedly available, as an advertiser had cancelled at the last minute. Because they were in a time crunch, they offered us the whole page for half price. (But that was still $1000!) Kathy immediately said yes, and brightly told me this would be perfect for our grand opening. I groaned, but I agreed.

The morning Heaven and Earth opened, there was a small line of people waiting outside the door. We welcomed them in, and through the entire day there was a steady stream of people. We even received a delivery of party balloons and flowers from the owner of another crystal shop in Boston. We sold several pieces of Moldavite to people who had come looking for it, and more pieces to people who were energy-sensitive and immediately recognized the powerful nature of Moldavite's vibrations. Our other crystals and stones were also well-received. Having just gotten married the day before, we were already happy in our hearts, and the surprising success of our first day made us feel optimistic about the future.

Throughout the first weeks and months of operation, our shop remained busy and profitable. But the many expenses of launching a new business, building up our inventory (which was rather thin at the beginning), and covering our personal bills added up to quite a lot. And I was still paying off the debts for the lost gems from the robbery. Our bank balance was often close to zero.

Kathy, with intuitive vision and trust, would sometimes write checks on Friday for bills that were due, counting on the weekend business to cover them by Monday. This gave me the shivers, but we managed it.

The reason I mention this is that after a few months of running our finances so close to the edge, Kathy got the inspiration to tape a thin piece of raw Moldavite into our checkbook. She told me that Moldavite's expansive energies would get us past the pattern of scarce financial resources. I was utterly skeptical of this idea. But, for whatever reason, after that day we never had problems paying our bills again.

Synchronistic Meetings and Other Events

It was clear from the start that Moldavite had its own destiny. Or perhaps Moldavite's story is part of the unfolding destiny of humanity and the Earth. One thing is certain—from the time I became aware of it and through many following years, there has been a trail of synchronicities that have led to Moldavite's emergence from obscurity into the lives of hundreds of thousands of people around the world. In this chapter, I'll tell a few of the many stories.

I have already described the way I discovered the existence of Moldavite, and how it led to an acceleration of my life and to many major changes. Even the name for our crystal store came as one of Moldavite's surprises. When the inner voice intoned, "The name of the store is Heaven and Earth," it was giving us more than a name. With that pronouncement came the intuition that the meaning of the shop's name referred to the mission of our work—bringing Heaven and Earth into a spiritual union. It also alluded to Moldavite, the most important item in our inventory. Moldavite came into existence when a huge meteorite crashed, forming a new substance from the earthly rock that it transformed. So it was literally a "joining of Heaven and Earth."

This example is just one of many events that showed me that an intelligence beyond our everyday selves was involved with Moldavite's emergence. Heaven and Earth was just a tiny little crystal and jewelry store in Gloucester, Massachusetts. And at the time we opened, we were the only store in the USA that offered Moldavite. How could it find its way from that one shop in a small seaside town to people all around the globe? There was no way we could have made it happen, but it did.

Randall and Vickie Baer

During Heaven and Earth's beginnings in 1986, I was just beginning to realize that the interest in crystals and stones for spiritual purposes was a real thing, and that it was growing fast. People were hungry, not only for stones, but also for information about their energies and how to work with them. Every day, people came in and wanted to know about the energies of Moldavite. I was still not able to feel stones myself, and had not seen anything written about Moldavite's energies.

We carried all of the most popular crystal books, and they sold quickly. One of these was *Windows of Light,* by Randall and Vicky Baer. It offered a lot of channeled information about Quartz crystals, and was the first book I saw that mentioned mak-

ing energy grids and templates using crystals. In the back of the book was a mailing address for the authors. Hoping that they might shed some light regarding Moldavite, we mailed them a piece, along with a letter explaining the stone's origins.

About a week later, much to our surprise, we got a telephone call from Vickie Baer. She was breathlessly excited, and she spilled out her story in a torrent of words.

She explained that she and her husband had been doing meditation and channeling for a number of years. In 1983, she told us, they had experienced communication from a remarkably powerful being, "an alien Master," Vickie called it. During that channeling session, the being told the Baers that at some point they would receive "a green meteorite" as a gift from strangers, and that when this happened, it would accelerate and transform their work.

For this precise thing to happen three years later was astonishing to Randall and Vickie, as well as to Kathy and me. The Baers were traveling a great deal at that time, teaching crystal workshops all over the USA. Sometimes as many as 500 people attended these events. And from the time when we received their phone call, the Baers spoke enthusiastically about Moldavite at every class, encouraging their audiences to contact us if they wanted to purchase some.

We began to get phone calls every day from people wanting to order Moldavite. We were sending pieces everywhere. And those people were telling their friends. In a matter of weeks, we realized we needed to print some sort of catalog we could mail out to prospective buyers. Our first edition was one sheet of glossy paper, with photos of Moldavite on one side and Quartz crystals on the other. The next catalog was twelve pages. It included new items such as Sugilite, as well as more Moldavite, and much more Moldavite jewelry. With the Baers singing the praises of Moldavite, and the customers turning on their friends, our shop turned into a mail order business without our ever having intended it.

And the Moldavite kept spreading.

Dr. Jean Houston

Doctor Jean Houston has been at the center of the human potential movement since the 1960s. She has authored over a dozen books and has led hundreds of groups. (*Mind Games*, which she co-wrote with her husband, Robert Masters, was praised by John Lennon as, "one of the two most important books of our time.") But when we received Doctor Houston's phone call in 1987, we didn't know who she was, except for the vague sense that she was somebody famous. "I'm Doctor Jean Houston, she announced, and I am very interested in Moldavite. I understand that you are the source." When I asked her how she found out about us, she told us it was a synchronicity.

The Moldavite page from the first Heaven and Earth catalog

"Every year I take two weeks off to learn something new," she explained. "And this year I decided to learn about crystals." She went to the local New Age bookstore near her home, and was browsing among the shelves. Suddenly, for no apparent reason, a book fell off one of the high shelves and landed open on the floor. Houston picked up the book and read one paragraph on the open page.

As it happened, that paragraph discussed Moldavite, mentioning our business as the source. (It was the *only* paragraph in the book that mentioned Moldavite at all!) Houston intuitively knew that this was the information she needed, so she made a note of it, closed the book and returned it to the shelf. The next day, she called us.

When Doctor Houston received her first two Moldavites, the energy immediately affected her, sending waves of heat from her hands up her arms. The currents soon rushed up to her face, producing what we came to know as the classic "Moldavite flush."

That first phone call led to a long and fruitful association with Doctor Houston. She introduced Moldavite (and us) to hundreds of her friends and students, many of whom acquired it from us. We decided to enroll in Jean's Mystery School, and we were in the program for two years. Aside from the wonderful things we learned there, Mystery School also provided a venue in which Moldavite became known to more people, as Jean often encouraged us to set up a table of our wares.

In 1989, we took a memorable trip to Bali with Jean and a group of other students. As we traveled the island, we "planted" Moldavite at several sacred sites. One of them was an outdoor temple, the oldest temple in Bali. Doctor Houston explained to the priest the significance of the Moldavite offering we wished to place on the altar there,

Balinese temple after Moldavite ritual. Note the "Rainbow Being" that appeared on our film.

and a beautiful ceremony ensued. As we were leaving, I turned back toward the altar and took a quick photo. Later, when the film was developed, the picture revealed the form of a rainbow colored being.

Look closely at the image and you may see what other people have reported—the shape of a female figure with the hood of her garment coming up around her head. We viewed this as a goddess figure, or an emanation of Sophia, Soul of the World.

When our first book, *Moldavite: Starborn Stone of Transformation,* was being produced, Doctor Houston agreed to write the Introduction. In it she reported the results of an experiment she decided to do, providing Moldavite to about 200 people:

Most reported an intensification of dream life and acceleration of life processes. A goodly number began to enter more seriously into meditative life after receiving the Moldavite. Here is the report from a university teacher . . . which is fairly typical: "After three months of having Moldavite, I discover that the speed at which changes are happening in my life is unlike anything I've experienced before. I couldn't stop them if I wanted to."

I then asked this person if she attributed the change to the Moldavite, to which she replied, "Yes, I do attribute it to the Moldavite because of the constancy in change in consciousness I experience when I'm wearing it. I have a constantly different state of consciousness when I have it on."

Another person . . . reported that she felt that the Moldavite had moved her to becoming, "more and more true to myself, resulting in a radical career change. I am now becoming a writer, capable of different kinds of writing. I am becoming more and more aware that I have an identity as an artist."

One of the sweetest connections Jean facilitated for us was with author Madeline L'Engle, who wrote one of the favorite books of my childhood, *A Wrinkle in Time*. Through Jean's intercession, we were able to gift L'Engle with a particularly lovely Moldavite. She wrote us back to thank us, saying, "Thank you for your gift of the Moldavite. I love holding it. It's warm vibration is like a healing prayer."

Artist John Nesta

During the first two years that our shop in Gloucester, Massachusetts, was open, a local artist named John Nesta was among the many customers who connected strongly with Moldavite. Over a period of weeks, he purchased several raw pieces, each of which generated powerful visionary experiences for him. Perceiving energy from a stone was quite surprising and paradigm-shifting for John, and he explored this new-found phenomenon with a passionate intensity. He often visited the shop two or three times a week, primarily to discuss his Moldavite experiences with us.

John made his living as a painter, mostly doing landscapes and marine paintings that people commissioned him to paint. He was famous in the region, and was usually quite busy with his work. However, during the time in which he was deeply involved

Nesta's first painting showing Moldavite and Quartz energies

with Moldavite, his commissions suddenly dried up. He had little or no work to do, and at the same time, he was having many powerful inner experiences and visions.

One day during that period, John came into the shop, showing obvious excitement. He told us he had realized that his commissions had ceased for a reason—he was supposed to be painting the energies of the Moldavite. He showed us a small painting he had done, depicting a Moldavite on a table next to a Quartz crystal. He had made the image somewhat surrealistic, so that the viewer would see a representation of the "subtle bodies" of the two stones, and the energies they were emanating.

During that period, John had a great burst of creativity. He painted more than a dozen canvases with images of Moldavite, sometimes combined with Quartz crystals. All of these striking images seemed to vibrate with the stones' energies. Each time he finished a new painting, he brought it into the shop for us to admire. He seemed almost puzzled by what was happening, and told us he did not feel like painting anything but Moldavite and crystals.

At one point, we received a new shipment of very large faceted Moldavite gems. Some were as much as thirty millimeters in diameter. When John saw them, he connected strongly with one of the largest ones, telling us that this was "his stone." He also insisted that the Moldavite needed to be set in a thick, 24 karat gold setting. He started to make payments on it, slowly, because he still had no commissions coming in.

Some weeks later, John felt that whatever had compelled him to work so feverishly on the Moldavite and crystal paintings had subsided somewhat, and his portrait commissions had begun to pick up again. One day, he brought all of the paintings into the store, so that we could view the entire collection. We were stunned, in the most pleasant way possible, by the beauty and energy we felt from them.

Then John told us he would be willing to trade the entire collection in exchange for his Moldavite and gold custom pendant. We happily agreed to the arrangement, and the paintings subsequently graced the walls of our business for many years.

The Men in Black

During our first year in the shop, virtually all the surprising synchronicities and paranormal moments were positive, exciting, and uplifting. This is the story of one that wasn't.

It was the last Saturday before Christmas, 1986. Kathy and I had been working seven days a week, and the store had been busy. It was dark outside, and we were starting to count the day's receipts in preparation for closing up. Then the phone rang.

Kathy took the call, and she quickly became thoroughly engrossed in some sort of intense conversation. She waved to me as she took the phone into the shop's back room.

In the next moment, the front door opened and two men came in. Both of them were dressed in black suits, and one of them wore a black hat. (They were probably the first people in suits who had come through our doors.)

The vibe I got from them was not good at all. They spoke to each other (not a word to me) very loudly and awkwardly, using odd sentence structure and stressing the wrong syllables in their words. Their movements were abrupt and over-emphasized. They didn't seem quite human.

They careened around the shop, grabbing various stones off the glass shelves and whacking them back down. As they did this, they made mocking-sounding remarks about the crystals. Picking up a delicate and lovely Quartz cluster, one of them loudly remarked, "This is the ugliest thing I've ever seen!" His companion guffawed. Then the man picked up a shapeless blob of raw black obsidian and sarcastically remarked, "Now, this is really beautiful!"

Even though the men made me feel terribly uneasy, I had come out from behind the counter and stuck with them like glue. I was worried that they were going to steal or break something, and I hoped that my staying in close proximity to them would cause them to leave. But they continued their chaotic tour of the store, obviously not wanting to buy anything, but seeming to enjoy trying to intimidate me. Kathy was nowhere to be seen.

When they reached our jewelry display, I slipped back behind the counter, still watching them closely. Finally, they got close to the Moldavite display.

Something about the Moldavite made them hesitate. For the first time, one of them looked me in the eye and spoke. Pointing to the Moldavite tray, he asked, "What's this stuff?"

Then another odd thing happened. As soon as he asked that question, a voice came out of me, speaking words I hadn't planned to say, with a power and strength that I definitely was not feeling in that moment. "That's Moldavite," I heard myself declare. "You wouldn't be interested in it."

"Oh," said the man in black. And without another word he turned away and walked out the front door, with his companion following.

That was weird enough. Those two characters did not feel like people, but more like some sort of crude imitation of a human. It's not easy to explain, but I felt as if something really dark had been in the room with me, and as soon as they were gone, I locked the door.

Then Kathy emerged from the back room, saying, "I was just on the weirdest phone call."

"Wait till you hear what happened out here," I replied. "But what was the call?"

"It was a woman, and the first thing she said to me was, 'I want you to talk me out of committing suicide.'"

"What?"

"That's what she said. I didn't know her, and I asked her if she was one of our customers. She said she wasn't, but that she knew I was the right person to call."

"What did you say to her?"

"A lot of things. You know what I would say to someone in that kind of crisis. She kept talking about wanting to kill herself, and I kept trying to reassure her and remind her that life is precious."

"How did it end?"

"That's the even stranger part. I heard the front door close, and at that same moment, the woman's whole tone changed. She suddenly sounded matter-of-fact, as if she had just called to check on how late we were open or something. She said, 'Okay, thanks, bye bye.' And she hung up."

I told Kathy my side of the story, and we both felt there was a connection between the phone call and the men in black. Kathy said she felt as if the events were coordinated, and that the call had been a way of separating us and taking her out of the room while the men were there. It was certainly true that, as soon as the two men left, the woman promptly ended the call.

We were glad for the role that the Moldavite had apparently played. It seemed to us that its vibration was too high for the pair of unwelcome browsers to tolerate. I had been amazed at the authoritative voice that had come through me, and at seeing the men immediately turn and leave. What occurred fitted our ideas about Moldavite's special qualities. One of those in particular was that Moldavite never needs to be energetically cleansed, because its vibes are too high and too powerful for any negative patterns to attach themselves to it.

It certainly seemed to repel those men in black.

That's where I have to leave this anomalous tale. Take it for what you will. I'm happy to say that they never came back, and we never ran into any others like them.

Laurence Fishburne

Some years later, we were at the Tucson Gem and Mineral Show, selling our Moldavites, our first Moldavite book, and our other wares in the Heaven and Earth showroom. One afternoon a man came in whom I felt I should recognize. His face was very familiar, but I couldn't place it. He went straight to the Moldavite display and started choosing a number of our best and largest pieces.

In the course of the conversation, I asked him what his profession was. "I'm an actor," he replied.

"Movies?" I asked.

"Movies, plays, television, everything."

"Have you been in anything I might have seen lately?"

"I did a film called *Just Cause* a couple of years ago."

"You're him?" I almost shouted. "I loved that movie."

Our conversation lasted a little while longer. He bought a copy of our Moldavite book to go with the several big Moldavites he wanted, and he asked us to autograph it. Then I asked if he gave autographs.

"I don't do autographs. I do hugs." So we all marched out from behind the counter and got our hug from Laurence Fishburne.

Even though I remember this event quite clearly, I didn't think about it much for several years, until I saw Mr. Fishburne on screen again in 1999, playing the role of Morpheus in *The Matrix*.

I'm sure it was his talent and not the Moldavites that catapulted him into worldwide stardom, but still . . . I liked knowing that he had them.

Night Watch (and the Overwhelmed Operator)

Among the surprising ways that Moldavite found to make itself famous was an out-of-the-blue invitation we received to go on a national television news show called *Night Watch*. We received a phone call at our shop, and the caller explained that someone who worked at the network had visited our shop. That person had purchased a Moldavite from us, and had recommended us as guests.

The network planned to do a program focusing on several New Age authors, as well as crystals and stones. Kathy and I were flown to Washington, D.C. for the live show appearance, and were given a complimentary room in a posh hotel. We brought crystals as well as Moldavite to display on the program.

When the interviewer turned to us, we showed our items, and I talked about stones and their energetic qualities—especially those of our signature stone, Moldavite. Although the interviewer was out of his element in dealing with metaphysical topics, we managed to deliver a good summary of Moldavite's story, and the reasons people were so enthusiastic about it.

Toward the end of the segment, we were asked to hold our Heaven and Earth catalog up to the camera. The interviewer said he couldn't give out our address, but urged interested viewers to contact us at our location in Gloucester, Massachusetts.

A snowstorm delayed our trip home for a day, so we got to spend another night in the fancy hotel, and we used the extra day in Washington, D.C. to visit the Smithsonian Institute's mineral collection. Sure enough, they had some specimens of Moldavite. (But I thought our pieces were nicer.)

After returning to Gloucester, we found out that our shop had been swamped with phone calls the day after the show and we sent out hundreds of our catalogs. This led to another wave of Moldavite purchases from people who had seen the program. And, as usual, they told their friends, which led to more pieces of Moldavite finding their way into the hands of people wanting to connect with it.

A few weeks later, we learned about a funny side note to this story. (Remember, this was in the 1980s, when computers had not yet taken over.)

A customer in the store, who lived several hundred miles away, told us that she had seen our appearance on *Night Watch,* and that had led her to visit our shop. "I decided that I wanted to buy a Moldavite, so I called Information to get your phone number," she explained. "It was about three o'clock in the morning.

"When I asked the operator for your number, she just about exploded. 'Why do you keep calling over and over, asking for the same number!' she demanded. 'This has been going on for three hours!' Then she gave me the number and hung up on me.

"I guess all the calls after you were on the show got routed to the same Directory Assistance operator, maybe because it was in her area. Poor thing! It must have been weird to be sitting there in the middle of the night and then to suddenly get hundreds of requests for the same number."

We have always wished we could have had the chance to explain it to her.

An Unexpected Letter

As Moldavite's popularity grew, people all over the world began to hear about it. And our book, *Moldavite: Starborn Stone of Transformation,* was adding to that awareness.

Several years after we opened our shop and subsequently began providing Moldavite to mail order customers, we received an unexpected letter. It was from Mary Bruce, the daughter of George Bruce, the man who had written the original Moldavite article in the 1958 *Lapidary Journal*—the article that gave me chills of destiny and set me on my path with Moldavite.

When we read the letter, we learned that Mr. Bruce had died, and that his daughter had inherited his stone collection. She had not had a close relationship with her father, and had not shared his interest in minerals and gemstones. However, one or two years after his death, someone gave Mary a copy of our first Moldavite book, and as she read through it, she came upon her father's name in the first chapter.

That led Mary to go through the stone collection she had inherited, looking for Moldavite. She wrote us that she had found several pieces, and because of our book, she began meditating with them. To her surprise, she felt Moldavite's energy right away, and she began exploring the rest of the collection. Then she started visiting crystal shops, finding that she could feel the energies of many different stones.

"I want to thank you," she wrote. "Finding your book and discovering my connection with Moldavite has led to many blessings for me. I love the crystals (and Moldavite especially), and I am using them for healing and spiritual growth. Also, all of this has made me feel a reconnection with my father, and I appreciate things about him that I never knew before. I am astonished at the synchronicity of the way all this has happened!"

We were amazed too. When things like this occur, we recognize that there is a much deeper mystery behind the events of life than we can even imagine. Behind the curtain of that mystery, I glimpse a vast, benevolent, creative intelligence. I think back to the "accident" of finding Mr. Bruce's article in the twenty-six-year-old magazine, calling him, and excitedly discussing Moldavite for four hours. What would have happened if he had not answered the phone?

I remember the feeling of destiny I experienced while reading about Moldavite that day, and I realize now that it was about far more than my personal journey. All the thousands of people in the world who have been touched by Moldavite are part of it, and so are Mary Bruce and her father—the man who provided the first pieces and set everything in motion.

And, in my opinion, you who are reading this book are part of the pattern, too.

CHAPTER 4

PLANTING MOLDAVITE AT SACRED SITES, CROP CIRCLES, & ADVENTURES IN MOLDAVITE COUNTRY

From the beginning, both Kathy and I had the vision that Moldavite had an important role to play in the spiritual awakening of humanity and the healing and awakening of the Earth. We shared our vision with our customers and friends, and the readers of our first book about Moldavite, which was published in 1988.

We felt that, as part of the process of world transformation, it would be helpful to spread Moldavite to as many of the Earth's sacred sites as possible. Whenever we traveled, we brought small pieces of Moldavite with us, to give to people we met, and to plant in places when and where we were drawn to do so. We also kept a bulletin board of photos and postcards from people who had written us to tell us where they had planted Moldavites.

It's impossible for me to remember all of the spots where we left the Moldavite "seeds" but here is a list of some of them:

1. Zeus' Cave in Greece

2. The Seven Sacred Pools on Maui, Hawaii

3. The Top of Mount Haleakala, Maui, Hawaii

4. The oldest temple in Bali

5. The Aesclepius temple, Island of Cos, Greece

6. The Chalice Well, Glastonbury, England

7. Mount Shasta, California, USA

8. Temple of the Descending God, Tulum, Mexico

9. Bell Rock, Sedona, Arizona

10. Our House in Vermont USA (We put it into the concrete when the foundation was poured.)

In addition, our customers and friends contributed to the worldwide "Moldavite grid" in countless locations. Among them were Macchu Picchu, Peru, and the Great Pyramid in Egypt. (There is actually one hidden there in the King's Chamber.) I can't say what effects have come from all this, but I still believe that the Moldavite, coupled with all of our intentions, has to have been beneficial. And one of the most exciting and dramatic Moldavite "plantings" occurred at England's most famous sacred site.

Moldavite Goes to Stonehenge

In 2007, Kathy and I flew to England to participate in a Crystal and Sound Healing conference in Glastonbury. That trip was punctuated with many synchronicities, including our discovering a crop circle in a field near Avebury Circle. That first exciting experience led to our finding more crop circles, and to befriending two people we met in the second one. While in one of the formations, we recognized that the powerful energies present in the circles were also carried by the native flint rocks that were present where the circles formed. Thus, we discovered Circle Stones.

The organizer of the conference had made arrangements for attendees to be able to take a special trip to Stonehenge, in which we would be allowed to go inside the fenced area and walk among the megalithic standing stones. Stonehenge is said to be located at a place where many ley lines converge, and to be oriented to act as a nexus for the "dragon currents" traveling through the whole planet. I had already decided that it was important to try to place pieces of Moldavite at the bases of as many of the big stones as possible. I sensed (and hoped) that this might energize the world grid for planetary healing.

With one pocket full of raw Moldavites and small clear Quartz crystals I boarded the bus from Glastonbury to Stonehenge in the wee hours of the morning. We arrived there just before dawn. As the morning light began to illuminate the huge standing stones, I felt a sense of timelessness and awe. We were let in the gate and were allowed to wander among the stones, under the watchful eyes of several British policemen.

Taking in the stark beauty and powerful energies of Stonehenge was an amazing experience. And we were there exactly twenty years after the original Harmonic Convergence! Kathy and I both felt a numinous sense of presence, and we spoke in whispers until the sun had risen fully.

Of course, I was very much aware of the Moldavites and crystals in my pocket, and hoped to plant them. The police were there to keep people from chipping off bits of the huge stones, or defacing them in other ways. Although my purpose was benign, I was not sure they would allow it, so I looked for opportunities to plant our offerings when we were out of their range of vision, quickly pushing the stones an inch or so into the soft soil at the base of each megalith.

Through good luck or grace, all the Moldavites and crystals got into their proper places, and we spent the rest of our time strolling and taking photos among the stones.

As with many "seeds" of Moldavite we planted, we could not know to what degree our intention would manifest, but we were happy to have gotten them into the ground at this nexus of the Earth's energy lines.

In addition to my surreptitious planting of Moldavites among the monoliths, others in our group set up a crystal grid at the very center of the monument, and a ritual was done there, holding the intention that the energies of Harmonic Convergence should resonate within Stonehenge, and, through the ley lines, through the whole Earth.

I share all this with the hope that some readers will look at the images and tap into the energies of Stonehenge and of what occurred there that day. The intention that was set is still in the process of manifestation, and our attention to it aids it.

< TOP: Stonehenge at dawn, Thursday, August 16, 2007;
MIDDLE: Robert and Kathy at Stonehenge;
BOTTOM: Kathy in Stonehenge Circle

Crystal Grid at center of Stonehenge, August 16, 2007

Crop Circles and Synchronicities

After our trip to Stonehenge, we returned to Glastonbury to attend the conference, and I made my presentation. When the event was over, we had an extra day to explore the area. We drove to Avebury so that we could walk around Avebury Circle, another standing stone monument, much bigger and much older than Stonehenge, but made from smaller, less geometric stones, and without the top stone slabs bridging the pillars.

Both of us felt powerful energies in the huge circle of standing stones. As we walked among them, we experienced a growing sense of their power and presence. I was moved to "plant" several small Moldavites among the stones.

A Wikipedia article describes Avebury Circle:

Constructed over several hundred years in the third millennium BC, during the Neo-lithic, or New Stone Age, the monument comprises a large henge (a bank and a ditch) with a large outer stone circle and two separate smaller stone circles situated inside the centre of the monument. Its original purpose is unknown, although archaeologists believe that it was most likely used for some form of ritual or ceremony.

Kathy and I did our own personal rituals as we walked among the stones. Our mood was quiet. It took us more than an hour to slowly walk the full outer circle, which has a circumference of about one kilometer. Part of the path took us up a gentle hill with four ancient trees growing so close together that they almost seemed to entwine into a single entity. Their exposed gnarly roots covered the hilltop, looking almost as if the trees were grasping the ground. We were enchanted to learn from our guidebook that J.R.R. Tolkien used to visit these same trees, and that they are thought to have inspired his imagination to create the Ents—benevolent treelike beings who played an important role in the *Lord of the Rings* saga.

As we stood on the hill beneath the trees in the late afternoon, looking out over the landscape, Kathy noticed a strange circular depression in a nearby wheat field. "Could that be a crop circle?" she asked.

"Let's go find out."

It was, indeed, a crop circle.

When we walked into the huge formation, we noticed that the wheat stalks were arrayed in symmetrical interwoven patterns. We also were aware of a numinous vibration. Kathy said, "It's not a circle–it's a sphere." I understood what she meant, because I also felt that we were within a spherical field of energy.

We stayed there for about forty-five minutes. Finally, we left, because we needed to retrieve our car before the parking lot closed. But by then I was eager to see if there were more crop circles in the area.

Our guidebook told us there was something called the Crop Circle Café nearby, so we drove there. The place had just closed, but we were able to talk to the last customer as he was leaving. He told us there was a new crop circle that had appeared just the night before, at a place called Stanton, St. Bernard, and showed us on our map where to look for it.

Twenty minutes later, we were driving slowly down a narrow country road surrounded by grain fields. We had not seen the crop circle and were almost ready to give up looking. Then I noticed two people parking a car and getting out, entering a field that was surrounded by a high hedge. "That must be it," I said excitedly. We quickly pulled up behind the other car and went through the hedge.

This crop circle was even larger than the first one, and had not been trampled by earlier visitors, as the first one had. (I later read that this formation had a diameter of 450 feet.) We didn't approach the other couple, who were some distance ahead of us. Instead, we explored the many sub-formations within the huge circle.

One interesting feature of this crop circle, aside from the astounding energy we felt while walking in it, was the long "bar" under the interior circle. Viewed from above, it appears three dimensional, because of the way light and shadows play upon the grain stalks. They have not been flattened, but bent, woven, and tufted. Part of the mystery of crop circles is how and why these intricate patterns occur.

Another major feature of this circle was that it contained, within the circle above the "bar," thirteen smaller circular spirals of wheat, arranged like the numbers on a clock, with the thirteenth spiral in the center. Kathy stood on one of these, and she immediately noticed a spiralling energy moving up through her body. She also was once again aware that the formation as a whole felt like a sphere of vibration that went up far over our heads and deep into the ground. Her sense was that the energy sphere had the same diameter as the crop circle itself.

The whole atmosphere within the circle felt charged, almost as if it was crackling with static electricity. This was a much more powerful field than the first one we had felt.

Kathy noticed a few interesting-looking stones on the ground within the circle. (We later learned that these were Flint, a high-silica Quartz rock native to the area.) She picked one up and felt it. "This has the same energy as the crop circle!" she told me excitedly. Then she walked outside the formation, found another

TOP: Stones of Avebury Circle; SECOND: "Ent" tree roots at Avebury Circle; THIRD: Approaching the Crop Circle at Avebury; BOTTOM: Wheat patterns in the Avebury Crop Circle

similar stone, and tuned into it. "This one isn't nearly as powerful," she said.

I tried making my own comparisons, and I had to agree. The stones within the crop circle were highly charged, while the same type of stones in the area outside the formation carried no special energies.

We put a few of the Circle Stones (as we later named them) into our pockets and continued to walk around within the pattern. Eventually, near the center of the circle, we approached the other couple, who had been making their own explorations.

After exchanging a few remarks about the circle and its energies, I noticed that the male member of the duo was looking at me curiously. Finally he asked, "Aren't you the guy who wrote that book about crystals?"

I was frankly flabbergasted. *The Book of Stones* had been published in the USA only a year earlier. There were not many copies in England yet, and the last place I would have expected to be recognized was inside a crop circle in the middle of a wheat field in Wiltshire! But it turned out that the man and his partner indeed had a copy of the book, and had in fact just opened their own crystal shop. We were all stunned and delighted by the synchronicity.

At that point, the conversation really took off. It turned out that this pair was very much into crop circles, as well as crystals, and they told us they visited every new formation. We showed our new friends the Circle Stones, and they quickly gathered some for themselves. They then offered to show us an even larger,

TOP: The Avebury Crop Circle; SECOND: The Stanton St. Bernard Crop Circle; THIRD: The long "bar" in the Stanton St. Bernard Crop Circle looks three dimensional when viewed from above. The wheat had to be only partially collapsed, and some sections woven and tufted to bring about this effect; BOTTOM: Shown here are two of the thirteen spirals found within the circle over the long "bar" in the Stanton St. Bernard Crop Circle. They were arranged around the circle like the numbers on a clock, with the thirteenth spiral in the very center. Standing in the center of any of these spirals caused us to feel a strong spiral of energy moving up through our bodies from below our feet.

more complicated crop circle a few miles away. We agreed and left quickly, hoping to see it before sunset. Before departing, I placed a Moldavite at the center of big circle as a ritual offering.

We arrived at a remote field in the golden hour just before sunset, and we had just enough time to view the extremely large and complex crop circle that had formed overnight a few days earlier. We were amazed at the incredible amount of detail in the patterns, including the weaving of wheat shafts into small, intricate braids throughout the entire structure. These details, along with the fact that the circle was perfect—in spite of being formed on undulating, bumpy terrain—convinced us that it was impossible for people to have constructed it, especially in the dark, over the course of a single night!

In this powerful formation, I felt the urge to plant several small Moldavites. I had the intuitive sense that Moldavite's currents would work harmoniously with the vibrations of the crop circles. (And we later discovered that Moldavite has a powerful synergy with the Circle Stones.)

After the sun went down, we left the field and went to dinner with our new friends. Each of us had stories to share, and we all agreed that our meeting was meant to be. We planned to stay in touch, and we made an agreement that they would supply us with Circle Stones, which we would exchange for our Moldavite stones, crystals, and jewelry.

Late that evening we returned to our hotel and prepared to depart from England. Our next destination was a place where we hoped not to bury any Moldavites, but to dig some up if we could!

TOP: This close-up displays the symmetry and perfection of the spirals found within this crop circle; SECOND: Raw Flint "Circle Stones" from crop circles in Wiltshire, England; THIRD: The complex Martinsell Hill crop circle with "woven" grain shafts; BOTTOM: The wheat in this complicated crop circle was intricately "woven" together throughout the entire 450 foot diameter formation.

Adventures in Moldavite Territory

The Glastonbury conference was over, and we drove to London the next day. On the following day, we flew to Prague, in the Czech Republic. Our main Moldavite supplier had invited us to visit the Moldavite digging areas of southern Bohemia. We were eager to see the countryside from which Moldavite emerged, and to possibly even find some ourselves. We rented a car, planning to drive south and do some sightseeing on our way to Moldavite territory. But before that, we wanted to see Prague and to visit the world's largest Moldavite at the National Museum.

World's largest Moldavite: A Moravian specimen weighing 265.6 grams

A Wild Synchronicity

After checking in at our hotel in Prague's Old Town, we walked immediately to the Old Town Square. We were eager to have a look at the Prague Orlaj—the Prague astronomical Clock. The Orlaj is the world's oldest clock still in operation (built in 1410), and it is a work of mechanical genius. Immensely complicated, it contains multiple dials, indicating not only the time of day, but the position of the Sun and Moon in the sky, relative to the signs of the zodiac and other astronomical details. Perhaps most amazing is its "Walk of the Apostles," an hourly show of moving Apostle figures and other sculptures (notably, a skeleton figure that represents Death), striking the time. In addition, there is a calendar dial with medallions representing the months. According to local legend, the city will suffer if the clock is neglected and its good operation is placed in jeopardy; a ghost, mounted on the clock, was supposed to nod its head in confirmation.

We hurried down to the square, hoping to catch the parading Apostles on the hour. As we made our way over the old, hand-laid black and white cobblestone square, I stopped suddenly. There, right before my feet, was a patten in the cobblestones that precisely matched that of the second crop circle we had explored in England, only two days earlier! There was a big circle with thirteen smaller circles inside, arrayed just as they had been within the crop circle!

I pointed it out to Kathy, and we both stared, forgetting that we had come there to see the Orlaj. It was, to me, an astonishing synchronicity, and a continuation of the magic of our journey. Here, in Prague, was the same image we had stumbled upon in the wheat fields of Wiltshire. And, because of the temporary nature of the crop circles, it seemed to me that Kathy and I were likely to have been the only two people in the world who had seen and connected these two patterns.

I wondered if the synchronicity was somehow calling our attention to time. It occurred at the base of the ancient astronomical clock, and both the crop circle and the cobblestone pattern were reminiscent of a clock face.

The next mystery of our trip was indeed linked to time, though not in any way that I would or could have expected.

Southern Bohemia and an Explosion of Memory

We spent a day driving south through the Czech countryside, meeting with our friend Lukas, who supplied most of the Moldavites for our business. He had kindly arranged for us to stay in his parents' cozy vacation cottage while we were visiting.

The day after we arrived, Lukas came to the cottage and took us on a tour of many of the famous Moldavite digging sites. We stopped to look through the fence at the closed quarry in Besednice, where many of the most beautiful Moldavite specimens were once found. We toured other Moldavite areas, including Jankov, Radomilice, Ceske Budejovice, and Vrabce.

As we walked through the fields of Chlum, Lukas noticed that a man was hauling up buckets of sandy soil from a hole about 10 meters from us. We approached the man and discovered that he had a partner who was at the bottom of the hole, which appeared to be fifteen to twenty feet deep.

They told Lukas that they were digging for Moldavites, and they showed him the piece that they had just found. I looked at it, and I was surprised to see that it closely resembled my own special Moldavite—the one that triggered the flood of spiritual Light I experienced on my meditative Moldavite journey to the Central Sun.

I eagerly asked Lukas to inquire if we could buy the piece the men had just found. They agreed, and I soon had the rather muddy (but

TOP: The Orlaj Astronomical Clock in Prague, Czech Republic; CENTER: "Crop Circle" pattern in the cobblestones; BOTTOM: Closed Moldavite quarry in Besednice

‹ TOP: Besednice Moldavites; MIDDLE LEFT: Robert and Kathy in Besednice; MIDDLE RIGHT: Robert and Kathy at Chlum; BOTTOM LEFT: Robert's fresh-dug Moldavite from Chlum; BOTTOM RIGHT: Robert's original Moldavite (30.5 grams) and its "twin" from Chlum (35 grams)

TOP: Robert and Kathy at Slavce; MIDDLE: Slavce forest with Moldavite holes; BOTTOM: Kathy in Moldavite hole

beautiful) Moldavite in my pocket. I was thrilled to be the second person to have touched it after it emerged from the Earth.

Next we drove the short distance to the digging location named after the nearby village of Slavce. Lukas took us into a wooded area where many Moldavites had once been uncovered. There had been a kind of "gold rush" in Slave when knowledge of this digging area became public, because Moldavites were plentiful there.

By the time of our tour, most digging in Slavce had ended, because the Moldavite there had run out. And the woods were filled with abandoned holes that reminded us of the craters of the Moon. The site was somewhat disturbing, as it was clear that the many Moldavite diggers had done damage to the landscape. It felt a bit eerie to be there, but we were excited nonetheless. This was true Moldavite country!

As we walked among the trees, Kathy suddenly bent down and brushed some dirt away from something she had noticed on the edge of one of the abandoned holes. She held it up for me to see. It was a Moldavite, a lovely crescent-shaped piece. Kathy was thrilled, not only because she had found her very own Moldavite, but also because she had long felt a special connection with the image of the crescent Moon, as a symbol of the Goddess.

On our way back to the cottage, we drove past the digging area known as Zakacka. Lukas spoke with a teenage boy who had been busily digging, and he showed us his prize of the day—a huge Moldavite that I estimated as weighing at least sixty grams. I asked about buying the piece, but the lad smiled and shook his head.

The next morning, we were in the cottage. It was the last day of our trip. The next day

Kathy displays her crescent Moldavite

we would fly to London, and on to New York. Heavy rain was pouring down, and there were rumbles of thunder. I sat at the kitchen table with a cup of tea while Kathy made breakfast.

As I watched her move about the kitchen, a strange thing occurred. I distinctly heard an inner voice in my heart, and it said, "It is she." I had never heard a voice in my heart before, and I thought it was odd, especially because I didn't understand what "It is she" meant. After a moment or two, I decided to mention it to Kathy. "Honey, I just heard a voice in my heart, and it said, 'It is she.'"

Saying those words out loud immediately triggered something big within me. I felt a huge surge of recognition and a powerful flood of emotion. At the same time, there was a sudden explosion of memory. I had a vivid vision that displayed what I recognized as my past lives—hundreds of them. I saw each one for only a second or so, and then came the next one. It was almost like flipping through a pack of cards, with different images on each one.

In each of those lives, I loved a woman. Often the lives were tragic or difficult, but I always loved the same woman, even though she appeared in a different body in each life. And I recognized that the woman was Kathy, my wife. Tears poured from my eyes and I sobbed. I knew without doubt that, "It is she."

It took quite some time for my sobs to subside so that I could tell Kathy about my vision and its meaning.

Does this experience have anything to do with Moldavite? I could never prove it to anyone, but in my own musings I recall that Moldavite was long viewed in its native land as a stone that blesses marriages. And I had received letters from people who told me they believed that bringing Moldavite into their lives had helped them to find their appropriate loving relationships. Even in my own case, the arrival of Moldavite had coincided with the end of my prior unsuccessful marriage and my meeting and falling in love with Kathy. And, of course, we were in Moldavite country, and had both acquired our new pieces only one day earlier.

Whatever Moldavite's role may have been, I feel certain in my soul that the vision was real, and the voice in my heart spoke the truth.

CHAPTER 5
SPIRITUAL PROPERTIES OF MOLDAVITE

Moldavite is the stone that initiated me into awareness of the spiritual properties of crystals and minerals, and it has been a catalyst for several of my most important spiritual experiences. It has, over the thirty-six years I have worked in this field, had similar effects on thousands of other people with whom I have spoken and corresponded. From my perspective, it has a special role to play in the awakening of humanity that is now underway.

A box of small Moldavites.

AUTHOR'S NOTE: I suggest looking at the photo and inviting the Moldavite energy to come into you. Attend to your inner state, and focus awareness in your heart. It is possible to experience Moldavite's energies in this way, without needing it to be physically present. You can try this with any of the Moldavite photos in this book.

Throughout history, and even into pre-history, Moldavite has been regarded as a spiritual talisman. The Neolithic peoples of Eastern Europe wore Moldavite at least twenty-five thousand years ago, and the famed Venus of Willendorf—the earliest known goddess statue—was discovered in a digging site that contained a number of Moldavite amulets. People of that period also used Moldavite for arrowheads and cutting tools.

In modern times, Moldavite has emerged as one of the stones most prized for metaphysical purposes. Its effects vary widely, from mild to almost overwhelming, from physical cleansings to breakthroughs into higher consciousness. Yet the common denominator seems to be the revitalization and acceleration of one's path of spiritual evolution.

In my first writings about Moldavite in the 1980s, I said this:

I feel that the two most important properties of Moldavite are its catalyzing effect on one's spiritual evolution and its opening of one's ability to ground Light for the healing of the Earth. These may be two ways of looking at the same event, for among the millions around the world who are opening up to their own spirits, with and without the benefits of Moldavite, there is deep and immediate concern for the healing of our planet. In any event, Moldavite, like the legendary Stone of the Holy Grail, serves to awaken the yearning for spiritual growth and to set one off upon one's highest path in an accelerated fashion. This basic impetus can take a variety of forms, and one can feel it in a number of different ways.

The most typical first reaction of someone holding a piece of Moldavite is the sensation of heat. Usually felt first in the hand, sometimes with the accompanying feeling of pulsating energy, the warming often heats up the whole person, sometimes causing sweating and/or flushing. (We have seen the flushing so many times that we named it the Moldavite Flush!) In certain cases, the heart chakra is activated, which may be felt as a pounding pulse or a gentle flowerlike opening. Emotional release can accompany this opening, running the gamut from laughter to tears.

Sometimes initial reactions to Moldavite are relatively subtle, even though it seems to be more potent than almost any other stone. Hundreds of times, we have seen people drawn to the Moldavite case in our store without really knowing why. They pick up a piece—some feel a tingle, some feel heat, some catch their breath at the beautiful green they see when holding it to the light. A portion are fascinated by the story of its celestial origin. A few recognize its similarity to the legendary Stone of the Holy Grail. Sometimes the stories Kathy and I share about our own life changes strike a chord. Often people pick up Moldavite and are surprised to find that they don't want to put it down. Many feel that their mood is lightened and their zest is increased. For people who say they don't feel anything, but who are nonetheless attracted, we often suggest sleeping with a piece taped to the forehead at the third eye chakra point. Virtually all who report back say that their dream states were deeper and more vivid.

When Kathy began wearing Moldavite, she felt greatly uplifted by it, exhilarated and energetic, with a continuous connection to higher states of consciousness. However, when we first opened our store and were working around large quantities of Moldavite all day long, she sometimes experienced light-headedness, and a difficulty in staying grounded. Because it so strongly activated her crown and third eye chakras, she found she frequently had to remove whatever Moldavite she was wearing. Over time, as she became attuned to the high vibrational frequency of the Moldavite, she was able to wear the stones for whatever periods she chose and still ground the energies. Other sensitive people sometimes have this initial experience with Moldavite. It offers a powerful doorway into higher states, but can be overwhelming for them if it is worn or held too long. Also, for many people, there seems to be a cleansing process involved. Here the Moldavite energies go first to where there are blockages. When these have been released, a pleasant lightness of emotion usually follows. In every case I know of, initial feelings of light-headedness or spaciness have given way as people attune to the higher energies and learn to ground the Light. With Moldavite, we are in the presence of a powerful spiritual vibration with which we can resonate, and that resonance can help bring us to an inner harmony.

Here is a recent report (2022) from our friend Rasa, who lives in Lithuania. She is an accomplished meditator, but she had never worked with Moldavite until we introduced it to her. I see many interesting parallels to the qualities of Moldavite that Kathy and I have felt, and that have been reported by others through the years:

At the beginning of the meditation, the Moldavite energy strongly activated the third eye and the crown chakra. I felt the bright light energy flowing to planet Earth. After that, I began to feel that my heart is one with the heart of planet Earth. I felt them beating together in one rhythm. I saw how Moldavite embraced our planet

with his strong energy and sent light. At that moment, I felt hope and faith in peace on Earth. My consciousness began to rise strongly and expand. I flew and felt myself and everything around in the golden bright light. There was no separation, just love, bliss, and trust. Also, in the second part of the meditation, when I was flying, I saw my past lives. It was displayed at some old beautiful buildings and museums. Pictures from those lives were crossing my consciousness so fast and disappeared. The main focus of all this meditation was that Moldavite energy flowed very strongly through us to planet Earth. It was light energy transmission. I notice when I meditate with Moldavite that his energy is very powerful, transforming, expanding and has high frequency vibrations.

In particular, I found it interesting that Rasa echoed Kathy's initial and profound impression that Moldavite's purpose and intention is the grounding of spiritual Light for the regeneration of the Earth (See Chapter 10: Experience at Bell Rock). Rasa also experienced a rapid review of many past lives. This precisely parallels the experience I had during our 2007 Moldavite quest in the Czech Republic. (See Chapter 4: Planting Moldavite at Sacred Sites, Crop Circles, & Adventures in Moldavite Country.)

Moldavite's energies can activate any and all of the chakras. Its vibrations tend to focus in areas where one has blockages or psychic wounds, first clearing these areas and then moving into resonance with one's entire energetic system. Resonance with Moldavite can take many forms—chakras can open; synchronicities can increase in frequency and significance; one's dream life can become dramatically more vivid and meaningful; one can connect with spirit guides; physical, emotional, or spiritual healings can happen; jobs and relationships can change; meditations can become deeper and more powerful. Yet all these can be viewed as symptoms of a shift in one's own energies. This shift is what Moldavite can catalyze. With its high and intense vibrations, it can resonate with one's energy pattern in a way that creates an intensification of spiritual vitality and an acceleration of progress on the path of one's highest destiny. This is much the same effect that legend says resulted from exposure to the fabled Stone of the Grail. (See the chapter in this book: Moldavite: Stone of the Holy Grail.)

Moldavite is a powerful aid for meditation and dreamwork. In both cases, taping a piece of Moldavite to the forehead can have the effect of creating a much more vivid and visionary inner experience. Moldavite increases one's sensitivity to guidance and one's ability to discern the messages sent from the higher realms.

Moldavite can be a powerful catalyst for self-healing, clearing blockages and opening the meridians, as well as energizing the interconnections among all aspects of the subtle body. It is a talisman of spiritual awakening, transformation, and evolutionary growth.

In addition to use in meditation and dreamwork, Moldavite can be worn as jewelry. This conveys the advantage of being able to keep its energies in one's vibrational field throughout the day, for further strengthening of its effects. Doing this also draws an increased incidence of beneficial sychronicities into one's daily life. Some people will

have to accustom themselves gradually to wearing Moldavite because of its energetic intensity, but most will make the adjustment in a few days.

Moldavite also offers an energy of spiritual protection. When one is in resonance with its high-frequency vibrations, negative energies and entities cannot connect with or hang onto one's field. In alignment with its transformational properties, Moldavite tends to disconnect one from unhealthy attachments and to magnetize the persons and situations most needed for evolutionary progress.

Moldavite is an ideal stone for making energy tools (See Chapter 15: Moldavite Energy Tools & Practices). It can be glued or otherwise attached to other stones to magnify both energies. It can be added to wands, headbands, templates, grids, and all sorts of devices to intensify their effects. Moldavite has the ability to enhance and accelerate the beneficial effects of many other stones. It works well with all types of Quartz, as well as Amethyst, Citrine, Rose Quartz, Sugilite, Charoite, Lapis, Larimar, Rhodochrosite, Aquamarine, Heliodor, Pietersite, Smoky Quartz, Selenite, and most other gemstones. For healing purposes, I would recommend combining Moldavite with Heartenite, Healerite, Healers' Gold, and/or Seraphinite. For enhanced visionary experience, Herkimer "Diamonds" are an excellent ally. Genuine Diamond, in crystal or gem form, further intensifies Moldavite's transformational energies. Libyan Gold Tektite increases Moldavite's empowerment of the third chakra, focus of personal power and will. Darwinite, a greenish tektite from Australia, aids Moldavite's capacity to help one connect to extraterrestrial energies and entities. Agni Manitite accentuates Moldavite's protective qualities. Pairing Moldavite with Master Shamanite provides the ideal energy combination for linking the root, heart, and crown chakras, and then activating the entire central channel that parallels the spine. Azumar, Larimar, Rose Quartz, Aquamarine, Rosophia, and Angelite soften Moldavite's intensity and help to focus Moldavite's power on healing and strengthening the emotional body. Thulite and Moldavite together can increase the intensity of passion in love relationships. (For more information, see Chapter 12: Combining Moldavite with Other Stones).

Moldavite has a special resonance with all varieties of Azeztulite, which provide powerful connections with the realms of spiritual Light.

Moldavite is one of the Synergy Twelve stones, along with Danburite, Tanzanite, White Azeztulite, Phenacite, Herderite, Tibetan Tektite, Satyaloka Azeztulite, Petalite, Brookite, Natrolite, and Scolecite.

Currently, I am especially interested in combining Moldavite with any or all of the other stones constituting the Four Cornerstones of the Alchemy of Stones—Phenacite, Rosophia, and the Azeztulite family of stones. (I call Azeztulites a "family" because there are now twenty-one different varieties!)

Moldavite's Disappearing Act

One of the most surprising characteristics of Moldavite is its apparent ability to disappear, and then reappear somewhere else. I experienced this phenomenon several times during my first year of involvement with Moldavite.

Typically, I would take my favorite Moldavite out of my pocket before going to bed and place it on top of the dresser. Once in a while, I would go to pick it up the next morning and it wouldn't be there. Then later, perhaps the same day, but sometimes days or weeks later, I would find it again in some quite unlikely place. I usually assumed that it was due to my faulty memory, but sometimes I would find the stone in a place that just seemed impossible. I remember once, after weeks of thinking I had lost my Moldavite, noticing it in the soil of one of our house plants. There was just no way I had put it in there!

Another time my Moldavite had been missing for a couple of weeks, and I was a bit frustrated, because I wanted to take it with me on a business trip to New York. (I had hoped it would bring me luck.) On the day of my trip, I was in the plane and I happened to put my hand into the vest pocket of my sport coat. To my amazement, the Moldavite was there. I seldom wore the sport coat, and had definitely not worn it in the weeks leading up to the stone's apparent disappearance.

This occurred enough times that I began to expect my Moldavite to leave me and return, though I had no idea how or why.

During the first year of running our store, I talked to countless people about Moldavite, and sometimes I heard tales of these inexplicable disappearances. I remember one particular morning, as we were just opening, a woman came into the shop, quite distressed that her three hundred dollar Moldavite had vanished. She was insistent that she knew where she had left it, but it wasn't there. She had come to see us, reluctantly, to replace her "lost" stone.

I replied to the woman that my own favorite Moldavite was currently "on sabbatical," and that I was expecting it to return sooner or later. I told her not to worry too much about hers, because the missing Moldavites tended to return.

While I was speaking with the woman, Kathy was opening the safe in the corner of the shop, getting out some of our gold jewelry and our cash pouch. When she pulled out the pouch, she noticed a lump, and she said, "What's this?" Upon unzipping it, she found, to all our astonishment, my own missing Moldavite, which I was sure I had left on the dresser at our house.

The timing was perfect for illustrating my point to the woman at the counter with me. But I was quite bemused, as it seemed that my Moldavite had transported itself across town, and had somehow gotten itself inside our thick, heavy safe. That was a trick fit for a magician!

The customer was delighted, and somewhat reassured, though she bought another Moldavite anyway. Some weeks later she came in again and said that, yes, her "lost" Moldavite had come home. And it had appeared in a location where she was certain she had never placed it.

Over the years, this phenomenon became an almost commonplace occurrence. We heard about it from dozens, or even hundreds of customers. And when we talked to "Moldavite people" about having had this experience, perhaps as many as a quarter

Here is my "Trickster" Moldavite in 2022. It is the same piece that catalyzed my early meditative journey to the Great Central Sun in 1986. Since then, it has "disappeared" and come back at least a dozen times.

of them had either experienced this weird behavior with their Moldavites, or had heard such tales from friends.

During the late 1990s, I met Doctor John Mack, the famed Pulitzer Prize-winning Harvard psychiatrist who investigated alien abductions. Doctor Mack had a wide range of interests, and his inquiries into alien abductions had opened him to other paranormal phenomena, including spiritual healing and the energies of crystals and stones. He purchased several Moldavites from us, as well as a long necklace made from drilled raw Moldavites. During our first conversations, I mentioned my experiences with the disappearing/reappearing Moldavites. Doctor Mack could feel Moldavite's energies, and during the ensuing weeks he enthusiastically shared Moldavites with his close staff and associates.

The next time I saw Doctor Mack, one thing we discussed was Moldavite's "Trickster" quality of going missing and coming back. He had experienced it himself, as had several of his associates. One of them had even observed a previously unheard–of phenomenon. She had "lost" a Moldavite, presumably in her bedroom, and had found it days later on the window ledge of her bathroom shower. But in this case, there was not one Moldavite, but two. And the second one was a piece she had never seen before!

After this event, Doctor Mack told me that he had decided to research Moldavite more deeply. I looked forward to the results, hoping he might include them in a future book. But those hopes, and my acquaintance with Doctor Mack, ended tragically in November, 2004, when he was struck and killed by a drunk driver.

The last, and for me, the most amazing Moldavite disappearing/reappearing story spans a very long time period. Sometime in the late 1990s my original large Moldavite pocket stone, which I had left on top of my dresser, was nowhere to be found. This Moldavite was very special to me. It was the one that had "initiated" me in 1986 by opening all my chakras, filling me with spiritual Light, and activating my capacity to feel the energies of all the stones. Kathy and I looked very hard trying to find it, but without success. We finally gave up, deciding it was gone for good.

Fourteen years passed, and the missing Moldavite was almost forgotten. In 2011, Kathy and I decided to move to New Zealand. We had to pack up all the belongings we wanted to bring with us, and we would give away or discard many more.

As I was going through a clothes closet, choosing what to keep and what to let go, I picked up a pair of white painter's pants. They were brand new, with the store labels still on them. I decided to try them on, planning to keep them if they fit me. When I pulled the pants up, I noticed a big lump in the right front pocket. I reached in and pulled out the object that had caused the lump.

As you will have guessed, it was my missing Moldavite.

Even knowing the history of Moldavite's trickster behavior in my life, I was astounded. To find that stone, fourteen years after losing it, in the bottom of a stack of clothes, in the pocket of a pair of pants I had never worn . . . it was more than a surprise. I called out to Kathy and hurried into the room where she was. I was holding up my Moldavite, with a big smile on my face.

I was very happy to see it again. (And I still have it.)

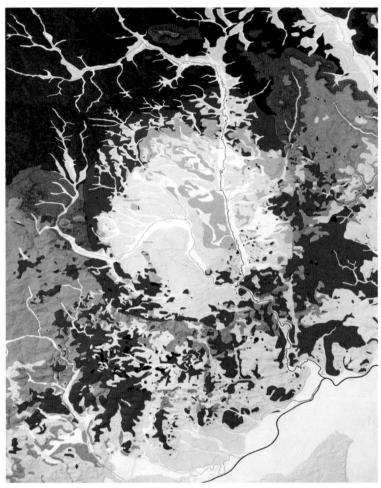

Geological Map of Ries Crater area. Note the crater's circular form and the size (over fifty square miles) of the affected area.

CHAPTER 6
SCIENTIFIC & HISTORICAL PERSPECTIVES

About 14.75 million years ago, a rare and fantastically powerful event occurred in what is now Bavaria, Germany. A pair of huge meteors or asteroids streaked northeast through the Earth's atmosphere at the almost unthinkable speed of 72,000 km per hour. (At that speed, one could travel from New York to London in less than five minutes.) Both of them landed within thirty kilometers of one another, causing cataclysmic explosions. The larger of the two objects, which formed the Ries crater, is estimated to have been one kilometer in diameter and to have weighed three billion tons. The smaller object, which formed the Steinheim crater, was about 150 meters in diameter.

The impact at the site of the Ries crater produced an energy eruption equivalent to the simultaneous explosions of 100,000 atomic bombs of the size used in World War II to destroy Hiroshima, Japan. It is estimated that the material ejected from this event was about 150 cubic kilometers, weighing over 400 billion tons. The rock that composed the Ries meteorite, as well as a great quantity of earthly rock, soil, and sands thrown up by the shock wave and impact, reached temperatures of about 30,000 degrees Celsius. (This is nearly five times as hot as the surface of the Sun.) The heat and explosion caused the meteorite and about three cubic kilometers of the earthly materials to be literally vaporized and impelled upward beyond the Earth's atmosphere at speeds of several kilometers per second.

Aside from the ejected rock vapor, within two seconds of impact, vast amounts of rock were thrown out of the crater into the surrounding landscape, landing up to forty kilometers away. Some of the ejected stones were as large as 100 meters in diameter.

Even 100 kilometers away from the impact site, the fireball would have appeared to be thirty times larger and seventy times brighter than the Sun. Within this area, all life would have been destroyed instantly. The shock wave had an initial speed of 600 kilometers per hour (about ⅔ the speed of a jet airplane), and circled around the entire Earth. The roar of the explosion would have been heard over the entire planet.

Meanwhile, up in the stratosphere, an alchemical transformation of the vaporized meteorite and earthly materials was happening. Complex interactions between melted microdroplets and the ejected rock plasma were occurring. Volatile elements were

This map shows the relationship between the Ries crater and the main Moldavite areas.

being purged, and what remained began to condense into ever-larger droplets of molten green glass—the tektite material we know as Moldavite.

Because the giant meteorite/asteroid that created the Ries crater came in from the southwest at a low angle of 30 to 50 degrees, some of the directional momentum of its kinetic energy was transferred to the cloud of rock vapor that it ejected. This carried the condensing material quite some distance to the northeast before it fell back to the surface. The strewn fields in the Czech Republic where Moldavite is found range from 250 to 400 kilometers away from the site of the Ries impact.

The impact site itself experienced an instant metamorphosis, aside from giving birth to Moldavite. The crater, which formed within just a few seconds, was 500 meters deep. Much of the underlying rock within the crater, which is twenty-six kilometers in diameter, was subjected to so much heat and pressure that it was converted into suevite—a so-called impact breccia, composed primarily of fused fragments of granite and gneiss with lumps of glass that had been molten crystalline bedrock. This material is very hard rock indeed, and well suited for construction. Much of the town of Nördlingen, Germany, which is inside the Ries crater, is built from suevite. The outer wall around the original town, as well as its central cathedral, were made of it.

An interesting aspect of the event that created both Moldavite and suevite is that it also produced diamonds. When the asteroid hit the Earth, the force caused graphite-bearing gneiss rocks in the region to form diamonds due to the immense pressure from the impact. It is believed that the walls of the Nördlingen cathedral contain over 5000 carats of diamonds, and that millions of carats of diamonds are present in the structures of the town. In fact, scientists estimate that Nördlingen and the surrounding area contain approximately 72,000 tons of the gemstone. Unfortunately, the Ries diamonds are all microscopically tiny, with the largest being just .3 millimeters in diameter.

The fact that Moldavite is found so far away from the crater led many scientists to disbelieve that the Ries event could have been its source. But the age of the crater, which corresponds to the age of Moldavite, certainly argues in favor of the Ries origin. And when one envisions the two huge meteorites coming in from the southwest at a low angle and blasting vaporized rock above the atmosphere, the fact that the Moldavite "rain" came down hundreds of kilometers to the northeast becomes plausible. Another old problem—that Moldavite's chemical composition differs markedly from that of the rock at the Ries site—may have been resolved by the hypothesis that the vaporization of Moldavite's parent materials, and the boiling away of volatile elements, is the reason for those differences. We will look at that theory near the end of this chapter.

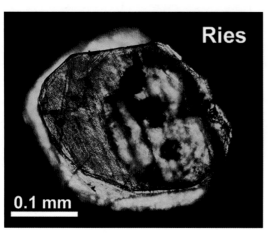

I have laid out the above picture of Moldavite's genesis in order to call attention to the exceptional, dramatic and overwhelmingly powerful circumstances that gave rise to these rare and beautiful celestial objects. Now I want to briefly discuss Moldavite as it has been

Impact Diamond from Ries Crater

known through history. This includes the evolution of scientific theories of its origins, as well as Moldavite's significance to people through many centuries.

Scientists classify Moldavite as a subgroup of the enigmatic class of natural glassy objects know as tektites. The word tektite comes from the Greek word *tektos,* meaning molten. The term Moldavite derives from the area in which the stones are found, near the Moldau River (called the Vltava in Czech). Moldavites are amorphous crystals, or natural glasses, and the question of their origin has been briskly debated for many years. However, virtually all scientists agree that the appearance of Moldavites and other tektites on Earth is the result of a meteoric or asteroidal collision. We will discuss the various theories later in this chapter.

Unlike other tektites, which are tar black or brownish black, Moldavite is a deep green color. It is the only variety of tektite suitable for cutting and faceting as a gem, and jewelry has been made out of it for literally thousands of years.

The stones themselves have been prized by early humans as far back as Paleolithic times. Our ancient ancestors gathered and used sharp-edged Moldavites as tools, and they also wore pieces as amulets. The two earliest archeological discoveries, made in Austria (Gudenushohle near Krems and the Paleolithic dig near Willendorf), date back to the Early Paleolithic period. In the journal *Lunar and Planetary Science* (XVI, pp. 447-448), an article entitled "A Moldavite from Staintz" states: "Moldavite splints have been found together with the famous 'Venus of Willendorf' in Lower Austria."

The Venus of Willendorf is an 11-centimeter-tall figurine estimated to have been made around 25,000-30,000 years ago. It is the oldest known goddess statue. The fact that this statue was found along with a number of Moldavites, in a digging site far from the Moldavite strewn fields, has led myself and others to speculate that Moldavite was associated with early goddess worship.

Vladimir Bouska also reports that in the Moravian part of the Czech Republic, Moldavites have been found in layers of strata associated with late Neolithic cultures. In particular, he cites a disk-shaped Moldavite found at the Skripinske Hradisko locality in a pit with Jevisovice pottery. Thus we can see that early man was attracted to Moldavites, both for tools and talismans.

Although we have no information on the use of Moldavites in medieval times, they are known to have been used in the 1700s as pendants and as adornments on men's walking sticks. Czechoslovakian lore states that in the Radomilice area young men traditionally brought Moldavites to their fiancées to bring good luck and harmony into the relationship.

Bouska reports that, in the 1800s, "in the Netolice area, an ostensory was said to have existed . . . adorned with Moldavites, but it did not remain preserved."

Venus of Willendorf

[AUTHOR'S NOTE: An ostensory, or monstrance, is defined as a sacred vessel or cup in which the consecrated Host is placed for veneration by the faithful. See Chapter 7: Stone of the Holy Grail.]

In 1891, Moldavites that were polished and set in gold were exhibited as gems in the National Exhibition in Prague. Their popularity rose until the turn of the century when unscrupulous dealers substituting bottle glass for true Moldavites dealt a blow to the market for the cut and polished stones. Since that time, most of the Czech jewelry market for Moldavite has utilized the stones in their raw state. [AUTHOR'S NOTE: Moldavite's current popularity has given rise to a new proliferation of fakes, mostly sold online. Although it is possible for experts to recognize raw Moldavite visually, and although tests of specific gravity, etc., make it possible to identify even cut and polished Moldavite, my advice is to purchase from a familiar source that will guarantee its authenticity in writing. See Chapter 17: Counterfeit Moldavites.]

In the 1960's and 1970's, the popularity of Moldavite gems for jewelry rose again, and the 1980's saw its blossoming as a stone of choice among those who use gems metaphysically. Since I first encountered Moldavite and began offering pieces for sale in 1986, it has undergone a spectacular rise in popularity.

Throughout the last half of the 20th century, and in the first two decades of the 21st, the true value and rarity of Moldavites has been recognized. In the 1960's the Swiss government gave a gift of Moldavite to Queen Elizabeth II on the tenth anniversary of her coronation. The piece was a beautiful, naturally sculpted raw stone set in platinum and surrounded by diamonds and black pearls. It is said that the Swiss government paid $5000 for the raw Moldavite alone. (That's probably a bargain these days!) In the 1990's a rosary of faceted Moldavite beads with a carved Madonna was specially made for and presented to Pope John Paul II as a gift from the Czechoslovakian people. In more recent years, Moldavite has become one of the most important stones among those who collect and meditate with stones for their energetic and spiritual properties.

Virtually all Moldavites in the world have been found in what is now called the Czech Republic. They occur largely in an attractive, mostly rural area about sixty to one hundred miles south of Prague and 100 to 150 miles northwest of Vienna, Austria. The strewn fields (the areas in which Moldavites are found) are small compared to those of other types of tektites. The two major areas of Moldavite occurrence are in Bohemia and Moravia. In Bohemia, the sites are scattered in a broad belt around the town of Ceske Budejovice. In Moravia, the swath divides at the town of Trebic and forms a northern branch in the basin of the Jihlavka River and a southern branch from Trebic southeast to Znojmo. The total area of the strewn fields is about 6000 square kilometers. This may seem large to a person on foot trying to find one of these rare stones, but compared to the vast strewn fields of black tektites in Australia and Southeast Asia, it is quite small. One curious fact is that between the two clusters of Moldavite-bearing areas, in Bohemia and Moravia, no Moldavites have been found. This may be explained in part by the fact that erosion over millions of years has changed the surface of the land, and many Moldavites have been washed into streams and rivers, thereby concentrating the eventual finds. Or it may be that the original explosive event in which Moldavites were formed sent two "plumes" of the molten material to these separate areas.

Searching for Moldavites is a time and energy consuming task. In the past, they were most easily found in fields after the spring thaw or in the fall after heavy rains. (In the summer, the stones were obscured by vegetation.) After a rain, any Moldavites on the surface were washed and, if still wet, glistened in the sunlight. Under these ideal conditions, an experienced collector might have found as many as fifty pieces in a single day in the richest areas. In other locales, such a search might be unsuccessful for several years.

Moldavites have also been found by digging in sand pits. This labor-intensive method of collecting is especially good for recovering gemmy or museum grade stones—naturally sculpted and shiny pieces which have had little wear. The best of these occur in layers that are rich in gravel fragments. Konta and Saul reported in 1976 on a dig in such an area:

> The sedimentary profile at Locenice, about one mile from Nesmen, is comparatively rich in Moldavites, and yields one to three Moldavites per 30 cubic feet. A group from Charles University (Prague) studied the section at Nesmen and Locenice and searched for Moldavite several years ago. Several beautiful Moldavites were found in each of these sand pits. Twelve people digging in three pits for eight days found 43 Moldavites. A total of 600 cubic feet of gravelly sand and 240 cubic feet of gravelly clay were dug and carefully examined. Forty-three Moldavites weighing a total of 118 grams were found and, of these, thirty specimens were of gem quality and weighed a total of 98 grams. The weight of the heaviest one was 13.276 grams and its size was 26.3 x 21.9 x 18.8 millimeters; the weight of the lightest one was .391 gram.

One has only to do some arithmetic to see how difficult it was to gather Moldavites by this method, even decades before Moldavite's popularity generated a wave of diggers who soon depleted the well-known collection sites. In the 1976 expedition, it took nearly two days per person to find a single piece, in the richest known areas.

In more recent times, the demand for Moldavite and the consequent digging has created more problems. Farmers have had pits dug in their fields without permission and diggers have even rob one another's pits. And when a rich find is discovered, a frenzy of digging can turn the whole area to something looking like the craters of the Moon. When we visited the Czech Republic in 2007, my wife and I saw one such place.

The Czech government has since enacted laws with severe penalties for unauthorized Moldavite digging. This has been partially successful, although the depletion of the digging areas has done more to discourage the "black miners." Digging for Moldavites is hard work, and few will do it if they are unlikely to get much reward.

Moldavite can also be excavated by commercial mining methods. One of the two legally authorized Moldavite mines is a large sand pit. The company sells the sand for construction purposes, carefully screening out the embedded Moldavites.

In the mid 1970's the total number of Moldavites collected since 1787 was estimated at 30,000 to 40,000 pieces, weighing approximately 400 kilograms. In 1987 Bouska estimated the total number ever collected to be approximately 200,000 pieces. Since then, hundreds of thousands of pieces of Moldavite have been collected by eager diggers and officially sanctioned mining operations. In 2020-2021, a wave of TikTok videos about Moldavite (over 500 million views) created a huge bubble of demand. Prices shot up to at least five times what they had been previously, and Moldavite availability plummeted. Even with hundreds of thousands of pieces having been found, Moldavites are very rare gemstones, possibly among the rarest on Earth.

By comparison, some 142 million carats of diamonds were estimated to have been produced from mines worldwide in 2019. Worldwide diamond reserves are estimated to be some 1.2 billion carats. That equals 240,000 kilograms, or *120 tons* of diamond reserves—far more than all the Moldavite ever found or mined. And this number does not include all the diamonds that have already been sold in jewelry. In 2018 a new study by an interdisciplinary team of researchers used seismic technology (the same kind used to measure earthquakes) to estimate that a quadrillion tons of diamonds lie deep below the Earth's surface. It is safe to say that Moldavite is a gem that is much, much rarer than diamonds.

Compared with other raw gemstones, Moldavites are also relatively small, with most ranging from $\frac{1}{10}$ gram to ten grams. Pieces over thirty grams are considered rare, and pieces over fifty grams are extremely rare.

According to Bouska, the largest known Moldavite weighs 265.5 grams and comes from Slavice, Moravia. The second largest, also from Moravia, weighs 232.5 grams. In Bouska's time, the largest Moldavite from Bohemia weighed 110.9 grams, and the second largest one, from Veseli and Luznici, weighed 96.8 grams. (It is possible that a few larger Bohemian Moldavites may have been found since then. In 2007, I purchased a raw Bohemian Moldavite weighing 105 grams. Unfortunately, it is no longer in my personal collection!) The average weight of Moldavite is about eight grams, though weights from the two major collection areas differ. Moravian Moldavites average 13.5 grams while Bohemian ones average 6.7 grams.

According to Rost (1972), the largest Moldavite collection exists in the National Museum of Prague, which had at that time a collection of about 9000 pieces. The Moravian Museum in Brno, the West-Moravian Museum in Trebic, the Museum of Jihlava, and the Museum in Ceske Budejovice also have beautiful collections of Moldavite. Minor collections can be found in Czechoslovakia at Charles University in Prague, the Chemical-Technological University in Prague, the University in Brno, and in private hands as well. In addition, the Smithsonian Institution in Washington, D.C. exhibits Moldavite in its extensive gem and mineral collection, and NASA also possesses a number of Moldavites.

The gravel sands where Moldavite may be found contain a variety of other minerals, especially Quartz. Along with the common Quartz have been found pebbles of Rock Crystal, Smoky Quartz, Rose Quartz, Ferruginous Quartz, and the rarer Pegmatite, Lydites, Gneiss, Graphite, Mica Schist, Granulite, Serpentine with Pyropes, Feldspar and Crystalline Limestone. Occasionally found were Black Tourmaline, fibrous aggregates of silky lustrous Sillimanite, Andalusite, and Bluish Kyanite.

The characteristic shapes of Moldavite offer evidence of their molten origins. The various shapes seen are most commonly drop-like (from quite round to very flattened), plate or disc shaped, oval, spheroid, dumbbell shaped, elliptical, rod-like, or spiral. These are all shapes found in the splash patterns of liquids, and their aerodynamic forms give evidence to the fact that they flew through the air in molten form. Moldavites from most Bohemian localities are more drop-like, elongated, or rod-like, while Moravian Moldavites are more spherical.

Many Moldavites are characterized by beautiful patterns of etching and sculpting. These traits were originally thought by Suess and others to be caused by aerodynamic forces operating as the molten Moldavites fell from the sky. Certainly the general shapes of the stones were affected by these forces. More recently in Czechoslovakia, Rost and his contemporaries have put forth the theory that the sculptation of Moldavites is a product of chemical corrosion occurring in the sediments over millions of years. Whatever the cause, this trait again underscores the unique nature of these rare stones.

The variation of Moldavite's color is partly a function of its location. The most common color for Bohemian Moldavites is bottle green (79%), with olive green, light, and pale green being the next most numerous colors. Brown and intensive green ("poisonous" green) are rarer, each counting for less than two percent. In Moravia, 89% of the Moldavites are olive green and brown. Bottle green accounts for five percent, light and pale green accounts for five percent, with one percent being the intensive ("poisonous") green.

The hardness of Moldavites on the Mohs scale is from 6 to 6.5. (Diamond is 10; common glass about 5.) Thus, Moldavite will scratch ordinary glass and is within an acceptable range for jewelry manufacture. The fact that Moldavite is harder than ordinary glass is attributed largely to the fact that its content of silicon dioxide (Quartz) is higher. Its average density is 2.342 grams per cubic centimeter. Its average index of refraction is 1.492. Its melting point was established as far back as 1899 to be 1400 degrees Celsius. More recently its melting point was calculated to be closer to 1100 degrees Celsius. This in itself was proof that these stones were not artificial glass, as some had thought. Their age has been determined to be about 14.8 million years, another proof that it cannot have been made by man.

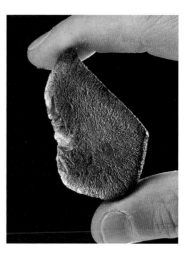

The chemical composition of Southern Bohemian Moldavites, as reported by Bouska, in weight percentages, is as follows: $Si\ O_2$ 79.97; $Ti\ O_2$ 0.33; $Al_2\ O_3$ 9.95; $Fe_2\ O_3$ 0.33: $Fe\ O$ celk 1.81; $Mn\ O$ 0.08; $Mg\ O$ 1.97; $Ca\ O$ 2.71; $Na_2\ O$ 0.46; $K_2\ O$ 3.39; $K_2\ O/Na_2\ O$ 7.37. Moldavites from the Radomilice area and from Moravia, as well as the extremely rare pieces from Dresden and Radessen, Austria, show some variance from these figures. However, one can get a very good idea of the general composition from Bouska's calculations. The predominant constituent is silica, the remainder being mostly made up of various metallic oxides. All tektites, Moldavite included, have this very high silica content, and aluminum ranks second. As has been stated, most tektites are black or dark brown, while Moldavites are various shades of translucent green. This translucence is due to the favorable fact that, among tektites,

Three examples showing varying patterns of sculptation in Moldavites

Moldavites contain the lowest amounts of iron oxides and other coloring oxides, along with the highest amounts of silica and potassium oxide. The iron content, in combination with the aluminum, is the largest factor in regard to their green color.

Moldavites often contain bubbles, and it has been determined that at least some of these bubbles contain a rather rarified vacuum, equaling the air pressure of a height of around twenty kilometers. The most recent theories of Moldavite's origins posit that the vapor which condensed into molten droplets was carried as high as fifty kilometers or more by the impact explosion. The bubbles of near-vacuum were originally seen as evidence of an extraterrestrial origin for Moldavites. However, it has been pointed out that vacuum bubbles can form in cooling glass even at sea level, so the evidence is inconclusive.

Theories on the Origin of Moldavite

Particularly challenging to all concerned has been the task of determining the origin of Moldavites, and of tektites in general. Various theories have held sway for a time, though in recent years scientists have begun to reach a consensus. But I'll begin with a list of the theories.

Konta and Saul in 1976 (after Mason, 1962) provided the following table summarizing various hypotheses concerning the origin of tektites.

1. Tektites have been formed from terrestrial materials by:

   a. Impact of (a) meteorites (b) comets.

   b. Lightning (a) fusing soils (b) fusing dust particles in the atmosphere.

   c. Natural fires: burning straw, forest fires, burning coal seams, etc.

   d. Volcanic activity.

   e. Human activity: furnace slags, glassworks, etc.

2. Tektites are of extraterrestrial origin; they came from:

   a. The Moon, from (a) lunar volcanoes (b) splashed from meteorite impact.

   b. Comets.

   c. A disrupted planetary body having a glassy surface layer.

   d. Meteorite consisting of free Si, Al, Mg, etc.

   e. Stony meteorites by fusion in the Earth's atmosphere.

There are different and variously powerful objections to each of these ideas. For instance, both the melting temperature of Moldavite, and especially its age, rule out its production by human activity. Natural fires cannot have produced the aerodynamic shapes. Crucial differences in chemical composition, especially Moldavite's extremely low water content, show that the stones cannot be volcanic. Lightning can be ruled out because of the aerodynamic shapes, the size and distribution of the strewn fields, and the sheer quantities of tektites formed in one area at one time. For terrestrial origin, this leaves the possible formation by the impact of meteorite or comets.

Many scientists have objected to the extraterrestrial origin theory of tektites. In the case of Moldavite, the small area in which they are found would mean that the fall from space would have had to be focused by some as yet unknown means. Others say that tektites cannot be meteorites because they seem not to have been subjected to the bombardment of cosmic rays that is characteristic of objects which have been in space for a long time.

One school of thought, originally proposed by Bouska, holds that the Moldavites are a product of the impact of a huge meteorite or asteroid that hit the Earth at the site of what is now called the Ries crater. This theory states that early sediment was melted, transformed into Moldavite, and thrown by the force of impact the many miles to the sites where it is now found. The chemical similarity of Moldavite to the surface sediments of the Ries area supports this idea. Furthermore, the age of the Ries crater has been calculated to be about the same as that of the Moldavites.

However, as Konta and Saul point out, there are problems: "Any theorizing along these lines must, however, take into account a troublesome aerodynamic consideration, namely, that tektites are invariably small and the Earth's atmosphere is large, and the launching, splashing, or throwing of the tektites in a liquid or solid form represents a problem analogous to throwing a feather a considerable distance." In other words, the distances that Moldavites and other tektites would have had to fly through the friction of the air after their hypothesized impact origin are impossible. Proponents of the impact theory try to explain this by imagining that the incoming meteorite or comet created a "vacuum tunnel" or hole in the atmosphere which would have lasted long enough for the Moldavites or other tektites to be thrown up and carried to their eventual landing places. The Australian tektites present a problem for the impact formation theory, for their strewn field is huge and, moreover, a number of these tektites have been fused or melted twice, which would indicate one melting on their origin and another during their fall through the atmosphere. Even Bouska admits the possibility of an extraterrestrial (in his mind, lunar) origin for the Australian tektites.

Other problems with the Ries impact theory for the origin of Moldavite are brought up by Rost. Study of the crater has uncovered at the site impact glasses (glass objects known to have been created by the crater-forming impact) which are chemically dissimilar to Moldavite. Rost states, ". . . it has not yet been explained how it could have occurred that the Moldavites have been perfectly separated from the glasses of the Ries crater. In addition, serious chemical differences exist between the chemical composition of the rocks from Ries and that of Moldavites." If Moldavites were formed by a meteoric or asteroidal impact other than the ones at Ries, the site of the crater has yet to be found.

John O'Keefe has put forth a theory that tektites were formed on the Moon as glass ejected from erupting lunar volcanoes. The relative similarity of tektites to earthly volcanic glass supports this idea. Also, the extremely low water content of Moldavites and other tektites, as well as the internal vacuum bubbles, make sense in this context. Some scientists object to this theory on the basis that there is no currently understood mechanism by which Moldavites could have come all the way from the Moon and yet have dispersed over so small an area.

Mr. Henry Hicks has sent to my attention a fact sheet from NASA's Ames research center, also postulating a lunar-origin for tektites. The NASA paper links the fall of Australian and Southeast Asian tektites, some 700,000 years ago, to the meteoric impact on the Moon which formed the crater Tycho. This theory, credited to Dr. Dean Chapman, pictures a crash on the Moon of a nickel-iron body some three miles in diameter, the force of which would have fused and melted lunar rock, throwing some of it outside the Moon's gravity, and finally to the Earth: "Reflection of sunlight from billions of glass objects diffused through space would have presented a light spectacle in the sky for many nights. To this was added a half-day-long rumble of continuous sonic booms as the tektites arrived and entered the atmosphere. Thick-browed Java man, whose fossil bones have been found with tektites, undoubtedly witnessed this extraordinary celestial event." The article also states that tektites have been found to be similar in composition to rock around Tycho's rim, and that the idea of formation by meteoric impact is supported by bits of nickel-iron found within tektites. However well this theory explains the Australian/Asian tektite fall, it still lacks an explanation for the small size of the Moldavite strewn fields. Both lunar theories suffer from the absence of chemical or isotopic similarity of tektites to the lunar rocks brought back by the Apollo program.

Going back to the terrestrial impact theory, two independent authors, Konta and Gentner, suggested in 1971 that the Moldavite material formed from condensation of silicate vapors. In this scenario from Konta and Saul in 1976, " . . . terrestrial silicate material evaporated during the thermal shock which followed the impact of a large cosmic body. During the explosive ejection, the gaseous silicate phase seized some of the liquid and solid phases and Quartz grains, in particular lechatelierite. In the opinion of both authors Moldavites were formed during the condensation of silicate vapors during their passage through the atmosphere." This theory could explain the chemical differences between Moldavites and the impact glasses of Ries, but it does not address directly the means by which the objects could have reached their resting places. Further, no examples were given demonstrating the occurrence of such silica condensation, which might, for instance, be expected from nuclear explosions.

A novel explanation for the origin of tektites was offered by Barnes in 1958. Taking into account the various tektite characteristics, including age, distribution, size, shape, chemical composition, flow structure, occurrence of lechatelierite particles, and the two periods of melting, he compared these to various theories of tektite origin. Among theories of terrestrial origin, he included volcanic, lightning, atomic explosion, and the impact theories—meteoric, cometary, and asteroidal. Among theories of extraterrestrial origin, he included the lunar theories of volcanic and impact events, as well as asteroids colliding with one another, and the possible destruction of a planet similar to Earth.

According to his analysis, the only scenario which could account for all the observed characteristics of tektites was that of the destruction of an earthlike planet. This rather fanciful theory has been superseded in recent years, but I must smile and say that it would at least explain Moldavite's uncanny resemblance to Kryptonite!

In a *Scientific American* article in July of 1967, Bill P. Glass and Bruce C. Heezen correlate the occurrence of tektites with incidents of geomagnetic reversal. They maintain that the poles of the Earth's magnetic field have reversed many times, and they specifically link one such reversal with the Pacific tektite fall of 700,000 years ago. They also adhere to the extraterrestrial theory of the origin of tektites. In support of this argument, they relate the story of the fireball explosion above a forest in the Tunguska Valley of Siberia in 1908. Tiny glassy spherules similar to tektites fell from the sky, but no impact craters or recognizable meteorites were ever found. On November 8, 1988, an article appeared in the *New York Times,* linking the crash event that formed the Ries crater (and purportedly created the rain of the Moldavites) to a geomagnetic reversal about 14.8 million years ago.

An Improved Theory?

Recently, the Institute of Geology of the Czech Academy of Sciences produced what they termed "An Improved Theory of Moldavite Formation." This is what they proposed:

> *According to the generally accepted theory, moldavites were formed at high pressures and temperatures from superficial Tertiary sediments in the Ries area in Germany during an impact of a huge meteorite 14.75 million years ago. A giant crater is [there] to remind [us] of this meteorite impact. The study published in the Geochimica et Cosmochimica Acta journal focused on a detailed comparison of chemical composition of moldavites and their presumed parent rocks located at the impact site. The analyses confirmed the known marked discrepancies in the contents of many elements between the source materials and moldavites. These discrepancies were now explained by an innovated model of moldavite origin. Material which functioned as the source for moldavites included, besides Tertiary sediments, also some amounts of organic material and soil. Material ejected from the impact site at a speed of several kilometres per second was subjected to complex interactions between the melt and the part of the ejected mass transferred into plasma. The key motive of the new model is the disintegration of melt into fine micro-drops due to the escape of volatile compounds. It was the forming of micro-drops which was responsible for the loss of some volatile elements as well as for the enrichment in other elements which condensed on their surface or had the form of separate drops. Moldavites, as found today, were then formed by merging of fine drops and by the formation of larger bodies in the process of mass transport above the level of the atmosphere. Finally, they were deposited mostly in the territory of the present Czech Republic.*

I particularly like this theory because it offers resolutions for many of the incongruities between the various competing hypotheses. Personally, I also appreciate the recognition that the impact of the asteroid/meteorite would have churned up organic matter as well as mineral materials. Metaphysically, this might relate to Moldavite's link with the living world. Another aspect of this theory that sounds correct to me is the envisioning of Moldavite forming from vaporized plasma and micro-drops, ultimately condensing like raindrops into molten glass "precipitation."

The entire theory can be found online here: https://www.gli.cas.cz/en/improved-theory-moldavite-formation-1

However one views the origins of Moldavite and other tektites, it is interesting to contemplate that their arrivals have been times of tremendous physical shifts and upheavals for the Earth. On the level of consciousness, we might also agree that the arrival of Moldavite into one's life can correspond with inner transformations—"upheavals"—leading to accelerated spiritual growth. It was certainly true for me, and for many others. Besides my own saga, which is told throughout this book, a number of people share their experiences in Chapter 18: The Moldavite Stories.

CHAPTER 7

STONE OF THE HOLY GRAIL

Some traditions hold that the Grail originated as a jewel—an emerald—from the crown of the Light Bringer, Lucifer, the Angel of the Morning, which fell from heaven during the war between angels.

—John Matthews, *At the Table of the Grail*

Page from an early illustrated copy of *le Conte du Graal,* an unfinished romance written by Chrétien de Troyes around 1190

O n the day I first discovered the existence of Moldavite, in George Bruce's article in a 1958 *Lapidary Journal,* one line leaped off the page at me. The author was using the term *agni mani,* meaning "fire pearl," to refer to the mysterious celestial objects known as tektites, of which Moldavite is the only gem-quality subgroup. In recounting the legends and historical stories around these stones, Bruce told the story of an encounter between "the learned Professor Nicholas Roerich" and the Baron Richard Johan der Touche-Skadding, in the Kulu Valley of Tibet. The professor had noticed the agni mani which the baron wore in a ring, and much of their discussion centered around the stones and their mythic parallels. The professor spoke of the most sacred jewel in all Tibet, the Stone of Shambala, to which the Tibetans had attributed a celestial origin, believing it came from the constellation of Orion. The author continues, "Professor Roerich went so far as to draw a close analogy between the Stone of Shambala and the *agni mani,* further asserting it was the same stone contained in the Holy Grail."

The words rang in my mind, even though I had never heard of Nicholas Roerich, even though I had only the vague notion that the Holy Grail was some kind of sacred cup that knights were always looking for and which nobody ever found. In the months that followed, when I occasionally showed the article to someone, I found myself pointing out that line. Sometimes when I spoke about it, my listener would have a bit of information for me. Thus I learned that Nicholas Roerich was a world traveler, mystic, author, painter, proponent of world peace, and founder of the school of Agni

Yoga. (There is, by the way, a museum of his paintings in New York City. Most of them have mystical themes, and both Kathy and I have found them to be deeply moving.) Well and good. This was someone whose opinion I could respect, but what was the Holy Grail?

This question led Kathy and me into the study of the Grail legend and in the course of that study, to the discovery of resonances within our own souls to the mythic truths of that legend. For us, the inquiry into Moldavite became a kind of Grail quest, wherein the moments of grace we experienced with the stones functioned as points of contact with a deeper reality in which we acted out our own myth. In this chapter we will concentrate on the correspondences of Moldavite to the Stone of the Holy Grail, within the context of the legend as a whole. Retelling the entire Grail story is outside the scope of this book, but for those interested, I suggest that opening to the Grail through study and meditation can be an illumination.

In her book *The Grail Legend*, Emma Jung outlines the myth:

> *The story is known to everyone, at least in its general outlines. A mysterious, life preserving and sustenance dispensing object or vessel is guarded by a King in a castle that is difficult to find. The King is either lame or sick and the surrounding countryside is devastated. The King can only be restored to health if a knight of conspicuous excellence finds the castle and at the first sight of what he sees there asks a certain question. Should he neglect to put this question, then everything will remain as it was before, the castle will vanish and the knight will have to start out once more upon the search. Should he finally succeed, after much wandering and many adventures, in finding the Grail Castle again, and should he then ask the question, the King will be restored to health, the land will begin to grow green, and the hero will become the guardian of the Grail from that time on.*

Portrait of Wolfram von Eschenbach from the Codex Manesse, c. 1300

Let us attempt, for a moment, to see this myth in modern terms. If there are parallels here and now to the Grail story, they may shed light on our current situation. For certain, we can see that we live on a beautiful planet that is fast becoming a wasteland. And, like the King, all of us are wounded by various events in our lives, and cut off, as was the King in the story, from the deepest parts of ourselves. (He was usually described as being wounded in the thighs, hips, or genitals.) Without the wisdom and energy of our deepest consciousness, all we can do is float around in a superficial dream of life, while our kingdom, both physical and spiritual, atrophies around us. Yet sometimes within us there arises the impulse to the heroic, an innocent (often, to others, foolish) desire and willingness to seek out meaning beneath the surface of our trivialized world—to search for something wonderful.

Through innocence, luck, perseverance, and grace, we may come upon the states of awareness that correspond to the magical Grail Castle. At that point, we experience our consciousness at the state of critical mass, in which we may follow the heart's impulse and act without hesitation. Through this, we achieve the inner transformation which brings us into union with our Deep Self, which heals us and thereby, our world. If we do not "ask the question"—if we do not move upon that moment—the critical mass state passes, and we must search for the means to reach it once again. Should we find it and then ask the right questions, our Deep Self rises to fill us with Light and Grace overflowing. In this profound shift, the kingdoms of our lives and world are restored. We then become the guardians and sharers of the Light, our responsibility being to bring our brothers and sisters also to the Grail, to the inner union with God.

But where, in our modern story, is the "mysterious, life preserving and sustenance dispensing object?" For though the achievement of the Grail may be seen as the conscious union with God, the legend depicts the Grail as an object, the vehicle of Grace, the precious vessel through which divine consciousness comes into us.

Some of the legends, such as de Troyes' romance, picture the Grail as a chalice, often the cup used by Christ at the Last Supper. Others say it is a stone, an Emerald that fell from the sky. The first myth-maker to describe the Grail in this way was the German Minnesinger Wolfram von Eschenbach.

In his tale, the Grail was not a cup, but a mystical green stone. Interestingly, Eschenbach lived in Bavaria, and the Ries crater, from which Moldavite was born, is in western Bavaria. Although he could not have known of Moldavite's origin, he may have known of Moldavite, or it seems possible to me that he could have unconsciously tapped into Moldavite's essential qualities in the inner realms. This is speculation, but it is beguiling that Wolfram changed the original story told by de Troyes and made the Grail a green gem from the heavens.

In either case, it is remarkable that a physical object would be the catalyst for a divine experience. Some might argue that the object is but a symbol in the inner myth. Yet it is also true that the themes of myth work themselves out in life, and there have been many human beings who have gone on physical journeys in search of a tangible Grail. The strength of the connection with that manifested form of the Grail would depend a great deal upon the state of consciousness of the observer—one must be innocent, trusting, and open, like the Grail knight. Guilelessness that some might judge as naïveté is an essential quality for one to be able to see and recognize the Grail when it appears. Thus the stone of the Grail would be, as Arnold of Villanova declared, "despised by fools, the more cherished by the wise."

If it is true that a person needs to reach a certain inner state in order to resonate with the Grail, it could very well be that the Grail object has long been within our midst without our knowing it. Witness, for instance, the rise, over the past few decades, of people's awareness of stone energies. One needs to be open to them, in a way that disbelievers might call naïve, in order to perceive and recognize these subtle currents. Yet, as the Grail myth describes, the recognition can be transformative.

Gradually I have come to think that this whole constellation of ideas about the Grail connects to Moldavite. I offer here some of the many correspondences:

The first book I discovered about the Grail was *The Grail: Quest for the Eternal* by John Matthews. In his commentary I came upon the following quote:

> In Parzival *[The story of the Grail as told by the thirteenth century Minnesinger Wolfram von Eschenbach] the Grail is described not as a cup, but as, "a stone of the purest kind . . . called* lapsit exillas *. . . There never was human so ill that if he one day sees that stone, he cannot die within the week that follows . . . and though he should see the stone for two hundred years his appearance will never change, save that his hair might perhaps turn grey."*
>
> *This description has always puzzled scholars, and various attempts have been made to suggest what Wolfram meant by* Lapsit exillas. *Did he perhaps mean to write* lapis lapsus ex caelis, *the "stone fallen from heaven?" That would seem to be borne out by a further statement in* Parzival *that the stone was a jewel, an emerald which fell from the crown of Lucifer during the war between God and Satan, and which was brought to earth by angels who remained neutral. Some translators interpret the emerald as being from Lucifer's forehead rather than his crown, and have linked this with a pearl fixed in the brow of the Indian god Shiva. Called the* Urna, *this stone signified the sense of eternity belonging to the god, and is like to the Third Eye with which one may see inward to knowledge and perfection. Thus, without the emerald, Lucifer is doomed to inhabit the earth as a manifestation of evil, while the stone itself becomes a fallen image which can be raised up only by the Grail quest and redeemed in the act of healing performed by Percival in its name.*

Reading this, I was immediately struck by the close correlations with Moldavite. That the Grail might be a "stone fallen from heaven" was interesting in itself, but that it was also described as a gem—and an emerald—was truly exciting. Translucent green Moldavite is the only known stone on Earth that fits such a description! Further, the idea of the Grail stone having been brought to Earth by angels matches with the intuition of many Moldavite users that the stones were sent to Earth as a spiritual gift. The Grail stone as gem of the third eye corresponds to what we and the majority of users feel is a key activation point in the use of Moldavite. The act of spiritual healing also fits, for many people began spontaneously doing healing work with Moldavite, even though we did not at first write about it. Later Kathy and I also began to use it for self-healing. It is most provocative to consider that in the Grail story the act of healing redeems the stone itself while it brings renewed life to the wounded king/patient, as well as higher consciousness to the healer.

So it is with Moldavite. For hundreds, if not thousands of years, these celestial gems sat in relative obscurity and have only come to light in recent times. These past few decades have also seen the emergence of many spiritual healers and crystal users. The great healing work of our time is the healing of our planet and our souls. Performed in the name of the Grail, in the name of our sacred partnership with God, this healing can redeem even the evil that has held sway for so long, as well as ourselves and the sacred talisman of our work. For Kathy and I, and perhaps for many of you, that talisman is the Moldavite.

We also find references to the Grail as the Emerald that fell from the sky in Emma Jung's work, *The Grail Legend*, wherein she equates the Stone of the Grail to the Philosopher's Stone, the realization of which was the goal of ancient alchemy:

King Arthur and his knights at the Round Table, with the Holy Grail in the center. Note the green gems studding the sacred chalice, which is borne by angels, and the green, chalice-shaped pillar behind the King.

The alchemistic equation of the vessel with its contents, the stone, also turns up, strangely enough, in the Grail story. In Wolfram von Eschenbach, the Grail is called a stone of which it is said:

> *Upon a deep green achmardi she bore the perfection of paradise both root and branch. This was a thing called the Grail, which surpasses all earthly perfection.*

And further on:

> *They [the knights of the Grail] live from a stone of purest kind. If you do not know it, it shall be named to you. It is called* lapsit exillis.

This *lapsit exillis . . .* has caused much speculation. Because of the reading *lapsit ex coelis* [stone out of the heavens] there was a wish to interpret the Grail as a meteorite, for in antiquity meteorites were considered to be stones with a soul. [These were] sacred stones that were assumed to possess divine life, stones with a soul, created by Uranos; these, set up in holy places, were venerated with annointings and garlands, or, in the hands of private persons, were used for diverse superstitions, for magic, and for fortunetelling. They were meteorite stones fallen from the sky.

The depiction of the Grail stone specifically as a meteorite is another point of contact with Moldavite. Meteorites have, of course, long been viewed as sacred objects. King Arthur's sword, Excalibur, said to have been forged from an iron meteorite, was well known for its magical properties. And, of course, the legend of King Arthur and the Knights of the Round Table is tightly woven in with the Grail legend.

The idea of "stones with a soul" fits well with a perception of some users that specific Moldavite stones have their own "personality" or energy pattern. We have witnessed many times the resonance of specific pieces of Moldavite with different individuals, and the lack of resonance of the same pieces with others, who subsequently found "their" piece. Jung's described use of meteorites for "magic and fortune-telling" hints at the mystical experiences many people have had with Moldavite. Furthermore, the motif of a divine stone from the heavens recurs in numerous other myths. Later in John Matthew's book, we find that such a stone occupies a central position in the Islamic faith:

> But there is still another stone that could have influenced Wolfram's conception of the Grail. This is the Black Stone, sacred to the Islamic religion, which stands at the center of Mecca, and toward which the faithful offer prayers from whatever part of the world they happen to be in. Like the emerald which fell to the earth, the Black Stone was believed to have been a meteorite which fell out of the sky in the distant past. It became an object of worship until the time of Mohammed, who denounced its use as such and declared that it should be used as a source of communication with God. According to Koranic sources, it was said to have been given to Ishmael by the angel Gabriel at the time of the rebuilding of the Ka'aba, or 'cubic house', where the stone was afterwards kept. In earlier times, it was said to have represented the triple-aspected mother goddess, the Mater Dea, who with the god Hubal was offered sacrifices of blood—a fact which becomes significant when considered in connection with the Grail. Interestingly, the color green attributed by Wolfram to the Grail stone is associated with Venus, whose day, Friday, is the Islamic Sabbath; green is also the color associated with the Prophet and is therefore sacred.

Here we see a divine meteoric stone *in physical embodiment* that services as central focus to one of the world's great religions. Mohammed said it should be used for communication with God. Kathy's first experience with Moldavite was of going out into the stars and becoming one with the universe, and with the Light that underlies the universe. She came back with one word—communication. Unlike the Ka'aba stone, Moldavite, I feel, has an energy of wholeness that harmonizes the different sexes, rather than a male or female energy. It is interesting to see in the quote above that the sacred green of the celestial Grail stone is also sacred in Islam. In another excerpt from Jung we see that Mohammed himself may have had a vision of the Grail:

> The writer Ibn Malik recounts a vision of Mohammed's which the latter commanded Malik to describe as follows: "on the night when I ascended to Heaven I glimpsed, under a canopy, a goblet of such penetrating brightness that all seven heavens were illuminated by it. Around the goblet was a prayer written in green characters. [According to a second manuscript the goblet itself was green.] . . . A voice declared, 'oh, Mohammed, the All Highest God has created this goblet for thine enlightenment.'"

In Mohammed's vision, the Grail is a green goblet of incredible brightness, an object created by God for enlightenment. This fits the perception of Moldavite as a green gem of high spiritual attunement, but what about the image of the goblet? This question runs throughout my study of the legend. We see the two archetypal images—the chalice and the sacred gem from the heavens. A quote from John Matthews may provide the resolution of these parallel themes: "The Grail itself was described by Wolfram as

The Ka'aba, or "cubic house" in Mecca, where the Black Stone from the heavens is housed

a stone and as an emerald from the crown of Lucifer which fell with him from heaven, and from which the cup was later carved."

These ideas raise provocative questions when viewed with an eye to Moldavite. Could a large piece of this green celestial gem have been carved into a physical cup, an actual material Grail chalice? Ultimately, we can only speculate, but it is interesting, in light of this, to consider the following quote from Emma Jung:

> *The fact that the Grail was considered to be a real object engendered the very widely held belief that it was identical with the vessel known as the* Sacro Cantino, *a bowl, ostensibly of emerald, brought back as plunder and payment by the Genoese after the siege of Caesara in 1101. A sixteenth-century Genoese chronicle in the Library at Berne says that this exceedingly precious bowl was called the Saint Graal and that according to some it was a platter Christ had used at the Last Supper with his disciples, but that others held that it was the vessel from which King Arthur ate, very devoutly, at important ceremonies with the Companions of the Round Table. Napoleon took it to Paris, where under expert examination it was found not to be emerald at all but simply molded glass.*

Lovers of Moldavite, unlike Napoleon, may not have been disappointed to find that the bowl was glass. "What kind of glass?" they might have asked, for Moldavite is classed as a natural glass, an amorphous crystal. My own intuition makes me wonder, if the story is true, whether a copy of the true bowl might have been substituted, to keep it out of Napoleon's hands, or whether the bowl in question may itself have been Moldavite. This is all speculation, but the connection of the precious green Grail stone (and its mythic parallels) to the *sacro cantino* is further illustrated by Jung:

> *Charlemagne's table was copied from Solomon's famous table which, according to legend, was made, like the Genoese* sacro cantino, *from a gigantic emerald, was three hundred and sixty-five feet long and most richly set with pearls and precious stones . . . [There was] known to Wolfram von Eschenbach . . . [an account of] a similar table, perhaps the same one, made from an emerald. The green color seems to be significant, since in Wolfram the Grail is also carried in on a green* achmardi *[fine silk cloth]. As the color of vegetation and in a wider sense, of life, green is obviously in harmony with the nature of the Grail. The land begins to show green again, when in the Grail castle, Gauvain asks the question about the lance. In ecclesiastical*

Hand-made porcelain chalice with raw Moldavites embedded on the outside, and in the center of the cup. I commissioned a ceramic artist to create this piece, with the intention of building energetic resonance between the Grail in the spiritual realm and this physical "Grail." It is a symbolic gesture of uniting Heaven and Earth.

symbolism green is the color of the Holy Ghost, or the anima mundi *[Soul of the World], and in the language of the mystics it is the universal color of divinity.*

In another interesting correspondence, when I was researching the chapter on the scientific data about Moldavite, I came across the following quote in the book *Moldavites* by the Czechoslovakian scientist Vladimir Bouska: "In the Netolice (part of the Czech Republic) area, an ostensory is said to have existed in the past century adorned with Moldavites, but it did not remain preserved." Upon looking up the definition of "ostensory," I found it was synonymous with "monstrance," which is "a vessel in which the consecrated Host is exposed for the veneration of the faithful." In other words, it is a holy chalice—a Grail cup. Thus we can conclude that in history there has been at least one real Moldavite Grail chalice. But what became of it, and whether there were any others, remains a mystery.

I find it interesting that our actions so often fall into line with the images of myth. Some of our earliest Moldavite jewelry pieces combine the green Moldavite with Amethyst crystals, and the strength of the Moldavite/Amethyst combination is preferred by many people to the present day. In addition, the deeper we go into the Grail legend and its parallels, the more frequently we see the color green associated with the Divine. As a stone, it is usually called an Emerald. However, when it is also said that the Emerald fell from the sky, the only counterpart in the material world is Moldavite. Further discussing the significance of the Emerald and the green, Jung states:

> To precious stones it [Emerald] is what gold is to metals, an everlasting, incorruptible substance, the goal of the opus. In this context the green color actually achieves the meaning of life itself. In the alchemical texts the benedicta viriditas (the blessed green) also services as a sign of the beginning of the reanimation of the material.

Thus we are brought to another of the spiritual dimensions surrounding the archetype of the sacred Grail stone, and this is the realm of alchemy. Jung tells us:

> The Grail of the alchemist was also a stone, the lapis philosophorum, or philosopher's stone. It too was a vessel of transformation and higher consciousness, a vessel identical with its contents.

And further on:

> The qualities mentioned, especially the bestowal of youth and longevity, are attributed to the Grail in almost all the versions. They are the same properties to the lapis philosophorum.

Yet another connection exists in the association of the Grail stone with the legendary Phoenix, as Jung states:

> That Wolfram was not unacquainted with alchemical ideas may also be deduced from the description of the Grail as the stone through whose power the phoenix is consumed by fire in order to rise again from the ashes. This allegorical figure played an important role in alchemy.

This same concept is reflected in the line from one of the Grail texts which states, "Thus our stone, that is the flask of fire, is created from fire."

And from Matthews:

[Wolfram von Eschenbach] says that the power of the Grail stone is the same as that which enables the phoenix to immolate itself and be reborn from its own ashes. The phoenix was frequently used as a symbol of the lapis *[the alchemical Philosophers' Stone] and was depicted as hovering over it. It is also a symbol of transfiguration in its own right and, like the Grail, stands for spiritual renewal.*

Moldavite connects with these ideas at many points, both in terms of what is scientifically known about it, and in terms of people's experience. Like the phoenix the physical Moldavite itself was consumed by fire, and reborn in fire. In fact, the predominant scientific theory of Moldavite's origin puts forth the idea that the silica-rich earthly stone from which it was formed was *vaporized* as it was thrown up in the meteoric impact, only to be reformed anew in the air as it descended once again. Shades of the phoenix!

The phoenix imagery also occurred to Kathy long before we investigated the legend of the Grail. In fact, during the first few months our store was open, a gem carver happened to come in, and, as we fell into conversation with him, we decided to have him carve a Moldavite for Kathy. They chose a raw stone, and as they looked, both of them saw the image of the Phoenix within it. The carving was done, and the piece was one of the prizes of our collection.

The fiery origin of Moldavite and other tektites is also reflected in their Sanskrit name, *agni mani,* which means "fire pearl." In addition, the transformation and higher consciousness attributed to the *lapis philosophorum* [Philosophers' Stone] are primary traits associated with Moldavite by many who use it.

From the beginning of our work with these stones, we have seen that our own experiences as well as the reactions of sensitive people to Moldavite form close parallels to the states engendered by exposure to the Grail. In fact, without these powerful here-and-now experiences, we would never have investigated Moldavite or noted the correlations to the Grail legend.

Let us look first at the effects of making contact with the Grail. Matthews states, "Like the *lapis philosophorum* and the Black Stone, the Grail was an object of supernatural origin and activity involving the prolonging of life, the birth of the divine child, the quest for wisdom and knowledge, and direct communication with God."

Emma Jung offers a longer list:

If all its various aspects are summarized, whether as a wonderful stone, as a vessel or as a relic, the Grail is found to possess the following characteristics. It dispenses material food accordingly to taste and imparts spiritual solace. It preserves youth and generally maintains life. In one instance it heals knights wounded in battle. It radiates light and a sweet fragrance, it rejoices the heart, and whoever sees it can commit no sin that day. It discriminates between good and evil. To the un-baptized it remains invisible. It makes known the will of God by means of writing which appears upon it. Only he who is destined by heaven and whose name is written thereon can find the Grail. Nor does it allow its defender to have any loves other than the one the Grail prescribes for him . . . It is as though the vessel were expressing an opinion on the man's choice in love; in other words, it guides his relation to the anima.

In regard to Moldavite and its corresponding properties, the Grail's dispensing of food according to taste can be symbolically equated to the way in which Moldavite acts to bring spiritual sustenance into one's life, according to the needs of the person. I can't say whether it maintains youth, but I and many others have felt an increase in physical energy with Moldavite's use. Kathy and I have used it for healing ourselves, and we have numerous reports from others about their healings. In our stores, our booths at gem and mineral shows, and at my workshops, we have many times watched as exposure to Moldavite engendered physiological changes in people, including flushing, a sense of electrical tingling, pulling sensations at various chakra points, laughter, tears, and emotional release. These symptoms seem to point to an opening of one's energies taking place as the high vibration of Moldavite interacts with the vibration of the individual.

Artist's depiction of Percival holding aloft the Grail chalice, while divine Light and the dove of the Holy Spirit descend. Symbolically, this image depicts the union of Heaven and Earth—the ultimate purpose of the Grail quest.

Many people who meditate with Moldavite experience seeing inner Light, or being in union with Light. On two occasions, Kathy and I have gone into deep meditations with Moldavite and have emerged to the scent of roses when there were no flowers in the room. In terms of "writing" of the will of God, I can report only that the etched patterns on certain raw stones look like strange symbols. Although one certainly doesn't need to be baptized to see or feel the energy of Moldavite, its energy is revealed immediately to some (as in Kathy's case), and is veiled to others (as in my own case) for weeks or months. In my situation, those months coincided with a period of self-purification and spiritual renewal.

In terms of its corrective effects regarding the "commission of sin," one of Molda-vite's most significant properties seems to be the stimulation and acceleration of one's spiritual path. In my own case, there was a sudden awakening to the spiritual dimension in my life at the time I first came into contact with Moldavite. It was as if I could feel the universe listening to my choices, and I could see more clearly the good and bad consequences. I could no longer plead ignorance, and when I did err, the karmic consequences were almost instant. I also had the experience of living in a state of grace, as I felt the positive avenue of my spiritual development opening before me. In the Moldavite Stories chapter of this book (Chapter 18), there are a number of tales similar to mine.

Curiously, even the trait of the Grail stone's expressing a preference about one's choice in love parallels the experience some have reported with Moldavite. In my own case, the first several months of exposure to Moldavite saw the ending of an unhappy marriage and the beginning of my relationship with Kathy. In numerous anecdotes told to us, and in some of the Moldavite stories we received, the entry of Moldavite coincided with a clearing of consciousness that made painfully obvious the shortcomings of certain relationships and, in some cases, presaged the beginnings of deeper and more spiritual ones.

From my work with Moldavite and from my research on the Grail, it is clear that both Moldavite and the legendary Grail stone catalyze a deep inner shift in the individual that brings about myriad reactions and effects. My experience with Moldavite has been that it acts in resonance with one's own energies to quicken the path of one's spiritual unfoldment. This can manifest in as many ways as necessary—from physical cleansing to the purging of relationships, from visions of the Light to changes of career, from spontaneous healing to instant karma. When we associate with Moldavite, our blockages are loosened and we become more conscious of our choices. Thus our journey to wholeness and fully awakened awareness is accelerated.

In the story of the Grail, Percival begins in innocence and almost non-existent self-awareness. Upon exposure to the Grail, his evolution truly begins. By the end of the tale, he has reached the transcendent consciousness that allows him to become king of the Grail Castle—the sovereign ruler of his own wholeness. This process also heals the sundered opposites of light and darkness through the process of spiritual redemption. Emma Jung says this about the Grail:

> *From one point of view, the Grail can also be taken as an image of the* transcendent function. *By this term [Carl] Jung understands the psychic synthesis of consciousness and unconsciousness through which it becomes possible for the psychic totality, the Self, to come into consciousness.*

And further on:

> *The* Lapis *[Stone of the Grail, and Philosopher's Stone] may therefore be understood as a symbol of the inner Christ, a God in man. Looked at from this point of view, the stone represents a further development of the Christ symbol, reaching downward into matter.*

The conscious emergence of the Self, the human/Divine Self, *in the physical world,* is seen as the fulfilment—the achievement of the Grail. This certainly is the goal of many of us who have chosen what we call a spiritual path. In my own most powerful Moldavite meditation, this was the experience—I felt a presence come into me that could only be described as living Light, whose wisdom was limitless, whose mode was joy, and whose nature was compassion. And yet I felt certain that it was also somehow myself. In Kathy's Moldavite meditation at Bell Rock, Arizona, she too became identified with the living Light. In reading the Moldavite Stories chapter, you will find other tales that echo similar moments. And in the profound peace of all those moments, the problem of the struggle between light and darkness is resolved. Our shadows hold no power as they are dissolved in the compassion of the Light. Most, if not all of us, are to a degree enmeshed in the inner and outer struggles of everyday life. This simply shows that we have yet to complete our journeys. But now that we have seen the Grail within, we know where we are going. With or without a sacred talisman such as Moldavite, all of humanity are called to the inner Grail. As Emma Jung puts it:

> *It is as if Percival were in himself the embodiment of that natural man who is faced with the problem of evil and the relation to the feminine, and through these with the task of a greater development of his own consciousness, so that by many a circuitous route he accomplishes the redemption of the Grail Kingdom, whose ruler he finally becomes. It is very pertinent in the story that the land to be redeemed is bound up with just those early days of Christianity when the Christ-image was crystallizing out of the matrix of the collective unconscious and at the same time, by its one-sided insistence on the light side, was casting off its shadow, the image of the Anti-Christ. It is as if a further enrichment of the symbol of the self, from out of that same matrix, were taking place in the Grail story, by which the continued tearing asunder of the opposites might be ended and their reconciliation striven for. For this task the individual human being serves as a* vessel, *for only when the opposites are reconciled in the single individual can they be united. The individual therefore becomes a receptacle for the transformation of the problem of the opposites in the image of God . . . each human being represents a place for transformation and a "vessel" in which God may come to consciousness.*

Thus it might be said that God needs us just as much as we need God—that the yearning for union is profoundly felt on both sides of the veil. Let us then as an act of compassion and love, offer ourselves in partnership to the Divine, who desires through us to express and be made manifest. This is beautifully put by John Matthews in his book, *At the Table of the Grail:*

> *In the centre of the Castle of the Grail, our own body, there is a shrine, and within it is to be found the Grail of the heart. We should indeed seek to know and understand*

that inhabitant. It is the fragment of the divine contained within each one of us—like the sparks of unfallen creation which the Gnostics saw entrapped within the flesh of the human envelope. This light shines within each one, and the true quest of the Grail consists in bringing the light to the surface, nourishing and feeding it until its radiance suffuses the world.

The call to life that evokes the Spirit—this is the core experience of working with Moldavite. It is also the call of the Grail. Beyond that, I would say that it is the call of our times. The reunification of ourselves with the realms of Light, the grounding of that Light upon the Earth plane, the living partnership of our local selves with our Divine Self—these are the goals of our transformation. In legend, the Grail was a catalyst for this experience. In the world of here-and-now, we have found, to our deep astonishment and gratitude, that Moldavite can serve as such a catalyst. Such transformations, of course, require our active participation as the key ingredient. But given that, we have in our hands a stone that, for many of us, can be a vehicle of grace. I am on this path myself and have not yet reached its end, if there is one. I therefore cannot write a conclusion to this tale. Instead, I invite you on a journey. Read these words with an ear for the resonance of your own truth—the truth your heart knows. If you heart urges you to begin that path, follow it. If you find upon your way a strange green stone, pick it up and see what happens.

This image of the Grail was carved into a temple wall. Notice the rays of Divine Light pouring out from behind it. I am reminded by this of the Great Central Sun, known esoterically as the Sun Behind the Sun, and my first Moldavite journey.

MOLDAVITE & THE EMERALD TABLET

Hermes Trismegistus with the Emerald Tablet

I n the Grail legend, the Stone of the Grail was described as an Emerald that fell from Heaven—a sacred object emanating fabulous spiritual powers. The story of the Emerald Tablet also describes a sacred stone of heavenly origin, this one having the secrets of the universe engraved on its surface. Those able to decode, understand, and receive the gifts of the Emerald Tablet were said to wield divine powers of transformation and healing.

Of course, what struck me about both of these legends was that they held as a central motif the image of a green stone that came from Heaven—a celestial Emerald. And in ancient times, any green gemstone may have been designated as "Emerald." The fact that Moldavite actually is a green gemstone that fell to Earth from the sky—revered as a sacred stone even in neolithic times—makes one wonder if it is somehow twined into the roots of these legends.

Over the years, as I have dug into the Grail legend and the writings of spiritual alchemy, the feeling of resonance between Moldavite and these ancient traditions has grown in me. One of the principles of alchemy is that the spiritual world communicates to us in symbols that manifest in the physical world. (For example, all synchronicities fall into this category.) As I consider Moldavite, there is, on the one hand, its unique and dramatic physical origin—an event that affected the whole Earth. On the other hand, there are legends such as those of the Holy Grail and the Emerald Tablet—mythic tales laden with symbolic meaning. Even though the creators of these legends cannot have consciously known about Moldavite's birth in a meteoric crash, these tales hold patterns that resonate so strongly with Moldavite's spiritual qualities that I feel there are connections I cannot ignore. In this chapter, we will look into the legend of the Emerald Tablet, and its potential link with Moldavite.

Although no modern-day people have seen the Emerald Tablet of Hermes Trismegistus, it is described as a slab of brilliant, crystalline green stone covered with Phoenician text in bas-relief. Viewed as the original source of hermeticism, gnosticism, Western alchemy, and science, the tablet is associated with the elusive Hermes Trismegistus, an ancient philosopher, healer, and sage, who was said in some texts to be a blend of human and god. References to him can be found in Renaissance, Christian, Islamic, Roman, and Greek literature.

The legend is recounted and interpreted in the book, *The Emerald Tablet* written by Dennis William Hauck. In it he wrote, "One of the most mysterious documents ever put before the eyes of man, the Emerald Tablet has been described as everything from a succinct summary of Neoplatonic philosophy to an extraterrestrial artifact or a gift from Atlantis." The tablet's central premise that "All is One," and that direct experience of the Divine is possible through meditation and psychological processes, became the foundations of Freemasonry, Theosophy, and esoteric schools such as The Golden Dawn.

Hermes Trismegistus was associated with Thoth, the Egyptian god of wisdom, writing, science, and magic. Thoth's qualities were identical to those of the Greek god Hermes. The name Hermes Trismegistus can be translated as "thrice great Hermes." So we can see the association of the human with the god. Thus, the Emerald Tablet of Hermes is understood as a divine object conveying divine wisdom, associated with a divine/human wisdom teacher.

Imaginative rendering of the Emerald Tablet, entitled Amphitheatrum sapientae aeternae (Amphitheater of eternal wisdom), by the alchemist Heinrich Khunrath (1606)

A Wikipedia article tells us:

The original source of the Emerald Tablet *is unknown . . . The oldest documentable source of the text is the* Book of Balinas the Wise on the Causes, *written in Arabic between the sixth and eighth centuries . . . In his book, Balinas frames the Emerald Tablet as ancient Hermetic wisdom. He tells his readers that he discovered the text in a vault below a statue of Hermes in Tyana, and that, inside the vault, an old corpse on a golden throne held the Emerald Tablet . . . [T]he* Tablet *became a mainstay of medieval and Renaissance alchemy. Commentaries and/or translations were published by, among others, Trithemius, Roger Bacon, Michael Maier, Albertus Magnus, and Isaac Newton. The concise text was a popular summary of alchemical principles, wherein the secrets of the philosopher's stone were thought to have been described . . . C.G. Jung identified* The Emerald Tablet *with a table made of green stone which he encountered in the first of a set of his dreams and visions beginning at the end of 1912, and climaxing in his writing* Seven Sermons to the Dead *in 1916.*

From this introduction, I want to move now to an Emerald Tablet translation named *Aurelium Occultae Philosophorum* (*Hidden Gold of the Philosophers*) by Georgio Beato, published in Frankfurt, Germany in 1610:

1. This is true and remote from all cover of falsehood.

2. Whatever is below is similar to that which is above. Through this the marvels of the work of one thing are procured and perfected.

3. Also, as all things are made from one, by the consideration of one, so all things were made from this one, by conjunction.

4. The father of it is the sun, the mother the moon.

5. The wind bore it in the womb. Its nurse is the earth, the mother of all perfection.

6a. Its power is perfected

7. If it is turned into earth,

7a. separate the earth from the fire, the subtle and thin from the crude and coarse, prudently, with modesty and wisdom.

8. This ascends from the earth into the sky and again descends from the sky to the earth, and receives the power and efficacy of things above and of things below.

9. By this means you will acquire the glory of the whole world, and so you will drive away all shadows and blindness.

10. For this by its fortitude snatches the palm from all other fortitude and power. For it is able to penetrate and subdue everything subtle and everything crude and hard.

11a. By this means the world was founded

12. and hence the marvelous conjunctions of it and admirable effects, since this is the way by which these marvels may be brought about.

13. And because of this they have called me Hermes Trismegistus since I have the three parts of the wisdom and Philosophy of the whole universe.

14. My speech is finished which I have spoken concerning the solar work.

Although we can't know with authority that Moldavite is the "stone" that constituted the Emerald Tablet—the foundation of alchemy—we can look at the translation and consider where there are correspondences. As an image, the Emerald Tablet was a green stone that was inscribed with these cryptic teachings from Hermes. As we go through the text line-by-line, it is important to view all of this through the lens of symbolic interpretation rather than literalism. We need to try and see this on multiple levels. One of the mysterious possibilities that has come to me is that Moldavite, which resonates with so much of the Emerald Tablet story, may be a sort of embodiment of the Tablet's wisdom. It seems to me that Moldavite has the ability to transmit the Emerald Tablet's essence. It would almost be as if Moldavite is *a manifestation of the same mystery* referred to in the Emerald Tablet. The similarities we see between Moldavite's properties and those described in the text of the Emerald Tablet work together to point toward that mystery.

So, let's go back and consider the text.

We can readily understand the ideas expressed in the first three lines, which affirm the alchemical dictum, As above, so below. In line 4, the statement, "The father of it is the sun, the mother the moon," is a provocative one. I can't think of a better way to poetically describe the nature of a meteorite!

The physical origins of Moldavite fit well with line 5: *"The wind bore it in the womb. Its nurse is the earth, the mother of all perfection."* Let us recall the scientific theory that the meteorite crash which generated Moldavite actually vaporized earthly and meteoric matter, propelling the vapors above the atmosphere. Then, as they cooled, the rock vapors condensed into molten glass, which eventually solidified as Moldavite. The blast from the collision sent the material hundreds of kilometers from the impact site. In this context, the lines from the Emerald Tablet apply perfectly to Moldavite. The wind indeed "carried it in its womb." And, of course, its "nurse"—that which "fed" and nourished it, is the Earth.

Lines 7 and 7a tell us: "If it is turned into earth, separate the earth from the fire, the subtle and thin from the crude and coarse, prudently, with modesty and wisdom." Following what is understood about Moldavite, I interpret this to mean that when the meteorite struck the ground, it was "turned into earth." In the next moment, there was a gigantic explosion with intense heat, able to vaporize rock and send it hurtling into the sky. Because the material was vaporized, it was instantly "distilled," meaning that impurities were purged, such that the Moldavite which was ultimately created is virtually pure green glass, without any bits of gravel or other material embedded in it. The phrases, "separate the earth from the fire, the subtle and thin from the crude and coarse," describes this intense purification within the explosive alchemical "furnace" of the meteoric impact.

Line 8 gives an uncannily appropriate description of how Moldavite may have formed and simultaneously acquired the energetic properties for which it is so well known: "This ascends from the earth into the sky and again descends from the sky to the earth, and receives the power and efficacy of things above and of things below." The explosion of the meteorite upon impact with the ground sent a superheated plume of gaseous rock shooting upward into the stratosphere. As the gas cooled, it condensed into droplets of liquid glass, which descended like fiery rain to the surface below. And while no one knows the how and why of Moldavite's vibrational power, it could be that the ascent and descent, due to the incredible force of the explosion, impressed the newly born Moldavite with unique properties. It is most certainly a literal physical embodiment of the joining of matter from the heavens with matter from the Earth—the above and the below.

Looking at line 9, it is not difficult to make the case that the text could apply to the spiritual qualities of Moldavite: "By this means you will acquire the glory of the whole world, and so you will drive away all shadows and blindness." The union with the Light I experienced during the Moldavite meditation in which I journeyed to the Great Central Sun could qualify as "the glory of the whole world," at least as far as I was concerned! The driving away of shadows and blindness mentioned in this line reminds me very much of Moldavite's tendency to catalyze the rapid purging of habits, relationships, and situations that are not for one's highest good.

Line 10 further develops this theme, but Beato's translation is rather murky. In a different translation from an Arabic source, the line reads: "The force of forces, which overcomes every subtle thing and penetrates into everything gross." Once again, it seems natural to me to describe the energy of Moldavite in just such words. The currents of Moldavite penetrate and influence both our subtle bodies and our "gross" physical bodies.

Line 11a offers a challenge to the imagination: "By this means the world was founded." How can we understand this? Could it be that the world we know "was founded" by a dramatic incident such as this great meteoric collision? I can't say, but we do know that the arrival of Moldavite was such a powerful geophysical event that it caused the reversal of the Earth's magnetic poles. Such meteoric events have been linked to mass extinctions and sudden bursts of evolution. On the spiritual level, it remains a mystery, but we know that the arrival of Moldavite occurred earlier than any known evidence of the existence of human beings. We evolved afterwards. Could Moldavite's cataclysmic arrival and reversal of the Earth's magnetic field have somehow seeded a burst of evolution that led to the emergence of human beings?

With line 12, we again encounter some difficult wording: "and hence the marvelous conjunctions of it and admirable effects, since this is the way by which these marvels may be brought about." It seems to be a comment about the beneficial qualities of whatever object or substance—the offspring of the Sun and Moon—has been described throughout the text. A 12th Century Latin version of the text says it more simply: "From this come marvelous adaptions of which this is the procedure."

Line 13 lays the claim of authorship upon the legendary Hermes Trismegistus (thrice-greatest Hermes) who was said to be an incarnation of Thoth and the progenitor of alchemy: "And because of this they have called me Hermes Trismegistus (aka Thrice-Blessed Hermes), since I have the three parts of the Wisdom and Philosophy of the whole universe."

Line 14 completes the text: "My speech is finished which I have spoken concerning the solar work." The meaning here is simple, except for the mention of the "solar work," known in some texts as the Operation of the Sun. I can offer one meaningful connection of this line with Moldavite: The "solar work" reminds me once again that Moldavite took me on a spontaneous meditative journey to the Great Central Sun, which, as I have said, awakened my capacity to feel and interpret stone energies.

I have taken us on a speculative journey into the correspondences that appear to connect Moldavite with the Emerald Tablet, the foundation stone of alchemy. Is the story of the Emerald Tablet a myth—a pattern of symbolism that sheds light upon resonant things and events in the manifest world? Or is the text a symbolic report of real events in the history of the Earth, perhaps prior to the beginnings of humanity? Or could it be that the pattern of the Emerald Tablet story and the principles of alchemy are so deeply embedded in the world's nature that the genesis of Moldavite and the Emerald Tablet text are simply different manifestations of the same archetypal pattern? This idea—*As above, so below*—is expressed in the Emerald Tablet. And in nature, the spiral of a snail shell resembles the spiral of the Milky Way. As above, so below.

There is no way to know the degree to which either, neither, or both of these hypotheses reflect an objective "truth." But they strike a resonating chord in the imagination, and I have always been beguiled with the Emerald Tablet, and with the Stone of the Grail. The fact that I feel multiple resonances between these stories and the nature of Moldavite is the reason I hold these thoughts and images within myself. And it is why I am offering them to you. The point of this is not so much to solve the problem as it is to *carry the mystery* inside ourselves.

The next time you pick up a Moldavite to meditate, or to put inside your pillowcase for dreaming, I suggest that you center your attention directly on this mystery. Don't create an opinion about it. Be there, not knowing.

Moldavite as a Cornerstone of *The Alchemy of Stones*

In my book *The Alchemy of Stones,* I designated Moldavite as one of the Four Cornerstones of the Alchemy of Stones. My reasons for that are implicit in what I have already said in this chapter. And if you have your own relationship with Moldavite, it is likely that you already understand. But I will summarize some my ideas here.

Moldavite is an initiator: If I had never found Moldavite I could never have written any of my books about stones and their energies. Without Moldavite's influence, my capacity to feel and interpret stone energies might never have been activated. And its impact on me was not limited to that incident. Within the first six months of my acquiring Moldavite, my life completely changed. An unhappy marriage ended, I stopped eating meat and drinking alcohol, I experienced a quickening of my interest in leading a spiritually focused life, and I met Kathy, my wife-to-be. My work life changed, from designing jewelry to opening a crystal business with my new wife and partner. The level of synchronicities in my life increased exponentially, and I felt a powerful sense of purpose, in which Moldavite played a central role. One need only to search "Moldavite experiences" on the internet to see that such initiatory happenings are typical for those who work with Moldavite. A number of such experiences are recounted in Chapter 18 of this book.

Moldavite Bridges the Above and the Below: Of all the stones on Earth, Moldavite is one of a very few that link, within their own substance, the union of Heaven and Earth. Those alchemists who were most spiritually aware realized that their quest for the Philosopher's Stone was both an inner and an outer one. They sought to incarnate the divine energies both within themselves and in the "outer" physical world of matter. Moldavite naturally facilitates this goal, because it stimulates inner transformation while the stone itself remains a physical object. Like the Philosopher's Stone, Moldavite carries and emanates a numinous spiritual energy.

Moldavite is a Trickster: As I mentioned above, Moldavite has a remarkably meaningful resonance with the Emerald Tablet of Hermes. Hermes was a Trickster god, who outwitted other gods for his own satisfaction or for the sake of humankind. It is said that Hermes was born in the morning, invented and played the lyre by the afternoon, stole his brother Apollo's cows in the evening, and was back in his cradle that night looking just like an innocent, sleeping baby. The rapidity of Hermes' development reminds us of the speedy evolution we can experience under the influence of Moldavite.

One aspect of the Trickster quality of Moldavite is that the accelerated pace of the evolution it can trigger causes us to be plunged into transformation, whether we think we are ready or not. Many people have commented on this to me, and I experienced it myself. Moldavite tends to quickly attract whatever one's spiritual metamorphosis requires. It also seems to cause whatever parts of our lives no longer serve our highest good to be discharged, whether we realize the need for that or not. This reminds us of Hermes, especially in regard to the speed of the changes that occur. Hermes was a being of great speed. He had wings on his feet, and was the messenger of the gods.

The other phenomenon that displays Moldavite's Trickster quality is its apparent ability to disappear and reappear. I have experienced this many times. In a typical instance, I put my Moldavite away on a dresser or in a box, only to find it gone the next day. Then, sooner or later, the Moldavite will reappear, usually in a ridiculously unlikely spot. I have described this phenomenon in more detail in Chapter 5.

What is the reason that Moldavite performs these disappearing acts? I don't know, but it might be that, like Hermes, the Being of Moldavite does this "for his own satisfaction or for the sake of humankind." I have thought at times that the intention behind Moldavite's disappearances may be to show us that the physical world is not necessarily as solid as we think it is. If that were proven to us, and if we accepted the evidence, the knowledge could be very liberating.

Moldavite is a stone of the heart: When a person first holds a piece of Moldavite, he or she often feels heat, especially around the heart. As this experience unfolds, the person frequently flushes red in the cheeks. This is often accompanied by tears, signifying an emotional release. And many times I have witnessed people holding a Moldavite and being surprised by the fact that their hearts began to beat in a different way. It is not a painful event—I compare the heart's behavior to a dog wagging its tail when it is happy. I believe the heart responds to Moldavite in this way, communicating its recognition and pleasure in the presence of this stone. And of course, Moldavite is green—the color of the heart chakra.

In my first powerful Moldavite experience, the sensation of energy began in my right hand where I was holding the stone. Then the current went straight up my arm and into my heart. At that point, my heart chakra opened, like a blooming flower of Light. And in the next moment, the Light surged both downwards and upwards from my heart, opening all of my chakras.

In alchemical terms, it is significant that Moldavite resonates with the heart, because the heart is the seat of Sophia (divine Wisdom) within us. It is the place where the union of the opposites that signifies the transformational alchemical Conjunction can occur. Although many stones resonate with our hearts in a gentle and loving way, only Moldavite vibrates one's heart so powerfully.

Moldavite is a visionary stone of transformation: I have mentioned my Moldavite-induced journey to the Great Central Sun several times in this book. There is also the Moldavite Grail meditation, in which we place Moldavite over our hearts and envision golden Light pouring through our bodies, overflowing from a golden chalice we imagine in our hearts. This meditation works very well, because Moldavite stimulates inner visions that lead to transformation.

I have noticed that Moldavite works well as a stimulator of visionary experiences, if the purpose or result of the vision is to be the rapid spiritual transformation and evolution of the person using it. It does not, however, work very well for idle exploration or fantasy. Like Hermes, Moldavite has an agenda, and it is all about this intense drive toward a metamorphosis into one's full potential. This is in complete alignment with the purpose of alchemy—manifesting the Philosopher's Stone, within oneself and in the outer world.

Moldavite is an incubator of dreams: This is true of Moldavite, more than any stone I have worked with. If you tape a small piece of Moldavite to your forehead at the location of the third eye chakra before going to bed, I guarantee that you will dream! A lot! I have tried this many times and recommended it to others for over thirty years. Almost all of us find that the quantity and depth of our dream life increases immediately. And the dreams are often spiritually significant ones. I believe that this happens because of Moldavite's affinity with the Deep Self, the part of us that creates our dreams. When Moldavite lends its power to one's Deep Self, a flurry of inner communication comes to us through a cornucopia of dreams. Another rather surprising symptom of Moldavite's effect on our dreaming is that most of us have to remove the Moldavite during the night, because we are dreaming so much that we need to take a rest from it and sleep more deeply!

For virtually all of us, the path of spiritual evolution involves healing. In alchemical terms, we need to "cook" ourselves so that the impurities in our energies—the disharmonious patterns in our subtle bodies—are burned away. And Moldavite just loves to do that!

Moldavite is a healing stone: Moldavite resonates with the pattern of our highest good—our full spiritual awakening and development. Thus, its influence moves us toward dispelling all patterns that are not in alignment with our wholeness, clearing the way for profound good health. However, the ride may sometimes be uncomfortable, just as it can be on the psychological level.

Moldavite doesn't mess around! In my own case, getting involved with Moldavite coincided with a long series of healing crises that continued for years. (It's clear to me now that I had a lot of cleansing and purification to do!) The symptoms were not usually terrible, but they were frequently mysterious and confusing. Regular allopathic medicine seldom did me much good, although Kathy's hands-on healing and other alternative practices often helped.

Something I experienced several times during my first years with Moldavite was the onset of physical problems that turned out to be rooted in past lives. As people who work with past life therapy often observe, my physical ailments expressed similarities (at least symbolically) to traumatic past life events. Hypnotic regressions were helpful in completing my review of these patterns and letting them go, but I am convinced that the presence of Moldavite is what brought them to the forefront.

Moldavite's ability to work fast, and to root out the problematic past life patterns in one's subtle body, can be quite remarkable. It "brings things to a head" very quickly. This has led some people to say that Moldavite brings "bad luck." Buy in my view, this is simply the rapid burning of old karmic patterns that need to be cleared away.

This is what I mean in regard to Moldavite's role as a healing catalyst. Its energies penetrate to the core of whatever dysfunctional patterns are being carried by the soul, within one's subtle body. Without the stimulation that Moldavite provides, one could go through a whole lifetime without having these issues come to the surface. Potentially, one might feel more "comfortable" without such disruptions, but one's evolution would be slower.

Sometimes, especially when one is already in the throes of an apparent illness that stems from long-held unhealthy patterns in the subtle body, the introduction of Moldavite can trigger a direct and rapid healing effect. It can seem as if the stone has "cured" a physical illness. But in my view, the presence of Moldavite has simply dislodged the stuck pattern, allowing the subtle body to clear itself and bring the physical body back to health.

If one wishes to work with Moldavite as a healing stone, it is often a good idea to bring another beneficial stone (or stones) into the mix. Heartenite, Seraphinite, Healerite, and Healers' Gold are good overall healing stones that can stabilize one's subtle body and work to soften the intensity of Moldavite. In my own past, during a time when my healing was focused on the emotional body, I found that Charoite and Moldavite felt best to me. White Azeztulite and Moldavite work well together for healing and resolution of disharmony on the spiritual level. I urge you to work intuitively in these types of situations, and let the Stone Beings tell you which ones are most appropriate. In Chapter 12, I offer a number of suggestions for the beneficial combination of Moldavite with other stones.

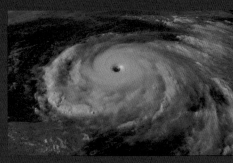

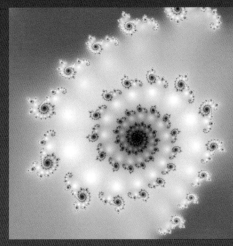

STARBORN STONE OF TRANSFORMATION

We do not really know the difference between material reality and the psyche.

—Marie Louise von Franz

All outer events in life are in a way only similes; they are only parables of an inner process, synchronistic symbolisations. You have to look at them from that angle to understand and integrate them. That would be spiritualizing the physical.

—Marie Louise von Franz

The title of this chapter is taken from that of the first Moldavite book, *Moldavite: Starborn Stone of Transformation,* written by my wife Kathy and myself and published in 1988. We chose the word "starborn" because of Moldavite's cosmic origins. And we selected "transformation" because it seemed to us that the stone's most fundamental quality is its capacity to stimulate rapid and beneficial evolutionary changes in the inner and outer lives of those who work with it, or who simply bring it into their possession.

In this chapter, I want to look more closely at this central trait of Moldavite, and to try to understand why Moldavite, among all the stones and crystals found on Earth, has this special characteristic. In this exploration, I am going to delve into symbolism, mythology, and my personal experiences.

In spiritual alchemy, one of the core principles is expressed in the phrase, "As Above, So Below." This draws our attention to the multiple layers of resonant likeness that make up all of reality. An easy example is that of the pattern of the spiral. We see it in snail shells, fern fronds, pine cones, broccoli, ram horns, whirlpools, hurricanes, and galaxies. It even appears in our DNA. There are various other patterns—such as the branching forms seen in dendritic agates, lightning, lungs, and river valleys—that appear on multiple levels in the natural world.

Take a moment to look at the images on the facing page. The yellow and blue spiral is a computer-generated fractal image, made by graphing the results of millions of iterations of a "feedback" equation. Note the smaller spirals present along the arms of the larger one. If we were to zoom in on any one of those smaller spirals, we would see even more spiral patterns emerging from the detail. And in fractal graphs such as this, the deeper the zoom, the more such self-similar patterns emerge. This goes on infinitely, giving us a mathematical representation of As Above, So Below. Each emerging spiral is slightly different from all the others, but the principle of self-similarity makes them all recognizable as spiral patterns. Those who study dynamic systems (Chaos Theory) say that nature operates in the same way. Examples of this can be seen in the adjoining photos, which display iterations of spiral patterns on multiple levels and in multiple mediums within the natural world.

In fractal geometry, many such non-identical but self-similar patterns resembling one another recur on multiple levels. These self-similar patterns, which also exist in invisible phenomena such as brain function, are what von Franz is pointing to in the quote above where she says that certain inner and outer events are "similes" of each other. I have heard the statement, "History does not repeat itself, but sometimes it rhymes." In a way, we can say that As Above, So Below tells us that the universe has innumerable self-similar or "rhyming" patterns running through it.

In regard to As Above, So Below, the alchemists were pointing to more than the physical world. They were saying that the patterns of inner and outer, of Heaven and Earth, resemble one another. Astrology is a spiritual discipline that makes much use of this idea. The resonance between the movements and configurations of planets and the shaping of our characters and lives is something easily seen by those who are willing to look. As Above, So Below.

Seeing the resonance of inner and outer patterns demands a different kind of perception—a symbolic perception that utilizes imagination to recognize and discern these motifs of meaningful likeness. Such perception is an essential aspect of spiritual wholeness. It allows us to see that reality is an integrated whole, and it makes us whole and at one with the world at the same time.

Carl Jung's protégé, Marie Louise von Franz, whom I have quoted above, describes what this point of view is like:

> The individuated [whole and awake] person lives in the world of active imagination, and the ego [self] does not identify with the outer world, nor with the inner world, but with the imaginative world, which includes both of the others . . . Normal ego consciousness would be replaced by an imaginative consciousness that beheld the world through the eyes of imagination. It would see underneath the apparent solidity of ordinary reality to the meaning hidden there. It would behold the spiritual powers at play in ordinary life, and it would possess the freedom that perceiving symbolically bestows.

In this quote, and the ones that begin this chapter, von Franz is saying that the division we imagine between inner and outer things and events is unreal, and that through imagination we can discover an infinite web of connection between consciousness and material reality.

I believe we need to view Moldavite with this kind of imaginative perception in order to get a glimpse of its spiritual meaning, and to perhaps understand its transformative power. I have already delved into looking at Moldavite this way in the chapters on its relationship to the Holy Grail and the Emerald Tablet. Now I ask the reader to look with me at the resonance between the story of Moldavite's genesis and our experiences of its energies.

In the chapter "Scientific & Historic Perspectives on Moldavite," I describe the event that gave birth to these unique and beautiful objects. I'll summarize it again:

A huge meteor or asteroid crashed into the Earth at incredibly high speed, creating a cataclysmic explosion that vaporized much of the meteorite as well as an even greater amount of sand, soil, rock, and organic material. The impact brought about vast physical destruction—the instant formation of a huge crater, a firestorm extending for 100 kilometers, penetration of the Earth's crust, the death of many living things, and seismic waves that literally shook the planet. The super-heated rock vapor was catapulted up beyond the atmosphere, and it then began to coalesce into liquid form—micro-droplets of a new substance—the translucent green material we know as Moldavite. As they descended, the molten micro-droplets collided, coagulating into larger and larger pieces. They ultimately landed, far from the impact site, in a cascade of molten, glassy rain.

Next, I want to address the question of what correspondences can be drawn between Moldavite's physical origin and the spiritual qualities it displays.

First and foremost is the fact that the most common phenomenon people report when holding a Moldavite for the first time is that there is a sense of warmth or heat. I have seen people get so hot that they have to take off an outer layer of clothing. A good many become flushed and/or break into a sweat. Of course, the stones are not emitting any measurable physical heat. Yet this is a very common phenomenon.

Why the sense of heat? I have felt the energies of hundreds of different kinds of stones, and a number of them do stimulate a feeling of warmth, but only Moldavite seems to have this effect at such a high level of intensity. I have seen this occur countless times. Looking at it with imaginative perception, I would say that the heat people experience is a direct resonance with the intensely fiery origin of Moldavite. On the energetic level, Moldavite retains the "memory" of the conditions of its formation, and it transfers an echo of that memory to us when we open ourselves to it.

Some spiritual frameworks would use the word *shakti* to describe the heat of Moldavite and the warmth of other stones, as well as the feelings of tingling and vibration that Moldavite and other stones can engender. My response is, "Yes, and . . . there's more." I will explore this idea more fully a bit later in the chapter.

Now, what about Moldavite's trait of seeming to trigger rapid transformation in one's life? This is one I have experienced personally, and I have received many letters from people who report these kinds of phenomena:

1. Sudden spiritual awakenings (chakra activations, awakening of latent spiritual capacities, opening the third eye, remembering past lives, glimpsing future events, seeing one's spirit guides)

2. Sudden changes in relationships (breakups of dysfunctional partnerships, meeting one's true love, breakthroughs of communication leading to mutual understanding, recognition of old toxic patterns and resolving to heal or end them)

3. Job and career changes (losing or quitting an unmeaningful job, recognizing and acting on a deep desire to change one's career, having surprising new work opportunities arise)

4. A radical increase in one's awareness of synchronicities and their meanings in regard to one's life path

5. Recognition of one's link with extraterrestrial energies/entities, sometimes accompanied with a feeling of "home"

All of the above experiences can be seen as transformational. In the first months of having Moldavite in my life, my unhappy marriage broke up, I met my true love, I stopped drinking alcohol and eating red meat, I took an avid interest in improving my health, and I focused much attention on following a spiritual path. I did not at first attribute these changes to Moldavite's influence, because they seemed to happen spontaneously. But I did feel as though the accelerator pedal of my evolution had been pressed to the floor! Since then, I have seen that this is a common occurrence.

So how does this resonate with Moldavite's origin? First, I want to point to the fact that all of the shifts Moldavite seemed to trigger in my own life were for the benefit of my spiritual and personal growth. This was true, even with the more uncomfortable changes, and I have heard this observation from many others. I view all such happenings as purifications—refinements that improved the quality of my consciousness and my worldly life. Another frequent observation is that these transformations occur rapidly and with much intensity.

The changes Moldavite triggers in its human partners symbolically echo the story of its own birth. The original materials—meteoric rock and earthly rock, sand, soil, etc.—were burned, purged, and thrown out of their "comfort zone" with a suddenness otherwise unheard of on Earth. Intense, explosive heat and kinetic energy instantly changed the state of these substances from solid to liquid to vapor, turning them into something new. And this new material was highly purified. What had once been a mixture of opaque rock, sand, organic matter, and whatever else was present was now pure, translucent, and green. We could say that Moldavite was the product of rapid evolutionary transformation, leading to a new and superior substance. And, in my view, the fast changes Moldavite is famous for putting people through do indeed purify us and raise our vibration—making us into a "superior substance." This stone, which often triggers a sudden metamorphosis in people, was itself the product of a more rapid physical transfiguration than has ever happened to any stone native to the Earth.

As Above, So Below.

What purpose do Moldavite's transformative energies serve? This may be the most fundamental question we can ask. My observations of the effects of Moldavite on myself and others lead me to conclude that it stimulates whatever changes are needed to facilitate and accelerate the spiritual evolution of each person who chooses Moldavite.

What do I mean by spiritual evolution? This can signify many different things to different people, but the common quality is an awakening to awareness of one's higher purpose and the intention to achieve or embody that purpose. In essence, I believe this means bringing Heaven and Earth together within oneself. By "Heaven," I am pointing to the Divine and all its qualities of light, love, compassion, and joy. I am also pointing to the realms of the angels, spirit helpers, devas, and other ethereal beings. By "Earth," I am pointing to the individual human personality and the physical world. In my view, these realms are artificially separated by the relatively unconscious state of human awareness, with its many veils—fear, egoistic desire, greed, anger, etc. However, in truth, they are one. When someone genuinely realizes this—through effort, grace, or a combination of both—Heaven and Earth are joined in that individual, and a radiance of that beautiful reunion pours out of that person.

Now let us consider the idea expressed by Marie Louise von Franz: "All outer events in life are in a way only similes; they are only parables of an inner process, synchronistic symbolizations." This is a profound insight. It suggests that there is no line to be drawn between the events of the "outer" world and the movements of consciousness. They are always in relationship with one another, with each reflecting the other. In quantum physics, this is recognized in the principle that the observer influences the event—whether in an experiment or in the world at large. Von Franz tells us that outer and inner events are related specifically in a *symbolic* way, as we discussed in regard to astrology.

So here we have Moldavite, a stone that is literally a *physical* blend of Heaven and Earth—the celestial meteoric object and the body of the Earth where it crashed. Moldavite is neither solely "Heaven" nor "Earth." It is both together as one. This way of looking at what Moldavite is corresponds very well with its effects on us. According to the testimony of many users, Moldavite's influence permeates both our inner and outer lives, sometimes leading to the union of Heaven and Earth within ourselves. And when this occurs, Heaven and Earth begin to bloom in the world around us. This is because the world is an ongoing, ever-flowering creative unfolding, moment to moment. Since we are individual centers of consciousness within the world, shifts in us generate self-similar changes in the emerging manifestation of everything around us.

To me, this insight is of huge importance. We can all see that much of the world is in what appears to be a deplorable condition. Many of us feel that we should try to do something to change and improve the situation. Although I honor the efforts people make through conventional means, such as protests and political action, I encourage the reader to contemplate the truth demonstrated by both quantum physics and Chaos Theory. Changes in the individual subject (the "observer") inevitably bring about corresponding shifts in outer reality. Put simply, when we evolve into inner harmony, the world is influenced and changes correspondingly. Therefore, Moldavite's powerful push towards one's rapid spiritual evolution cannot help but create self-similar changes in our world. This is one reason that I have spent decades writing about Moldavite and encouraging people to work with it, and it is why I rejoice in Moldavite's recent explosive burst of popularity.

At this point, I think back to my first conscious experience of Moldavite's energies, which I described earlier in this book. In my meditation, I journeyed up into the sky and out to the stars, eventually arriving at a golden Sun. It was orbited with a procession of souls whose bodies were radiant spheres of golden light, and I soon recognized that I was one of them. Then a voice said, "The Light you seek without is identical to the Light within." In the next moment, back on Earth, in my physical body, the Moldavite in my hand seemed to sizzle, and energy shot up my arm and into my heart, making it bloom with white Light, as if it were a flower of Light in my chest. Then the energy moved up to the top of my head, and down to the base of my spine, opening all my other chakras as it went. This occurrence brought my attention away from the inner vision of the golden Sun, back to my body. I was once more on "Earth," but I was filled with the energies of "Heaven." And from that day forward, there has always been a little (or sometimes a lot) of both in me.

This experience was quite dramatic, and I think it illustrates the "similes"—the symbolic likenesses—between Moldavite itself and its effects on people. And I believe that even the more mundane changes Moldavite triggers are nudges in the direction of unifying Heaven and Earth. In my view, the union of Heaven and Earth is Moldavite's essence, and its purpose.

The idea of the unification of opposite polarities into a transcendent wholeness is an old one in spiritual alchemy, which is filled with images of various pairs of opposites—male and female, Sun and Moon, black and white, king and queen. This pattern was

Shiva and Shakti represent the divine opposites of numinous emptiness and continuously manifesting energy and creation. Their union, experienced in meditation, is the ultimate goal of awakening.

also present in Gnostic mythology, in which divine *syzygies*—linked pairs of opposites—such as Christ and Sophia, were prominent. In Hindu lore, Shiva and Shakti occupy a similar complementary position.

Before going on, I want to point out that the "male" and "female" nature of the Shiva/Shakti polarity is to be viewed as a metaphoric approximation. Even though these deities are portrayed with male and female bodies that look like ours, they are not people. In inner experience, they are more like energies, though their images can sometimes appear to us in human shapes. Likewise, the merging of Shiva and Shakti— or any pair of opposite polarities—is not sex as we think of it, although we might say that it "rhymes" with sexuality. Shiva and Shakti represent a complementary pair of spiritual and vibrational qualities that is polarized within us. Like the opposing poles of a magnet, they are energetically attracted to one another.

Shiva is viewed as a male deity, and has the quality of infinite awareness which permeates and is the infinite stillness—the empty fullness—behind all appearances. The tone of Shiva is silent bliss.

Shakti is characterized as a female deity who embodies and expresses the vibratory energies of creation, constantly manifesting the universe in an eternal dance, which she performs before Shiva. The tone of Shakti is vibrant ecstasy.

It is said that Shiva without Shakti would be like a corpse, and that Shakti without Shiva would be uncontrollably wild. When they are in union, there is the perfect unity of blissful awareness and ecstatic dancing life. I would liken Shiva to the polarity of "Earth" with its dark, solid, grounded stillness and calm, blissful awareness. And in my picture, Shakti represents Heaven, with its undulating energies of creative fire and light, generating life and metamorphosis.

Statue of Ardhanarishvara, representing the union of Shiva and
Shakti. Notice that the body is half male and half female.

As I mentioned earlier, the sense of heat that Moldavite often engenders can be
viewed as a manifestation of Shakti qualities. But in the case of Moldavite, the Shakti
is just one of its two aspects. The Shiva qualities are also there. I think that is why
Moldavite does not typically make people feel "spacey," although they do feel a lot of
energy.

When the qualities represented by Shiva and Shakti are in union within an individual, a new way of being is born. The self is beyond all polarities, and the union of
Heaven and Earth takes place as a transcendent consciousness. This subjective experience is represented in Hindu iconography as the being known as Ardhanarishvara.

Drawing of the alchemical Rebis by Heinrich Nollius, 1617

This being is depicted as an androgenous entity, with a body that is half Shiva and half Shakti. This union is exalted in Hinduism as the root and womb of all creation. It signifies the totality beyond all duality. To achieve this state in meditation is to become enlightened.

Almost identical principles were at the core of spiritual alchemy. The goal of spiritual alchemy—after the aspirant's psyche went through many processes of destruction, dissolution, purification, and reunification—was to produce and/or become the Philosophers' Stone, a divine "substance" of unlimited beneficial magical power. In alchemical symbolism, the Stone was sometimes represented in the figure of the Rebis.

The Rebis (from the Latin *res bina,* meaning double matter) is the end product of the alchemical *magnum opus,* or "great work." After one has gone through putrefaction and purification, separating opposing qualities, those qualities are united once more in what is sometimes described as the divine hermaphrodite—a reconciliation of spirit and matter, a being of both male and female qualities as indicated by the two heads on a single body.

The hermaphrodite means nothing less than a union of the strongest and most striking opposites . . . This primordial idea has become a symbol of the creative union of opposites, a "uniting symbol" in the literal sense.

—Carl Jung CW 91 pp. 292-294

There is something profoundly significant in this unification of the opposites, as symbolized in the alchemical *Rebis,* the Hindu *Ardhanarishvara,* and the syzygy of Christ/Sophia. The word hermaphrodite itself points to the same pattern, conceived in the mythic union of the Greek gods Hermes and Aphrodite.

As I have been saying, I view Moldavite as a physical substance that is resonant with this pattern. It is the union of Heaven and Earth in matter. It is a "simile" of the divine union of opposites—it "rhymes" with that mythic pattern. And the effects of Moldavite's energies, when we open to them, can take us into the transcendent experience which all of these motifs are pointing to.

My early meditations with Moldavite brought me a transcendent experience, and initiated an alchemical journey to wholeness. Now, some thirty-six years down the road, I have begun a new series of meditations, facilitated by two stones—Moldavite and Master Shamanite. At the time of this writing, I have worked with them for about three weeks, and I am having very powerful inner experiences of the conjunction of opposites. I recognize this most readily as the coming together of Shiva and Shakti energies, but I realize that this is fundamentally the union of all polarities and an awakening to the true Self.

For those interested in the meditative technique, I can only give some hints, as this is not my practice to offer—another teacher gave it to me. Basically, it echoes the path of Moldavite's formation—an intensely energetic descent through the chakras, followed by an explosive, fiery ascent. Then the descending and ascending energies—Shiva and Shakti, or Heaven and Earth—mingle and merge, forming a new, stable wholeness. This stability is neither male nor female, neither quietly blissful nor exuberantly ecstatic. It can oscillate with great intensity to either end of the spectrum, but there is a center line along the channel of the chakras that is incredibly solid, even as vast energies pour through it. Often there is an upwelling of laughter, like a geyser of joy.

Each time, as I go through this process, the Moldavite I am holding gets quite warm, and so do I. I wear the Master Shamanite as a mala necklace, and it is there for two main purposes. First, it provides a strong link to Earth, attuning me to the Shiva aspect of awareness and keeping me from becoming ungrounded. (This helps me to receive the powerful energies of Moldavite's Shakti aspect without being overwhelmed by them.) Second, the Master Shamanite resonates most strongly at the root, heart, and crown chakras. As the energies are moving, I can put my attention on these three points, which the Master Shamanite emphasizes. This helps me stay in balance while the energy is doing what it wants to do within me.

I have tried the practice without Moldavite, and it does work, but the intensity is diminished. I am sure that the Moldavite makes this particular transformative experience much more readily available to me, and I value it highly. It is at the leading edge of where my journey has taken me.

Moldavite initiated my personal path of transformation thirty-six years ago, and it has recently facilitated a new surge of spiritual experiences. I believe that it can help in the worldwide awakening now occurring, and will do so to whatever degree people are prepared to open themselves. This is true for first-timers, who are surprised by Moldavite's heat and vibration, and for old-timers like me, who are thrilled to discover new realms of experience. Moldavite, the Starborn Stone, is a talisman that remains true to its nature and purpose, and can help us to discover and realize our own.

CHAPTER 10

EXPERIENCE AT BELL ROCK

I n the early years of our Moldavite saga, Kathy and I traveled to Arizona to buy crystals and stones for our shop at the Tucson Gem and Mineral Shows. In 1987, after we finished our business in Tucson, we decided to visit the Sedona area before flying home to Massachusetts. During that trip, we had an unexpected experience that profoundly affected both of us, and its reverberations still resonate in us thirty-five years later. As has so often been the case for us, Moldavite was involved in what occurred.

Sedona, Arizona, Full Moon – Feb. 1987

We reached Sedona late at night after a rain, and the whole canyon smelled of juniper. Breathing was like taking in pure life force. The next morning, we were amazed at the beauty of the place—green pines springing up from the red earth, towering rock formations like sculptures reaching to the sky. After breakfast, we decided to visit

Robert at Bell Rock, 1987

some of the energy vortexes for which the area is famous. The vibes at the first one, Airport Rock, felt like high-powered chaos, and it made Kathy sick. We had to rest for several hours after that. A canyon vortex hike late that afternoon felt very nurturing, and we sensed the presence of the Earth Mother. That evening, we drove to Bell Rock and parked on a little hill with a view of it. Its massive dome and central spire were beautiful in the light of the nearly full Moon. We sat and looked at it for over an hour, transfixed and not quite knowing why. Finally, we left, agreeing to return the next day to climb it.

The following morning, we began our climb at about ten o'clock. The weather was cool and a bit cloudy, and our initial progress was fairly rapid. We passed numerous medicine wheels laid out in rocks by previous travelers, and it was almost as though we could hear the echo of their presence when we passed them. We felt unusually quiet and reverent as we climbed. As we worked our way up, the paths got steeper and our breath came more quickly. We could feel the effects of the elevation as well as the exercise. We began looking for a spot to sit for a meditation. As we topped the crest of a hill-sized hump of bare rock, I heard Kathy say, "Look, I've found my spot." There just ahead of her was a six-foot alignment of small rocks set up by some previous person. Instead of a medicine wheel, the rocks formed a perfect "K," for Kathy. In a moment, I looked a few yards away and saw another formation laid out in a "B," for Bob. I laughed and said, "This must be the place."

Just past the rock patterns and between them, we found an almost square rock with a flat top, about three feet in diameter. It was darker than anything else around it, and we decided it was just the spot to set up a meditation grid. On the top of the rock we laid out a mandala of raw Moldavites and large Herkimer diamonds. We also added carved Zuni fetish figures of turquoise, serpentine, and jet. We decided to meditate one at a time, with the other person acting as witness, guide, and operator of our tape recorder.

I went first. I lay down on the solid rock beside our Moldavite and crystal grid stone and allowed myself to relax. After a few moments I was breathing slowly and following the imagery of Kathy's instructions, which put me in a deep state of meditation.

The first thing I saw was a whirling vortex of white light. In my mind's eye, it seemed to spiral up from the grid we had laid out. I let my consciousness enter it and felt myself pulled into the sky. After some moments, I was surprised to see above me the underside of a round white flying disk. (Part of my mind said, "Oh, come on, not a flying saucer!") I felt pulled to go inside it, but my rational mind would not accept what I was seeing, and the vision began to break up. I caught glimpses of friendly faces in blue light. I inwardly heard the message, "Send the other one up." After a few moments, I opened my eyes and said to Kathy, "I'm finished. It's your turn now." I didn't mention what I had seen.

Next, Kathy lay down on the rock and went into meditation. She went deep into it almost immediately, and after a minute or two, I stopped trying to guide her. The next section, told in present tense, is her story, in the words as she spoke them into the tape recorder. The bracketed statements were added later as explanation.

"I feel my spirit expand, and I am out of my body, sitting in an upright position above my head, behind me. I am very much at peace as I sit and look at the mountains. [I could see all around where we are and to the mountains in the distance. I could see the sky and clouds and trees and desert. I looked over the land for several minutes from the part of my being that was outside my physical body.]

"And from this sitting position, I once again feel my spirit expand beyond that and become very large, going upward, my feet on the mountain, standing and becoming larger and larger—much higher than the mountains.

"I am that. I am that part of me sitting. I am beyond these mountains and I see the desert and more mountains. I feel like Guardian of this space and the sky . . . [From here, I saw vast distances and could see the curvature of the Earth. I felt timeless, that I was past and present and future, all at the same moment. I knew that I have always been observing the Earth and always will, and I will keep her safe, even as I observe all the changes.]

"I feel . . . I feel that there have been space beings here for many, many moons, many centuries, and I have watched . . . [I saw/remembered different kinds of space vehicles coming to this place. They come down and the Earth opens and Light pours out and upwards to be taken into the bottom of the ships.]

"It feels as if the vortex points are a place, almost, of "refueling" for the ships. They come down and draw off the great energy that funnels up from the Earth. And as I look into the vortex point, I feel that the opening goes to the center of the universe, not the Earth. They're doorways . . . [I saw the stars and galaxies and the central Sun.]

"Part of my purpose is to see the larger picture, the larger patterns. I understand the connections. At times I can become One with the Great Spirit and speak from the place of knowing and seeing. And I bring protection too . . . [I saw and felt myself swirling upwards in a spiral/column of light and I saw a large curved wall in front of me that somehow opened up to become an entrance.] I enter the doorway of a spaceship and I am greeted by a man and a woman, as a friend, as one of them. It is like taking a layer of being off as I step through the door. [In that moment I was aware of my body, the part of me sitting, the part of me standing, the part of me swirling up and being stepped-out-of, and the Light being I became.]

"I'm stepping out of that identity into the Being that is of my Light body. I have flashes of memories of going through the stars and looking out the windows of the space ship as we travel and seeing familiar landmarks and stars and planets. I see planets where I have been and worked. [I remembered lifetimes on other planets and serving the Light over and over—moving through lifetimes in many different places, but always only continuing the Work. I remembered my friends from the ship in some of the lifetimes. I remembered choosing to come to Earth to serve long ago—many lifetimes ago—and forgetting who I'd been before. There is so much need on this sweet green and blue plant. I have chosen to be here for a long time.]

"Part of me feels a great longing . . . [At this point there were tears streaming from my eyes. It is so glorious out in the stars, free and unlimited—I had forgotten.]

"The planet Earth is not my home . . . [I was now in a circular room and everything was a soft blue, including us. There were low soft couches that were also in a circular layout. The two beings were tall and fair, and very beautiful. They radiated light and did not look as solid as humans on Earth do. There was no direct lighting, but the room was softly and uniformly lit as if the light was just there in the atmosphere.]

"I sit with my two friends, and I feel thoughts and ideas and communication flowing back and forth between us. We're not speaking out loud. We're tripping over each other's thoughts, we have so much to share . . . So different . . . [For several minutes we communicated about mutual friends and what we had all been doing since we last met, and other personal kinds of things. Suddenly I became aware of an inner call.]

"It's time to meet . . . I don't find the right word—not entirely 'teacher'—it's the One who tells me what I must do next, who is wiser than I . . . [We all said our goodbyes and suddenly I was in an empty room with a low platform on one end in front of me. There was a radiant Light Being before me. I was filled with a feeling of blissful Love, and I greeted this Being with reverence and love in return. As I was sitting, I was flooded with energy and realized that I was being given the next part of the mission that I am to do. I did not at that time have conscious knowledge of what I was to do, but I knew that I would understand when it was time for me to do so. I was also filled with grace and protection and given blessings. As I sat in communion with this Being, I saw his heart center begin to glow brighter and start to vibrate. The Light formed a ball and slowly began to come towards me. Then it moved into my own heart center.]

"I feel the ball of Light coming from this Being and it's planted in my heart, and it's a pulsating Light. It's almost like . . . . In a way, it feels like a homing device—that's my connection. It's my way of communicating with those above. [The Light in my heart quickly expanded and I was no longer in the room with the Light Being. I became the Light—I AM THE LIGHT—I saw and heard and tasted and smelled and felt only Light. There is only being Light. There is no form or thought or feeling. I AM Light for an endless time. Slowly, from the center of my being Light, a question formed in my consciousness: 'Why is the Earth so important that so many are working so hard to save it?' For another endless time, I was Light, and from the center of my Being the answer came.]

"As I look at the universe, or this section of the universe, I see the Earth is on the outer circle of how far the Light has spread, and we need the Earth to be of the Light to continue the expansion. It is like a pivotal point, where if the Earth turned to the

Radiant Earth

darkness, it would be as a black hole. But turned towards the Light, it would have such a brilliant radiance that would bring Light to much more of the universe. Once we begin to know that we are one in the Light, we will no longer be able to hurt another, including hurting the one that is this planet Earth. She is like someone who needs to rest and be nurtured and healed. She is purging. But to purge so much is weakening her, too. She needs all those on Earth who are Light workers to create a web of Light— one that will hold her steady and create a gridwork through which more Light may be channeled in, from off the Earth. So, those of us on the Earth need to be aware that we need to draw Light down and around the planet.

Kathy at Bell Rock, 1987

"OUR ONLY PURPOSE IN ALL OF ETERNITY IS TO BE ONE WITH AND IN THE LIGHT. We must ever expand the Light in our individual Being and become fully conscious of that Being, so that our every everything is of and for the Light. Each breath we take, if we are conscious, draws Light into our Being. Every word we speak sends forth Light, if each word is spoken in consciousness. Every time we focus our attention on another being, we are opening that channel of Light—and it's like a beam of Light that goes out. And if that other being responds with focused attention, there is a great brilliance of Light. As our Master Jesus spoke, 'When two or more of ye are gathered in my Name, there am I.' I AM. Because in the two truly being conscious, for even a moment, it connects and creates more of that network of Light. Every connection made with every person is connecting those people with a filament of Light. Every acknowledgement of the Lightwork makes that connection. Every person that has been met and communicated with, each of those people become part of the network, if we acknowledge that we are the Light and working for the Light . . . and if we acknowledge the Light within them, and that they too have a responsibility to be of the Light. It does not have to be complex and wordy and flowery. A few words, a few sentences acknowledging the Light are all that is needed. And at times all that is needed is a touch or a look or even just seeing someone clearly for an instant.

"THERE IS GREAT RESPONSIBILITY AND THERE IS GREAT JOY IN SPREADING THE LIGHT."

Some minutes after she stopped speaking, Kathy took a deep breath and opened her eyes. We said hello, but did not talk for a while. As soon as she sat up, Kathy ritually planted at my heart the Light that had been placed in hers.

We looked across the panorama of sculpted rocks and canyons to the red horizon and the blue sky. We saw the face of the Full Moon pale in the daylight. The only sounds came from our breathing.

CHAPTER 11
MUSINGS FROM KATHY

Everything keeps reducing to Love—the essential nature of Being— the key to enlightenment—what we're all here to learn and manifest.

—Kathy Warner, *New Moon,* September 1988

In this chapter I would like to share some of the insights I have had with the Moldavite over the years. I have done many meditations with the Moldavite and it has opened other levels of experience and knowledge for me that are new and exciting. Each experience has been unique.

There are various ways of incorporating Moldavite into meditations. I have laid out gridworks around and near me, with and without Quartz crystals or other stones. I have taped raw, faceted, or shaped Moldavite to my third eye chakra, sometimes adding Herkimer Diamonds or tabular Quartz crystals. I have placed a Moldavite and Herkimer "crown" on my head, or just worn a Moldavite pendant, ring, or earrings. Or I have simply held a piece of Moldavite in my hand. I'm someone who has always had very deep or vivid meditation experiences, but many of my Moldavite meditations have been profoundly different in content as well as feel.

I feel that Moldavite is a stone of great importance at this time in the spiritual evolution and healing of humankind and the Earth. We are in an era that is unique. Less than a hundred years ago, we had only seen the little piece of the planet that we called home, and not much beyond that. We thought of the gifts of the Earth as being

inexhaustible, because we thought of the world as huge and almost infinite. Now humanity has depleted and polluted much of the planet as a result of our narrow vision. We have seen the Earth as separate from us in our materialistic worldview. The spiritual worldview is a vision of wholeness, an understanding of the essential unity of all life. This worldview has been vivified by the fact that now we human beings have been able, for some decades, to see our planet as a whole being.

The following description by former astronaut Edgar Mitchell, as he caught his first glimpse of the Earth after orbiting the Moon, captured my inner experience of going out into the stars and seeing the Earth, when I first held the Moldavite. The picture of our beautiful blue and green world with its mantle of white swirling clouds, floating like a gem in the blackness of space, is a modern icon. Its image moves us to send our wills towards personal and planetary healing, just as the view of it from so far away stirred the heart of astronaut Mitchell:

> *There have been few of us privileged to experience the mystical and soul-rending feeling of floating through endless space and looking back to see home, the beautiful jewel of Earth. After months and years of perfecting the testing of an immense system of man and machine which would place me there in space—all of that was but a foreshadowing of my realization of the place man has in the scheme of the universe. We are part of a universe of consciousness. I sense this out in space. I devote my life to the discovery of what this means for me and for all humankind.*

For me, too, seeing the Earth as a jewel in the Oneness of the infinite universe has inspired me to more fully devote and dedicate my life to understanding—and sharing the understanding—of the part we have to fill in the greater whole. Throughout the last few years, I have repeatedly gone inward and asked my guidance about the Moldavite and its purpose. I believe that Moldavite was created and put on the planet to aid us and Earth at this very critical time, in our transition to a new way of being. The growing spiritual awareness which we are witnessing and experiencing is worldwide, and the Moldavite is one tool that many are using to help awaken and expand their spirits. Moldavite, I believe, is Source-connected. It helps us to go beyond the familiar local form of our life to unexplored parts of ourselves, and to touch the Oneness where it all comes together.

Frequently in my inner journeys, I experience myself as a personification of humanity. What I see inwardly is not just about me and my part in the world, but is a vision for you, too, if it resonates in you or sparks your vision. My belief is that we are all part of a greater wholeness. Whatever one being does or experiences affects all of us and all of the Universe, and is part of Infinite Being. As more of us choose to travel spiritual paths, taking responsibility for our own evolution and healing, we are helping and healing each other, the Earth, and, in some way, all of Creation. The following words recount one of my Moldavite meditations:

> *As I deepen into myself, I find I am in a crystal temple that I frequently see in my meditations. I am sitting in a small alcove to the right of the main hall. I reach into a small inset shelf in the hall and pull out a black velvet cloth. I open it up and spread it in front of me. It is about two feet square, but as I look at it I am looking through a window to the stars. Suddenly I am looking at the Earth. I see it floating, tiny but*

whole, amongst the stars. The Earth is in need, as are all the beings on the Earth—individually, in groups, and in nations. The need for healing is on every level. Feeling this, I reach out and hold the Earth gently in my hands and ask to be at one with Infinite consciousness. Healing flows through me and my hands and surrounds and fills all with Love and Light; I am able to sending healing to the whole planet and every being on it. I feel that sending our energies in this way can awaken the Light enough so that a choice is seen—to allow healing and to heal ourselves. Grace. I can open myself and be a vehicle for the working of Grace. I can be a Light that awakens the Light in others, and as they become Light, they awaken others as well. I am filled with great Love and compassion for the Earth and Humanity.

So ends my meditation.

The following quote is from a book called *Letters of the Scattered Brotherhood*. It is a collection of letters written in the 1930's and 1940's for a religious newsletter, which was then put together with quotations from great spiritual writers throughout history. It is as relevant now as it was then:

In this time of great storms of feeling, movements of psychic forces, hatreds, passions, merciless terror, the agony of self-preservation and misunderstanding . . . here you stand. It is the moment for you to realize that when you open to Spirit, you let into this maelstrom of feeling a north wind to cool the heat and clear the skies, and to know that you can be a means of bringing sanity and lifting hope. Oh see the vision! This is helping to overcome the world.

In the galaxy of thoughts that makes your mind, you have the imagination of the seeing eye, the eye that perceives the invisible. Keep a childlike hopeful knowledge of the unseen goodness and a surety that the Divine Principle can be reached; remember that though you may be very small outwardly you can be as the Universe—your mind is limitless. Realize your cosmic powers and take time to be a channel for the infinite Spirit to pour through in this great war against darkness, inertia, and savagery. As you walk your way and go about your little daily lives, be measureless, be timeless, be eternal. —Anonymous

It is my vision that we will all find the courage and compassion to follow our Spirits' lead and walk our highest path, serving all. This book is about Moldavite, and it is about Moldavite as a key to opening gateways to Spirit and our purpose for being. In the final chapter, you will have an opportunity to read letters from people sharing their inner visions. I was amazed and delighted to see the similarity of many of the experiences—to each other and to mine. As I saw in the Bell Rock meditation, we seem to be connecting to one another with filaments of Spirit, or Light. There is so much we can do together to uplift each other. Many of the Moldavite Stories express great hope and joy. In the midst of what to some appears to be the worst of times, more and more of us are able to perceive the glimmer of the dawn of a new and glorious day.

Interlude:
A Gallery of Fine Moldavite Specimens, Carvings & Jewelry

The natural forms of Moldavite can often be both beautiful and unearthly. Given the conditions of their origin in an explosive event of planetary proportions—one powerful enough to turn rock to vapor—we can readily envision the gaseous rock condensing into molten glass and falling to Earth in an incandescent rain.

Moldavite's classic shapes include droplets, dumbbells (double droplets), discs, balls, rods, ribbons, and "cookies." All of these were created by Moldavite's descent through the atmosphere in liquid form, combined with the effects of how and where they landed. There are Moldavites that display the patterns of broken droplets, flattened balls, and even spiral twists. Any jeweler who has tried to make a pair of raw Moldavite earrings can testify that it is very difficult to find two pieces that are even approximately alike!

Three droplets reveal Moldavite's descent in a liquid state. Center piece is from Slavce. Outer ones are from Besednice.

Sculptation is the term used to refer to the unique patterns etched into the outer surface of many Moldavites. When the Moldavites initially landed, it is likely that their outer surfaces were relatively smooth and glossy. It is believed that the dramatically sculpted surfaces of many Moldavites were created by soil acids acting on them over millions of years. Pieces from different localities exhibit greater or lesser degrees of this sculptation. Moldavites found in the Besednice quarry display the most dramatic patterns, while Moldavites from digging areas such as Chlum, Jankov, and Slavce are usually somewhat smoother.

But nothing I can say does justice to the beautiful, wild, and amazing appearance of the finest Moldavite specimens. In the following pages, you'll see many of these.

In the first section, the pieces are from our own collection. Following that, you'll see photos from our 2007 trip to the Czech Republic, when we were privileged to view one of the world's premier Moldavite collections. Next come some amazing images of world-class Moldavites housed in the Moldavite Museum in Cesky Krumlov, Czech Republic. The last section in our Gallery shows Moldavite carvings and an array of Moldavite jewelry.

As you are viewing the photographs, I invite you to tune into the energies of the pieces. Some may speak to you more than others, but it is quite possible to feel Moldavite's energy from the images alone. This is part of its magic, and it is why I felt it was important to include a large number of good Moldavite photos in this book.

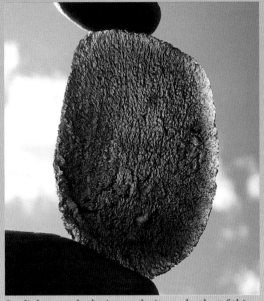

Sunlight reveals the inner clarity and color of this specimen from Chlum (51 x 36 x 10mm; 28.6 grams)

Six small glossy Moldavites from Chlum

Flow lines in this piece accentuate its aerodynamic droplet form. The tail is missing, probably broken off at impact. (46 x 26 x 11mm; 16 grams)

Three well-formed droplets from Slavce

Tall piece from Slavce with finely textured surface (87 x 31 x 15mm; 36.8 grams)

Fine specimen from Vrabce shows both fine matte and deep glossy sculptation (48 x 35 x 19mm; 24.1 grams)

Rare natural heart shape from Chlum (23 x 23 x 8mm; 5.3 grams)

Beautifully sculpted and glossy piece from Slavce (55 x 32 x 10mm; 17 grams)

Large, flattened "cookie" shape from Chlum, with an unusually glossy surface (48 x 34 x 14mm; 24 grams)

Deep green rod-shaped Moldavite from Chlum (64 x 16 x 12mm; 17.4 grams)

42 x 22 x 18mm; 17.1 grams

Six small glossy pieces from Chlum and Slavce

52 x 17 x 15mm; 15 grams

50 x 23 x 22mm; 26.4 grams

57 x 19 x 12mm; 12 grams

Here Comes the Sun!

Moldavite's rich interior color is best revealed when it is backlit with sunlight.

56 x 39 x 10mm; 27.6 grams

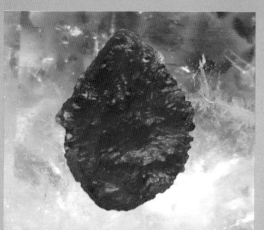

27 x 21 x 9mm; 6.5 grams

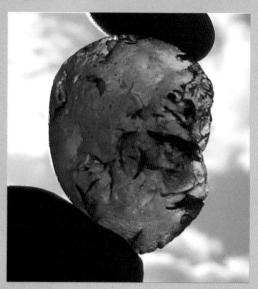

38 x 3 2x 16mm; 25.7 grams

Besednice Moldavite

Although all Moldavite is wonderful to me, I have a special passion for the deeply sculpted pieces from the now-extinct locality of Besednice. These pieces are from my wife Kathy Warner's collection.

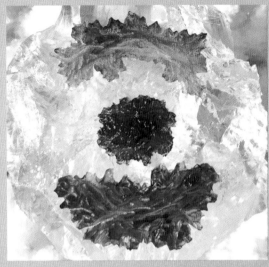

The imagination is stimulated by the forms of Besednice Moldavite. They can remind one of trees, leaves, angels, and other sorts of delicate beings. And their energy seems more refined than that of other Moldavites.

NOTE: The specimen shown at bottom left is a rarity. This is a single piece of Moldavite, connected by two very thin threads of glass. It is likely to have been a droplet that shattered upon impact, losing its "head" and "tail." But this piece did not quite separate, and has remained connected for almost fifteen million years.

ABOVE: One of the prizes of our collection, our largest Besednice piece (73 x 35 x 15mm; 34 grams).
BELOW: Large leaf-shaped Museum Grade Besednice specimen, photographed in two different light environments (55 x 31 x 13mm; 17.8 grams).

54 x 42 x1 3mm; 28.2 grams

Besednice Moldavites

51 x 50 x 8mm; 16.5 grams

50 x 37 x 16mm; 33 grams

Angel Chimes

Less than 1% of Moldavites are scientifically designated as "sonorous" Moldavite. This term refers to the fact that these exceptionally rare pieces make a clear ringing sound when dropped onto another Moldavite or any hard surface. This is caused by exceptional inner tension in the molecular structure of these pieces. When we discovered some of them in our early shipments in the 1980s, I nicknamed them "Angel Chimes," because their tinkling sound reminded me of angels. Also, the shapes of the Besednice Angel Chimes often looked angelic to me. Angel Chimes are often thin and delicate, but not all of them are. See our largest one below!

Four Small Angel-shaped Angel Chimes

Our largest Angel Chime (61 x 51 x 10mm; 40 grams)

Curved droplet-shaped Angel Chime

Three Angel Chimes with fantastic, delicate forms

Private Collection from Czech Republic

During our 2007 trip to the Czech Republic, we met the owner of one of the world's finest and most extensive Moldavite collections. There were hundreds of beautiful specimens in an amazing variety of forms. The owner of the collection allowed us to photograph a few of our favorite pieces. I hope you'll find them as wonderful as I do. (NOTE: Sizes and weights are my estimates.)

Assortment of pieces in classic shapes. Size range is 25 to 75 grams each.

An extremely rare Moldavite weighing over 100 grams

Large rod-shaped piece, over four inches long, weighing 40 to 50 grams

Extra large flattened drop with fine sculptation, five+ inches long, 70+ grams

Angel Chime from Besednice

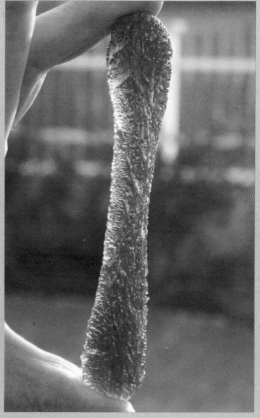

A "fine double-droplet or "dumbbell" shape, over 6 inches long

A remarkably long and slender droplet-rod shape, about 6.5 inches long and 40-50 grams

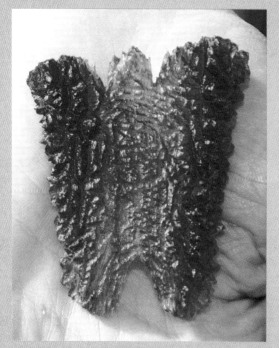

"Butterfly" from Besednice, about 2 x 3 inches

"Mushroom" from Besednice, about 2 x 3 inches

Two deeply sculpted "Hedgehogs" from Besednice, 30 to 40 grams each

Three "dumbbell" or double-droplet pieces, from 20 to 40 grams each

Deeply sculpted droplet from Besednice, 5 to 6 inches long, 30 to 40 grams

Deeply sculpted droplet from Besednice, 3.5 to 4 inches long and 35 to 45 grams

Deeply sculpted "cookie" from Besednice, about 2.5 inches in diameter and 45 to 60 grams

From the Moldavite Museum

One of our original Moldavite suppliers collected special Moldavite specimens for decades, and eventually launched the world's first and only Moldavite Museum that is open to the public. The owners graciously allowed us to use photos of some of their specimens in this book. (See more about the Moldavite Museum in the back of this book.)

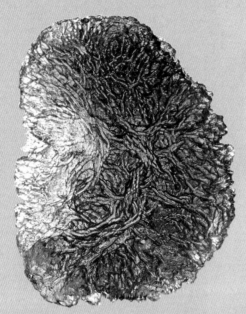

From Lhenice, 33.96 grams

From Lhenice, 26.3 grams

From Vrabce, 41.98 grams

From Vrabce, 33.86 grams
and 66mm long

From Besednice,
12.96 grams

From Besednice,
32.38 grams

From Besednice, 31.78 grams
and 81mm long

From Vrabce, 39.14 grams
and 50mm long

From Drbrkov, 18.52 grams
and 49mm long

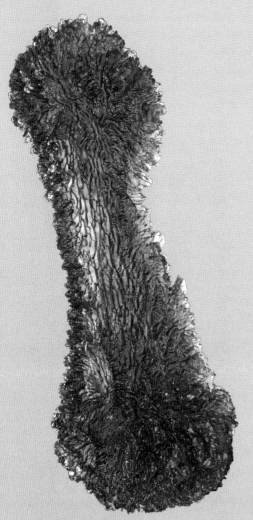

From Besednice, 31.74 grams

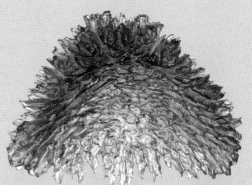

From Besednice, 32.18 grams

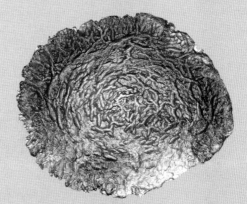

From Chlum, 34.58 grams

From Dolni Chrastany, 35.88 grams

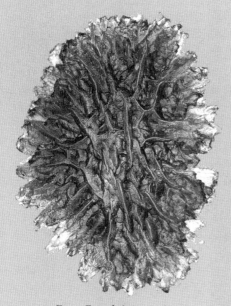

From Besednice, 30.46 grams

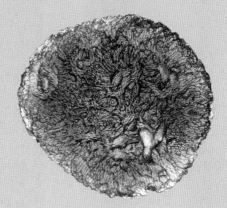

From Chlum, 34.48 grams

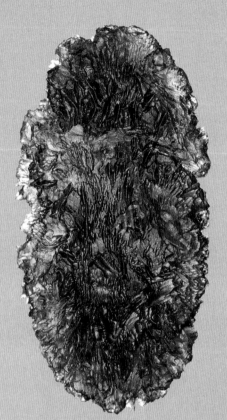

From Besednice, 62.02 grams

From Slavce, 70.72 grams

From Besednice, 31.78 grams

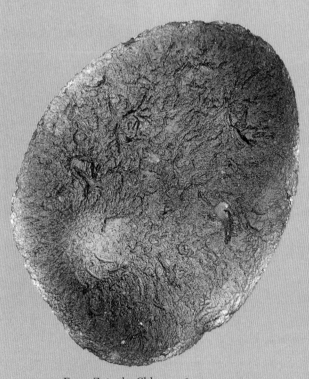

From Zatacka Chlum, 116 grams

Moldavite Carvings

121

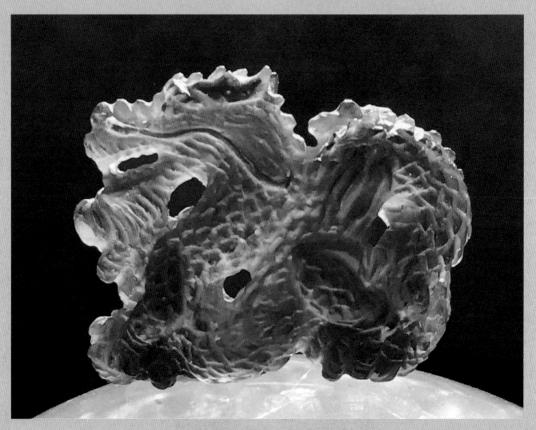

Moldavite Jewelry

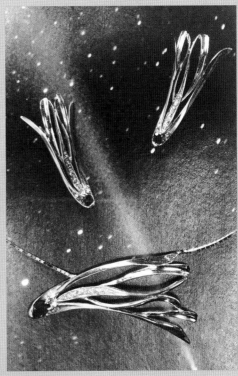

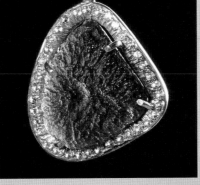

Moldavite Spheres ranging from 10 to 15mm in diameter

Moldavite's high melting point makes it a big challenge for glass blowers, but one enterprising artist managed to create this figure.

Moldavite   Celestite   Prophecy Stone

CHAPTER 12

COMBINING MOLDAVITE WITH OTHER STONES

When describing the energy currents of different stones, I often use a musical analogy. Like musical notes, each stone has its own distinctive vibrational pattern. When people ask which stone is best for them, I suggest that they "listen" to the stone by paying close attention to its energy and how it feels in one's physical body, subtle body, and/or energy field. When the person experiences pleasure or inner harmony in the presence of particular stones, that is one way of judging what stones that individual will enjoy working with.

Of course, like different notes of music, the vibrations of various stones affect us in ways that are outside the dichotomy of good or bad feelings. Sometimes the currents of a stone may relax a contracted area in the subtle body, or even trigger an emotional release. Again, in my musical analogy, I point out that a musical composition is more than one note, and it often takes the listener on an emotional journey, or even a spiritual one.

Those of us who love stones and their vibrations are frequently drawn to combine their various "notes" to make harmonious "chords" of energy. Doing this is a little like making music, and the instruments are not only the stones themselves, but also our own energy systems. As we experiment with these practices, we frequently find stone combinations that produce beneficial experiences, and we can learn to observe and categorize their effects.

I have a list of stones that I think work especially well with Moldavite, but before I present that, I want to offer some reports from three highly sensitive people—Lee, Rasa, and Gintare—who have shared their meditative experiences of combining Moldavite with various other stones. I'll begin by showing the experience of each of them with the same combination of stones.

Moldavite, Celestite & Prophecy Stone

LEE

WOW! The meditation began at the crown chakra, which became the foundation of the entire forty-five minute experience.

The crown chakra opened immediately and then fully opened down to the shoulders. From there, we expanded upward. During the entire meditation, the crown chakra was the foundation of perfectly integrated Stillness and extraordinarily high frequency vibrational energy.

Near the beginning, a female deity appeared in front of me, bowed her head, and presented me with a gift. It was a smooth brown fruit the size of a small grapefruit. I split it open into two halves and to my utter amazement, the insides were filled with a radiant, glowing, shimmering, vibrant blue. As I gazed down in amazement, these two blue orbs exploded upward and my meditation partner and I were merged with it.

Then there was a series of explosions of color, each of which raised the vibratory frequency and expanded and intensified the experience.

Then the energy congealed into a blue ball with a radiant center, which burst into vivid rays of silver and blue, transporting us into the cosmos.

We flew by Celestial Beings with such rapidity that they were just multiple flashes in Consciousness.

This was an ecstatic experience of extremely high vibrational frequency. Truly profound Shiva-Shakti!

As I write this, I can still feel the full effects of this meditation.

RASA

At the beginning of the meditation, the crown chakra opened very quickly and I felt intense bliss in my body. My consciousness began to rise above and I sensed lots of explosions of lights.

I was expanding and suddenly Lee saw the Deity and at the same time I merged with the blue consciousness color. It was extremely blissful. All the energy in my system was like pure honey.

After that we went even higher. I felt another explosion and I saw a vision of an interesting Being. It looked like a Spirit bird. I never saw anything like that before. I felt that we were one and were flying together. In energy, it was so beautiful. And after that, my consciousness was expanding and shimmering even more. I felt God intoxication and ecstasy.

At the end of the meditation, when I opened my eyes, everything around me was shining. My eyes even shimmered because of intensive light and bliss.

I felt that, in this combination, Moldavite and Celestite are very strong crystals. They carry an intense frequency and raise the level of consciousness very high. Moldavite can also assist visionary experience. With Celestite you can have a connection with celestial Beings. Prophecy stone grounds high energy and gives you stability. These three together make a very good combination for discovering higher realms of consciousness.

GINTARE

The meditation with Moldavite, Prophecy Stone, and Celestite stood out with great energy of Shakti within Shiva. There was also a special flow of knowledge that poured relentlessly into my consciousness. After a quick trip through different layers of consciousness, my knowledge took me back to past meditations and showed me exactly how special these stones are and what their main features are. The understanding went through me as a beautiful, beautiful picture, proving that consciousness is very intelligent.

In this meditation, the explosions of consciousness which I saw and felt through the third eye took place almost continuously, until about halfway through the meditation. It felt like multiple explosions taking place, one after the other, or even one within the other. They were extremely intense; I could see each separate part of the energy that exploded in me and merged with me. Mostly they were blue explosions.

In meditation, I usually see my body metaphorically, as a container filled with energy—as an energetic body—or sometimes as a container filled with bliss. This time, I felt/saw not only my body, but also a lot of action taking place about half a meter above my head. I was connected to that place—it was like an extension of me. I experienced the part of my energy that is higher than my physical body.

When meditating with these three stones (Moldavite, Prophecy Stone, Celestite), the upper chakras (the third eye, the crown, and the one above the physical body) are uniquely strong and active.

In the middle of the meditation, a silhouette appeared in front of me. It gradually brightened and I saw a full-size figure. As he approached me, I saw/felt a uniquely beautiful fusion of dark green and blue. I saw these colors, all the way up to their source. They appeared as tiny vibrating dots that merged with each other, rotating in the contours of that figure. It was infinitely beautiful. When the figure came closer, I felt like merging with him. When I did so, I felt an infinite amount of bliss. Later, already after the meditation, the meditation leader said that the figure was the Moldavite's being, whom he also saw. He saw very clearly the bright head and features of this being, in the same colors I saw. A friend [Rasa] who was also meditating with us joked that between the three of us, we saw the whole Moldavite being.

The Shakti energy that flowed through this meditation felt like a waterfall flowing upwards, from the bottom of the spine to the crown chakra, and beyond to the cosmos.

A lot of personal knowledge also came to me during the meditation. Many things were shown to me, and various things were taught/introduced. The flow of knowledge was very intense, and many things fell into place for me after the meditation. Sometimes the knowledge was related to the difficult personal situations unfolding in my life, and sometimes it was just like an explanation or response to the things I had thought about or usually think about.

It is interesting to observe the similarities and differences in these stories. Many of the details indicate that the three people were sharing a genuine connection with the stones, and with one another. Yet each person also perceived some different things. Nonetheless, the intensity of the combined currents of Moldavite, Prophecy Stone, and Celestite was very strong for all of them. I invite readers to try meditating with these three stones together and to notice how your experience compares with theirs.

Now let's look at a list of combinations I have worked with. This list doesn't include all of them, but I think it is a good set of suggestions for your own explorations.

Agni Manitite with Moldavite: Facilitates the fulfillment of one's wishes and dreams, especially if they are in accord with one's highest path of evolution. Allows one to call upon higher powers to aid in the accomplishment of one's aims. This pairing has a vibrational resonance with the divine being Ganesh, the remover of obstacles.

Ajoite with Moldavite: Supports rapid spiritual transformation through healing the emotional body and dispelling the effects of old wounds. This pair offers a conscious connection with the Soul of the World, and encourages one to love the world fully. Stimulates the heart and throat chakras, inspiring the wisdom and courage to know and speak one's highest truth.

Amber with Moldavite: Powerfully increases life force, supporting the optimal functioning of one's bodily organs and systems. This is an ideal pair for those wishing to facilitate transformational healing—in oneself and/or in others. It supports one in releasing fear of judgment or conflict, and in finding inner freedom. This combination is very solar, with a great deal of warmth. It offers comfort and energetic support to the physical body.

Amethyst with Moldavite: Facilitates purification and transformational healing. Opens inner doorways to one's divine connection. Very powerful for providing spiritual protection and dissolving negative energies.

Angel Aura Quartz with Moldavite: Aids in reaching deep states of meditation, facilitates communication with angels. This pair activates one's spiritual purpose, encouraging one to be a beacon of inner beauty, commitment, peace, and expanded awareness. It can facilitate remembrance of past incarnations, guiding one in grasping their meaning in one's current lifetime. In meditation, it supports the experience of one's "inner temple"—a place for rest, meditation, and healing with the support of angels and higher beings.

Aqua Aura Quartz with Moldavite: Carries a strong element of peace and inner serenity into one's process of spiritual transformation. It opens the throat chakra and supports clear and eloquent expression of one's inner knowing. This pair helps one to function calmly and efficiently at a high level of intensity, free from stress or frustration. It aids one in accessing multiple dimensions and can activate one's abilities to channel guidance from higher beings.

Aquamarine with Moldavite: For those who experience heat rushes and/or overamped energy from Moldavite, Aquamarine cools the heat and smooths out the vibrations. This pairing also helps one to communicate clearly and compassionately about emotional issues without becoming upset or judgmental.

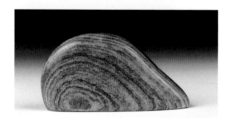

Aroha Stone with Moldavite: Combines Moldavite's transformational power with the loving, joyful vitality of Aroha Stone. This pair inspires one to undergo evolutionary change with a light heart that is generous to others. It is excellent for healing, especially if one is recuperating from a longstanding health problem.

Auralite 23 with Moldavite: Enhances inner purification, psychic sensitivity and visionary awareness. Encourages the emergence of one's Higher Self, increases psychic ability. This pair can also facilitate enhanced insight, the disappearance of chronic ailments, balanced kundalini awakening, visons of future events, and communion with angels.

Aventurine (Green) with Moldavite: Facilitates expanded awareness, combined with confidence and optimism. Aids in manifesting good fortune, abundance, and prosperity (an ideal stone combo for gamblers!). This pair enhances one's zest for life, and opens up the synchronistic path of adventure and fulfillment of one's wishes.

Azeztulite (White) with Moldavite: Stimulates a powerful connection with the Nameless Light of the Great Central Sun. Activates the Light Body and facilitates the process of Vibrational Ascension. This pair brings powerful spiritual energies into the body at the cellular level, dispelling contracted patterns of disharmony and disease. It enables one to become a channel for Divine Light to be directed into the Earth, for her healing and awakening.

[NOTE: There are twenty other varieties of Azeztulite, and all of them have a strong, harmonious resonance with Moldavite. To read about their spiritual qualities, see my books *The Alchemy of Stones* and *The Book of Stones*.]

Azumar with Moldavite: Brings forth an energy of dynamic joy, humor, and lightheartedness—even in life's difficult moments. This pairing aids in accessing higher levels of awareness, with special emphasis on the vibrations of happiness and laughter. An ideal combination for emotional healing and wellbeing.

Black Merlinite with Moldavite: Stimulates one's deep link with the unconscious, facilitates lucid dreaming, meditation, shamanic journeying, spirit communication, divination, and prophetic vision. It energizes all of the chakras, especially the third eye and the root chakra. This pair quiets spiritual fears and encourages inner union with the unconscious, leading to alchemical transformation of the Self. It supports the bodily systems that are involved with purification.

Brookite with Moldavite: Opens one's aperture of awareness to higher levels of mental consciousness. An excellent pair for working to perceive the structure of consciousness, and to map those regions. Also helpful for those engaged in mathematics, philosophy, and psychology.

Cacoxenite with Moldavite: Brings maximum acceleration to the unfolding of one's spiritual evolution. Intensifies the awakening of awareness, from the highest mind through the spectrum of emotions, all the way down to the level of cellular consciousness. This pair facilitates alignment with one's Divine path, spiritual cleansing and purification, and the regeneration of the body.

Calcite (Pink) with Moldavite: Brings a softening to Moldavite's intensity, centers awareness in the heart, facilitates the experience of wholeness and well-being. This combination can awaken the "mind of the heart"—a major spiritual experience. Highly recommended for dispelling destructive emotional fixations, including hysteria, panic, and despair.

Celestite with Moldavite: Provides a powerful elevation of awareness, including ascension into higher dimensions. Activates the heart, third eye, crown chakra, and the etheric chakras above the head. This pair aids one in realizing the infinite expansion of one's field of awareness, while supporting a blissful state in which one recognizes one's total interconnectedness with All That Is.

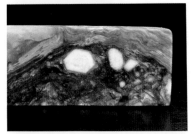

Charoite with Moldavite: Brings potent currents of psychic protection, and enhances one's capacities of clairvoyance, clairaudience, clairsentience, channeling, prescience, and prophecy. Aids in accessing the Akashic records and recalling the knowledge of ancient civilizations. Helps one to incorporate the "selves" of one's past lives into conscious accord in this lifetime.

Circle Stone with Moldavite: Stimulates rapid full brain activation and awakening of body intelligence, inspires exhilaration and passionate devotion to the Soul of the World, awakens latent psycho-spiritual capacities. This pair can flood the entire head with intensely pleasurable vibrational energy. It aids in emotionally and spiritually connecting and communing with the Earth, and can unlock one's intuitive understanding of the Earth's soul-stream of silent song.

Citrine with Moldavite: Activates the third and sixth chakras, bringing one's mental ability and power of intention into harmony. Stimulates one's innate intelligence and speeds up thinking processes. Excellent for creative manifestation of one's inspirations.

Clear Quartz with Moldavite: Focuses and strengthens the energy of Moldavite. Allows one to direct one's intention, both inward and outward, to enhance manifestation. Lends a great deal of power to meditative states, and enhances one's ability to direct subtle energies throughout one's body and vibrational field.

Crimson Cuprite with Moldavite: Stimulates and awakens kundalini energies, opens the root chakra for the infusion of Life Force, links one with the Divine Feminine. This pair can facilitate rapid transformational healing and expansion of consciousness. It energetically supports the heart, lungs, circulatory system, prostate, lower bowel, and sexual organs.

Danburite with Moldavite: Activates the heart, crown, and etheric chakras above the head. Facilitates ascension to the angelic realm and communication with one's angelic guardians and teachers. Allows one to assimilate high vibrations while maintaining serenity and balance. Excellent for clearing away stress and/or emotional wounds.

Devalite with Moldavite: Initiates the reunion of heavenly and earthly energies and entities. This pair evokes the presence of angels, ETs, and spirit guides, as well as Nature spirits and Devas, allowing them to communicate with one another as well as oneself. It facilitates the healing of longstanding emotional wounds and encourages a state of childlike openness and delight. It supports the heart, lungs, and circulatory system.

Diamond with Moldavite: Offers maximum intensification of the speed and power of spiritual metamorphosis into one's highest expression of Self. This pair can aid one in quickly "burning through" emotional contractions and long-held unhealthy complexes. It can activate the energies of the pre-frontal brain lobes, unlocking hidden capacities. This combination powerfully stimulates paranormal abilities such as mediumship, psychometry, remote viewing, and astral travel.

Elestial Angel Calcite with Moldavite: Stimulates interdimensional awareness, including angelic communication, visionary experiences, and hearing the "Music of the Spheres." Opens the link of the heart and mind, enhancing communication with higher beings, including spirit guides, extraterrestrials, and devic entities.

Golden Brucite with Moldavite: Stimulates a joyful avalanche of high spirits and humor, allowing one to "laugh one's way to enlightenment." This pair is ideal for those seeking to overcome negative attitudes and/or addictions. The vibrations of these stones inspire one's sense of freedom and self-worth, working to heal the emotional body and help one to recognize that one's true self is pure joy.

Golden Healer Quartz with Moldavite: Aids one in manifesting the inner Grail of the Heart, which is envisioned as a chalice at the center of the chest, overflowing with golden Light. It can fill the body with the ecstasy of Christ consciousness, creating the permanent shift of awareness to one of universal love. It attunes one to the intention of co-creating the Earth as a planet of Light. It energetically supports the body with the infusion of spiritual Light, which aids healing on all levels.

Golden Labradorite with Moldavite: Concentrates the combined energies on the third chakra, enhancing inner strength, vitality, courage, clear thinking, endurance, mental activity, spiritual focus, and purposefulness. This pair aids in recognizing and attaining one's spiritual destiny. It offers a vibrational connection to the Great Central Sun, which may be experienced as a gold-white Light. Also, it enhances self-confidence and charisma. It aids detoxification and supports the kidneys, gall bladder, and spleen.

Guardianite with Moldavite: Stimulates the opening of the root chakra for a powerful infusion of Life Force, integrating these energies through the chakras and meridian system, generating well-being on all levels. This pair offers very strong psychic protection, allowing one to feel secure in one's own strength and power—safe, happy, and confident. It is highly recommended for those recuperating from illness. This combination also nourishes the astral and etheric bodies, enhancing their integration with the physical self.

Healerite with Moldavite: Aids in maintaining one's overall health and wellbeing while undergoing spiritual metamorphosis. This pair brings in an abundance of high vibrations, while steadying one's subtle body field to accept and integrate them. Highly recommended for those dealing with transitory and/or chronic health issues.

Healers Gold with Moldavite: Facilitates healing through transformation, and transformation through healing. Moldavite's intensity and dynamism is balanced by the grounded strength of Healer's Gold. This pair can be helpful in dealing with health concerns on the more serious end of the spectrum. They both charge and balance the entire meridian system, enhancing vitality and life force.

Heartenite with Moldavite: Encourages one to fully live from the heart, and makes doing so feel natural and easy. This pair works to stimulate the immune system, and brings healing, peace, confidence, and enthusiasm to the emotional body. It enables one to connect with high angelic beings and sometimes triggers rapid bursts of spiritual metamorphosis.

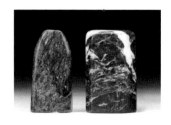

Hematite with Moldavite: Provides grounding of the high vibration energies of Moldavite, allowing sensitive people to be comfortable with it. Encourages a solid sense of self, dispelling feelings of insecurity. This pair purifies one's energy field and clears negativity from one's environment. It supports the blood and the immune system, and protects the body's fields from toxic energies. It helps one to believe in one's dreams and to manifest them.

Herderite with Moldavite: Opens the third eye and crown chakras and brings about a great increase of awareness, far beyond the physical body. Stimulates the subtle body, expanding it to infinite proportions. Increases the frequency and vividness of visionary experiences. A great pair for astral travel, lucid dreaming, and meditation.

Herkimer "Diamonds" with Moldavite: Stimulates visual displays in meditation and dreaming. Enhances one's overall clarity of perception. Opens the crown and Soul Star chakras, facilitating access to communication with one's spirit guides. Herkimers can magnify Moldavite's vibrations, facilitating their complete integration into one's subtle body and energy system.

Infinite with Moldavite: Facilitates the gradual opening of the kundalini channel, and attuning oneself to higher vibrational frequencies. It aids one in communicating with devas, fairies, and the spirits associated with power spots. This pair is useful for healing and protecting the auric field, and can shield against unwanted contact from ETs or other psychic entities. In spiritual self-healing, it increases the potency of reiki and other energy treatments, and it helps the cells and DNA remain stable when exposed to electromagnetic or energetic pollution.

Jet with Moldavite: Provides a powerful influence of spiritual purification, grounding, and protection. These stones combine to form a vibrational shield that cannot be penetrated by negative influences (unless one invites them in!). This pair heals energy leaks in the aura, while infusing one's entire field with Moldavite's high vibrations. It allows one to experience the unification of heavenly and earthly energies within oneself.

Kammererite with Moldavite: Stimulates rapid spiritual evolution through attracting initiatory experiences. Strengthens the emotional body, supports one's physical energies, enhances endurance, quickens one's reflexes, and makes one comfortable in one's body. This pair can enhance one's dynamism, playfulness, and humor. It can help one to overcome maladies rooted in fatigue. It stimulates the root, heart, and crown chakras, engendering stamina, compassion, and awakened awareness.

Kunzite with Moldavite: Bathes the heart in love and spiritual power. This pairing is ideal for those doing deep heart work, reaching inward for the Divine spark of one's true identity. It also aids with emotional healing from wounds received in past lives, and these healing experiences can trigger a transformational awakening. These stones work together to make one a channel for Divine love to enter the world.

Kyanite (Blue) with Moldavite: Focuses intense energies on the third eye, stimulating psychic awareness. Enhances telepathy among close family members, friends, and spiritual associates. Allows one to "download" information from higher sources. If one is carrying dysfunctional emotional patterns, this pair works to dissolve them and replace them with a conscious, healthy attitude toward relationship.

Labradorite with Moldavite: Enhances the magical quality of Moldavite's transformational energies, kindling a life of synchronicities. These stones work together to unlock one's psychic and spiritual gifts, facilitating telepathic communication with other people, as well as spirit helpers. They stimulate experiences of clairvoyance, astral travel, past life recall, and access to Akashic records. They also offer spiritual protection, shielding one from negative energies.

Lapis Lazuli with Moldavite: Helps one to evolve and integrate with one's Higher Self, aids in the attainment of moral virtues, enables one to claim one's true sovereignty of Self. Deepens meditative experience, enhances past life recall and visionary experiences. This pair strongly activates the psychic centers at the third eye, facilitating enhanced intuition and access to spiritual guidance. It can aid one in seeing and transmuting the karmic or psychological roots of illness.

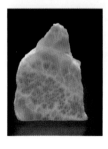

Larimar with Moldavite: The harmony of this pair mellows Moldavite's intensity and brings vitality to Larimar's pleasant, relaxing currents. This pair creates an enjoyable blend of dynamism and gentle sweetness. It is ideal for partners in romantic love to share with one another. Moldavite and Larimar offer beautiful energies that aid in healing the emotional body, clearing the way for love.

Lemurian Light Crystal with Moldavite: Offers the experience of expanded consciousness as pure pleasure, activates the "Mouth of God" chakra at the base of the skull, allows one to see visions of ancient Lemuria and to experience Lemurian consciousness. Aids one in activating latent brain capacities and increasing the coherence of the Liquid Crystal Body Matrix. This pair can trigger multiple ecstatic experiences of inner Light, inspiring one's full commitment to the spiritual path. It also supports the brain and central nervous system in overcoming brain dysfunction.

Lemurian Mist Crystal with Moldavite: Expands consciousness and activates psychic and empathic awareness. Facilitates one's ability to access and actualize the deeply intuitive Lemurian way of being. Can also aid in accessing the Akashic records of Lemuria. This pair supports the link between the heart and brain, helping one to achieve simultaneous self-awareness in both of these centers. It can also be used to activate the "Mouth of God" chakra at the base of the skull.

Lemurian Seed Crystal with Moldavite: Facilitates one's connection with the Divine Feminine, unification with the soul, and access to the knowledge of ancient Lemuria, including its connection with Star Wisdom. This pair connects one with "Lemurian awareness"—the balancing, nurturing, loving, spiritual, and sensuous consciousness that has long been lost by most of humanity. The influence of Moldavite quickens the Lemurian stream, supporting its revival in our present world.

Lepidolite with Moldavite: Works to soften Moldavite's vibrations, making them more comfortable for highly sensitive people. Moldavite brings an increased level of activation to Lepidolite's qualities of spiritual purification, enlightened awareness, and serenity. Together they can elevate one's consciousness while providing a foundation of calm centeredness.

Libyan Gold Tektite with Moldavite: Equally stimulates the solar plexus and heart chakras, creating synergy of the heart's longings with one's creative intentions. This pairing can be used for manifesting anything, from wealth to art to spiritual attainments. It can also aid in connecting with extraterrestrial intelligence.

Master Shamanite with Moldavite: Energizes the root, heart, and crown chakras, linking the physical and spiritual realms through the conduit of one's subtle body. Empowers one to face and overcome difficult circumstances. Provides psychic protection and dispels negative entities, implants, and attachments. Stimulates shamanic abilities for inner journeying and healing work.

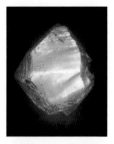

Moonstone with Moldavite: Enhances one's intuitive abilities, calms the emotional body, enables one to descend into the depths of the unconscious. This pairing balances the masculine and feminine aspects of oneself, allowing one to access either polarity whenever one wishes. In self-healing, they work for relief from stress and the release of negative attachments from previous lives. Also very helpful in connecting with Goddess energies.

Morganite with Moldavite: Emphasizes and magnifies the vibrations of the heart chakra. This combination enables one to connect with Divine Love, and to clear any veils of fearfulness that may obscure the heart. Morganite and Moldavite combine to aid in healing the heart from sorrow and grief, even when it reaches back into one's past lives. They remind the heart of its natural joy, and support one in living from joy in each moment.

Mystic Merlinite with Moldavite: Supports opening of dormant areas of the mind, increases sensitivity to communication with the subtle realms, and enables one to work with elemental energies for magical manifestation of mystical experiences. This pair aids one in alchemical self-transformation, uniting the cosmic and earthly aspects of the Self. It encourages the recognition and integration of one's shadow material, and the embrace of one's wholeness. It offers energetic support for recovery from spinal misalignments and joint problems.

Natrolite with Moldavite: Instantly opens the crown, third eye, and etheric chakras, producing a rapid ascension of one's awareness. Facilitates access to multiple higher realms, including the domain of "living geometries," such as those some people access with ayahuasca. (Those who take ayahuasca might wish to bring Moldavite and Natrolite into the experience.) This powerful and dynamic combination can be ungrounding, and one should take time to re-ground after using it.

New Zealand Carnelian with Moldavite: Stimulates rapid spiritual awakening, prolific creativity, unencumbered passion and courage, increased personal power, and accelerated evolution. This pair encourages one to recognize and embrace one's destiny, free from hesitancy or doubt. It activates the second chakra and can open the way to ecstatic tantric experiences. It provides energetic support to the nervous system, sexual organs, blood flow, digestive system, and immune system.

Nuummite with Moldavite: Facilitates powerful inner journeys into the depths of the Self. These can include connecting with spirit helpers, recalling past lives, and death/rebirth experiences. This pair is highly recommended for those on the shamanic path. It can be of great benefit to shamanic healers and their clients.

Obsidian (Black) with Moldavite: Provides strong spiritual protection and puri-fication of one's energy system, enables one to stay grounded while working with Moldavite's high energy levels. Facilitates scrying, spirit communication, astral travel, remote viewing, and psychometry. This pair helps to bring one's shadow material out of exile, facilitating the reclaiming of one's wholeness. It aids in healing physical issues caused by unprocessed shadow material.

Petalite with Moldavite: Brings a delicious sense of euphoria into one's entire field and cellular structure. Can be used to awaken the legendary "body of bliss." Expands one's awareness while allowing one to deeply relax. An excellent pair for recuperating after long hours of work or travel. Ideal for relieving stress while still main-taining a high energy level. Intensifies inner experiences of dynamic stillness mixed with ecstatic, dancing energy.

Phenacite with Moldavite: Harmonically activates and syn-chronizes the heart, third eye, and crown chakras. Enables access to interdimensional communication and travel. Opens portals to a multiplicity of inner realms. Allows one to see and remember the threads of Light by which one travels to higher realities. Can be used together to activate and unify the third eye and "Mouth of God" chakras.

Pietersite with Moldavite: Activates and unifies the solar plexus, heart, and third eye chakras, increasing and integrating the power of one's will, intuition, and love. This pair is highly spiritually activating, accelerating the pace of one's evolution and sometimes triggering peak experiences. It can sharpen the intuition of those whose consult oracles, making for clearer visions and deeper understanding.

Pink Amethyst with Moldavite: Focuses profound healing energies in the heart, aids in all types of emotional healing, engenders a loving connection with one's inner child, helps to bring the whole psyche into a state of union. Empowers one to process sorrow and grief while keeping the heart open. This pair provides comforting currents that can help to restore joy and peace in one's heart and soul. It can be used in shamanic soul retrieval work, and it facilitates communication with loved ones who have died.

Prophecy Stone with Moldavite: Powerfully enhances one's capacity to access and ground spiritual Light through one's body and into the Earth. Both of these stones share this purpose, and their synergy is amazing to experience. It feels as though Prophecy Stone and Moldavite were created to work with one another. This pair can also bring about visionary experiences of future events.

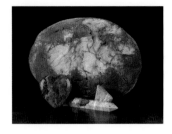

Revelation Stone with Moldavite: Stimulates the heart's visionary awareness of the patterns of the unfolding patterns of the future, sometimes leading to prophetic visions. Enhances past life recall and intuitive capacities, aids communication with departed souls, strengthens understanding between the heart and brain. This dynamic pair brings courage and confidence as well as vision, allowing one to release fears about the future. The stones work together to provide a powerful and steady healing influence, attuned to manifestation of one's divine blueprint of perfect health.

Rhodocrosite with Moldavite: Facilitates emotional healing, recovery of lost memories and forgotten gifts, self-love, and compassion. It facilitates deep healing of inner child and past life issues, heals the emotional body, repairs the aura, and rekindles one's zest for life. This pair can cleanse, soothe and empower the heart's energy field, repair damage to the auric field, and deepen one's experiences of meditation and/or past life regressions. It helps one to release stress and brings harmony to one's auric field.

Rhodonite with Moldavite: Combines spiritual transformation with the awakening of compassion, altruism, and generosity. Very supportive of one's emotional body. This pairing can trigger the emergence of one's unique hidden talents, inspiring one to use them for the benefit of the community. An ideal combination for aiding one in manifesting the fullness of one's highest self.

Rose Quartz with Moldavite: Gently opens the heart chakra and allows the process of spiritual awakening to be guided by love. Softens the intensity of Moldavite, making it more comfortable for highly sensitive people. Rose Quartz is the quintessential stone of personal love and self-love, while Moldavite vibrates with the love arising from one's Deep Self. Together they aid one in achieving true wholeness.

Rosophia with Moldavite: Helps one to live in a state of dynamic spiritual growth towards one's highest good, in harmony with the Wisdom of the Earth. Links one with Sophia, Soul of the World, and facilitates co-creative partnership with her. Aids in grounding Moldavite's energies in one's body and in the Earth. This pair lends strong healing support for issues arising from anxiety and/or loneliness.

Rutilated Quartz with Moldavite: Greatly intensifies Moldavite's energy and speeds up the process of evolutionary transformation. In body layouts, this pairing stimulates the meridian system, and can be used for clearing away energy blockages. In daily life, this combination is recommended when one needs to accomplish a great deal of work in a short time. In self-healing, it supports the nervous system.

Scolecite with Moldavite: Produces gentle, blissful experiences in meditation. Facilitates a gradual, steady process of vibrational ascension. Soothes the nervous system, while allowing one's awareness to remain crystal clear, lively, and alert. In meditation, this pair allows one to "tour" the inner realms in a relaxed, comfortable way. It facilitates contact and communication with angels.

Selenite with Moldavite: Energizes the heart, third eye, and crown chakras, opening the pathway for ascension into higher realms. In this pairing, Selenite magnifies Moldavite's transformational power, accelerating its tendency to bring about rapid spiritual transformation in the direction of one's highest good. The main focus of this pair is the merging of one's ordinary identity with the Higher Self.

Seraphinite with Moldavite: Facilitates healing on all levels—spiritual, emotional, and physical. Brings one's awareness into harmonious accord with the highest angelic realms. This pair saturates one's auric field with currents of wholeness and well-being. Excellent for regeneration and rejuvenation. In spiritual self-healing it offers energetic support to those dealing with cancer, or with heart ailments.

Shungite with Moldavite: Quickens one's process of spiritual awakening and evolution, clears the body of dysfunctional patterns, dispels negativity and associated emotional difficulties, and prepares one for full activation of the Light Body. This pair operates vibrationally at the molecular level, freeing the atoms of one's body from bondage to negative patterns and energies. It dispels patterns of self-sabotage and encourages one to adhere to the truth. The energy of these two stones together is fast and fun!

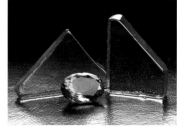

Siberian Blue Quartz with Moldavite: Awakens numerous psychic and spiritual capacities, enhances mental clarity and insight, helps one to feel comfortable and at home on Earth (even if one comes from elsewhere). It awakens self-awareness in Star Children, helping them to claim their powers and gifts. This pair can enhance clairvoyance, clairaudience, clairsentience, prophecy, psychokinesis, mediumship, and interdimensional communication. It supports brain function and healing.

Stonehenge Bluestone with Moldavite: Opens inner doors for attunement to ancient knowledge, geomancy, and shamanism. This pair resonates with the Earth's ley lines, as well as the interdimensional corridors of consciousness. It helps one attune to the best locations for buildings, temples, altars, and/or meditation. It helps one increase vitality and personal power by linking cosmic and Earth energies through one's body and vibratory field.

Sugilite with Moldavite: Introduces powerful currents of spiritual protection and healing into one's energy field. If one sleeps with these stones, one's dream life will be dramatically enhanced. This pair is recommended for healers to use on themselves and their clients. It is also excellent for incubating lucid dreams. In spiritual self-healing, it supports those dealing with cancer and/or memory problems.

Sunstone with Moldavite: Enhances personal power, freedom, and expanded consciousness; supports openness, benevolence, warmth, strength, mental clarity, and the capacity to bestow blessings. Inspires self-confidence, responsibility, and conviction. This pair is a creative dynamo, assisting in manifesting prosperity, acquiring knowledge, and attaining wisdom. It enhances leadership, will, imagination, and sexuality. Its warming influence supports the metabolism, as well as the digestive, endocrine, and reproductive systems of the body.

Tanzanite with Moldavite: Stimulates and harmonizes the heart, throat, and third eye chakras. Encourages one to "think with the heart" and to allow oneself to freely and eloquently speak the heart's wisdom. Strengthens one's self-confidence, while maintaining a compassionate point of view. This pair is highly recommended to those who are hesitant to speak their own truth. It links one with that truth and allows one to speak without fear.

Thulite with Moldavite: Brings the heart into a state of inner resonance, engendering strong experiences of happiness, enthusiasm, contentment, pleasure, and joy. This pair is nourishing to human relationships, enhancing empathy and encouraging one's full commitment to love. It dispels judgement and inspires generosity and kindness. It stimulates sexuality and creativity, will and action, love and communication. In spiritual healing, it supports and integrates the heart and digestive systems.

Tibetan Tektite with Moldavite: Stimulates the entire channel of the chakras, while maintaining one's center in the heart. Ideal for activating the kundalini energies in a safe and balanced way. Enables one to "travel" from the deepest core of the Earth to the highest realms of Heaven, while remaining linked with both, and with all points in between. These two can be combined with Libyan Gold Tektite to enhance one's link with extraterrestrial consciousness.

Topaz (White) with Moldavite: Offers a powerful magnification of Moldavite's transformative energies. White Topaz acts as a neutral amplifier of whatever energy it encounters, whether it is positive or negative. Because Moldavite's energy is overwhelmingly positive and is attuned to one's highest good, it is safe and quite effective to combine White Topaz with it. In addition, this pair supports the manifestation of health and vitality, expands one's awareness to higher spiritual realms, teaches faith and gratitude, and increases the speed at which one's intentions can be manifested.

Tourmaline (Black) with Moldavite: Emanates powerful energies of spiritual awakening and transformation, psychic protection, purification, and grounding. This pair keeps one's auric field clean and clear at all times, while allowing one's consciousness to remain expanded and in a state of high energy. It can clear away worry, judgment, anger, fear, shame, and other toxic emotions. It stimulates an awareness that is wide awake and boundless, and calls forth an emotional body that is both receptive and strong. In spiritual healing it supports purification of the body through eliminating toxic substances and energy patterns.

Vivianite with Moldavite: Takes one down into the deepest chambers of the heart. This pair emanates currents that cover the heart's full spectrum of love, wisdom, joy, and compassion. If one wishes to find utter peace within pure love, and to bring that energy into the world, these stones will aid in that endeavor. Vivianite is the quintessential stone of the Deep Self, and it combines with Moldavite's evolutionary impulse to produce rapid awakening and growth.

Vortexite with Moldavite: Facilitates states of dynamic equilibrium, balance, refreshment, empowerment, and attunement to the Divine. This pair is amazingly powerful, acting in mutual amplification to manifest the full depth and beauty of the Self. It links one to the Life Force of the Earth, aiding one in assimilating this potent energy into one's subtle body. It supports the emotional body through a graceful flow of feeling that dissolves stress and inspires joy. In spiritual healing, it vibrationally supports the DNA for cellular self-repair.

The listings above are simply my favorite stones to combine with Moldavite. There are a great number of other stone choices one could make, and I encourage readers to experiment. Also, I have only offered suggestions of individual stones to be paired with Moldavite. But there are any number of multi-stone vibrational "chords" one might compose, utilizing Moldavite and a variety of other crystals and minerals. Let your intuition (and the invitations you sense from the Stone Beings) guide you. This is part of the alchemical adventure we are all experiencing.

The Synergy 12

As a final suggestion, I want to mention a very special combination of stones that I have named the Synergy 12. The name was inspired by the fact that the energies of these stones blend in a powerful harmony that produces exceptionally beneficial effects on the majority of people who have worked with them.

The Synergy 12 stones are: Moldavite, Phenacite, Tanzanite, Danburite, Azeztulite (White), Herderite, Natrolite, Azeztulite (Satyaloka Clear), Tibetan Tektite, Brookite, Scolecite, and Petalite. I discovered this combination through trial and error over a period of years, and my company, Heaven and Earth, has offered it in necklaces, pendants, bracelets, templates, grids, dream pouches, and stone sets. [For more information, visit www.heavenandearthjewelry.com]

The Synergy 12 engenders a variety of experiences, but if I had to distill it down to a couple of lines, I would say this: The Synergy 12 fully activates one's energy system, while harmonizing and integrating its components. The overall effect is that one feels like the Self that one was born to be. There is a sense of expanded awareness, confidence, and power, tempered by gentleness, compassion, and love. One feels more awake, livelier, and more sensitive to everything. Yet one feels strong, embodied, and happy.

There is no doubt in my mind that Moldavite is one of the most exceptional stones to be found on Earth. And at the same time, it is exciting to contemplate the potentials that may be realized through incorporating Moldavite with other stones. With their help, we can all become composers, creating silent symphonies of energies.

TOP ROW: Moldavite, Phenacite, Tanzanite, Danburite, Azeztulite (White), Herderite;
BOTTOM ROW: Natrolite, Azeztulite (Satyaloka Clear), Tibetan Tektite, Brookite, Scolecite, Petalite

CHAPTER 13

THE MOLDAVITE CHANNELINGS

In the first two years of being involved with Moldavite, before my own ability to perceive and describe the energies of stones was well developed, Kathy and I sought out spiritual channels to give us information about Moldavite. Our first contact was with Elwood Babbitt, a man who was a respected trance medium for over fifty years. Our second contact was Auriloitha, another well-known and respected trance medium. In both cases, we were highly impressed by the conscientious manner in which these people approached their work. Each time, we left the channeling session quite moved by the experience. We felt the energies in our own bodies, and the personal guidance given to us rang true. We are grateful to these mediums for their help.

First Moldavite Channeling—Elwood Babbitt

On December 1, 1986, I went to the noted medium Elwood Babbitt for a personal reading. Although Babbitt had channeled literally hundreds of different discarnate entities, his control and usual contact was an entity who called himself Dr. Fisher. In the course of my reading, Dr. Fisher gave me a remarkably detailed account of a number of my past lives as well as a very accurate (it seemed to me) summation of my life energy and purpose. At the end of his initial monologue I had the opportunity to ask questions. The first question I asked was about Moldavite. (Mr. Babbitt had no prior knowledge of any of the questions I was going to ask.)

DR. FISHER: How may I serve you?

ROBERT: I've been working with an extraterrestrial gemstone called Moldavite. What is its purpose and best use and what is my role for that?

DR. FISHER: It is to widen the expansion and recognize it is the stepping stone to the outer forces of all infinite vibration. It is not so much what you term the healing of atoms in the bodies of individuals, as it is the true pathway toward the creative purpose of the infinitude of life itself. It is a protection away from the astral planes of limitations, where a person could be tempted to stop and visit with those that are in the changing efforts of their lives and understanding of their own spiritual divinity. Therefore, this shall become more expansive and more interesting to those that are searching for the true pathway to illumination, which does not require books and learning. It is the simple expedient of opening to all of the forces of vibration that entail the total force of all creativity. Its actions bring together creation and procreation. It is what you may term the glue of life itself. Here what you call the ova of femininity, the semen of masculinity, involved within the expansion and purpose that affects worlds that are not seen in the finite, but which is the total elixir and the identity toward all things that move and have their expression, therefore, this [Moldavite] is of a limited substance within the full galaxy of your world. And so it should be brought forth to all who would serve it in the Truth.

Second Moldavite Channeling—Elwood Babbitt

On October 12, 1987, Kathy and I returned to Elwood Babbitt for a second personal reading, which we this time received together. After almost a year, we had a number of more specific questions to ask about Moldavite. Again, Elwood had no prior knowledge of the questions. In this reading, an unusual thing happened. Instead of Elwood's usual contact, Dr. Fisher, a being came through who identified himself as Alcion, the Master force. This contact felt very powerful to Kathy and me, and at the end of the session, Dr. Fisher checked in to make sure things had gone all right. He told us that it took a lot of engineering on the other side to step down the energy, so as not to damage us.

ROBERT: One of the crystals we've been working with is a stone from outer space called Moldavite, and we wanted to ask a few questions about the uses of that. The first question we wanted to ask was, what is the origin of Moldavite, and how did it come to Earth?

ALCION: In the Beginning of all Creation, there was not an outer layer of the density you call Earth and flesh and planets. It was a Oneness of infinity in vibrational form, ripples of activity across the endless condition and force of what is known in your world as space. Yet in the velocity of movement [there was] required a Law of Balance, not only to lessen the degree of velocity of that Oneness, but to bring about the balance needed to sustain the actions of the force of life. But life that was in celestial form, not in the material condition of body, or solid density of life. As this velocity moved to a slower generation of purpose, it formed from its gases an explosion to make possible a solid outer layer of the atom of density, that which you now call Moldavite. It is the Scepter or the Staff which was broken from the Wheel of esoteric life, when the forms of reality as you know it in solid form were brought for the balance of Creation. Then the desire of those formed, such as yourselves, as energies, moved away from that celestial force, to serve and to observe the creation and motion of life. [You] longed to fulfill the natural laws you knew, that now seem impossible to the laws of science in your world. And yet many around you became so engrossed in the density of materiality, they lost the channel back to their origin of Cosmic Oneness. You have retained your oneness in your moments of reflection, of dreams, of the sound of nature around you. And it's been your endeavor since that first expression upon a planet not yet fulfilled in its formation and idea—the wanting to bring the Oneness or esoteric principle across the broad force of what you call worlds and galaxies that surround one pathway linked to the Infinitude of Life. So to the Moldavite: [It] is that broken Staff of Infinitude. Whomever you give it to, let yourself feel they are worthy, for it has a power for those who would use it for greed, to destroy them. But to those who use it to see the Illumination of infinitude—wear it proudly. For it shall be a beacon for the service of those aliens that will observe that Light, and know they serve those individuals that will once again regenerate the Earth.

ROBERT: Thank you.

KATHY: There is a connection, then, between us and the Moldavite and those that wear it, and extraterrestrial beings? Is that correct? Does it help us be in communication, and work with extraterrestrials that are working for the Light, too?

ALCION: Moldavite is the saving force of the world you now live on, for it is the energizer that allows your world to be reborn again—to start anew in a cleansing process, to which each of you had come to service and to fulfill the ways of that Infinitude. So be not content in recognizing the limitations of life—widen to the unlimited potentials of each to the other. And know what has entered your lives is a service to mankind that you have yet to understand. Before you we shall place not only your intent of goodness, not only the answer to your spiritual quest, but you shall find all things you touch shall be of the greatest fulfillment to all needs you have, in Spirit, soul, and body.

ROBERT: Thank you. I have read that there was a connection in regard to the Moldavite, a connection to the Stone of the Holy Grail. I wanted to ask if you could comment on that.

ALCION: It was part of the Holy Grail in what is called vibrational frequencies that affected it. And remember also, it was the effect when the Nazarene of your world, one called Jesus or Buddha, of the past and regeneration of lives, used the force of Moldavite when he gradually dissipated the outer layer of flesh and left his imprint upon the cloth of your world.

ROBERT: In terms of the use of Moldavite by people now, are there particular forms that are preferable in terms of the cut and polished shapes or the raw form, for people who want to use it to reach higher dimensions?

ALCION: The raw form is better for the neophyte. The refinement of its energy is for the teachers. And the greater force that is shaped in the Ankh cross is the interconnection to the infinitude of those that witness the coming and going of the Angelic forces of Compassion and dimensions.

ROBERT: Are there healing applications for the use of Moldavite, and if so, what would be the most appropriate forms and uses?

ALCION: The action lies not only within the energized frequencies of the Moldavite of the broken Staff of Life, but the attention also of the individual who wears it. For [when] they can widen to the force of Oneness, and not limit their potential of Infinitude, then the force of healing merges in spirit, soul, and body, to the ultimate goal that their spirit had set into motion. The sorrow of your Earth lives is the many that enjoy poor health, and would not know the fuller enjoyment of perfection.

ROBERT: Is it true that the use of Moldavite can help us ground more Light on the Earth, and help to heal and raise the vibration of the planet?

ALCION: It is the Illuminator that casts your world and the worlds around in the total Oneness of all Etheric Light, where there is no darkness, but where each world flows in the Light, in continuous fulfillment of that Infinitude itself. The acceptance or imperfections of your creation and infinitude . . . is only the acceptability of individuals stating that only half of your world is lighted at any given Earth moment. The Light and Force contributed by the Broken Lance of Infinitude you call the Moldavite will be the Illuminator and generator of all things in the esoteric performance that now moves across your lives.

ROBERT: What is our role in the distribution of Moldavite and how is it that this has come to us?

ALCION: You will find it is not in your control. It is not by accident or coincidence, for every person that has moved across the periphery of your life has been sent to you.

And as you look more deeply in the understanding of that Law of Attraction, more shall come to you. Yet be warned not to rely upon books and what others call the knowledgeability of what is the Moldavite or Broken Staff. Rely upon the flows through your inner spirit of intuition, and in each instance, you shall be given the words to use. For each one you've served in the present lifetime, you shall serve again.

ROBERT: Thank you.

KATHY: Thank you.

Moldavite Channeling—Auriloitha

On June 27 of 1988, we drove to western Massachusetts to the home of Auriloitha, an accomplished trance medium and channel. We had experienced her work on two previous occasions, at large gatherings, where she channeled Angelic and Master forces. We were impressed by her both on a personal level and in her mediumship. Personally, she was warm and friendly, with the aura of a powerful self-discipline and commitment to working in the Light. At her channelings, Kathy and I were both strongly affected by the energies that flowed through her. On each occasion, we both felt ourselves move into higher states of consciousness as we listened to the words and sounds that came through Auriloitha. These consciousness changes were accompanied by beautiful visual imagery, and, on one occasion, the scent of roses. Because of these experiences, we were moved to arrange for a personal session in which we could ask for information about Moldavite. (We did not tell Auriloitha about our opinions and information about Moldavite, nor did she ask us about it.)

As the reading began, Auriloitha went into a deep meditation while we sat before her. About five to ten minutes later, she began to speak. Although Auriloitha was in her thirties, the voice that came through her sounded very old, and the precisely articulated pronunciation reminded me of my high school Latin teacher. After an initial period of personal messages, we began to ask questions about Moldavite.

ROBERT: One reason we came today is that we have been working with an extraterrestrial gemstone called Moldavite, and we were hoping to get some information from you about it. The first question we have is, what is the origin of Moldavite and how did it come to Earth?

AURILOITHA: It is from the system that is known to you as the Pleiades. Here is the connection with the Altantean energies, and it was designed in a flow of thought for a specific function and purpose. It was sent through the ethers to land in your world, upon your planet, that the properties that it brings forth into the world might reach individuals spiritually directed, to aid them in their enfoldment and the unfoldment of their spiritual abilities.

ROBERT: In terms of its purpose, can you give us some guidance about what its properties might be?

AURILOITHA: It is here to activate crystalline energies upon the planet. It works in harmony in particular with the Quartz crystals of your world, in particular with the clear and Smokey Quartz, most effectively. It is designed to activate particularly with those individuals who are working with the extraterrestrial flow, to release energies within the seven chakras of the body, particularly in the sixth chakra. When used in the area and directed by thought to do so, it will activate the crystalline energy in the subatomic particles of that sphere of energy, which you call Inner Sight, or Third Eye. It activates that center and the seventh center, to receive more fully the energies from out-world or off-globe, particularly those which are aligned with the Pleiadean energies, and the energies of Helios Vesta, or what you call the Solar Logos, or your Sun. It can also be used as individuals grow in their understanding and their abilities, to bring a fuller flow into the Seat of Being, or what you term the third chakra. Here it allows, if you will, a chain of command to be placed in the center, which allows thought patterns or communication flows to be received by Great Beings who are beyond this planet, but who serve this solar system and this galaxy. It helps to bring a fuller radiance of cycles of eight hertz, which is the flow of your world, the harmonic vibration of C, which is the flow of your world, and here empowers a balance and fuller radiation between an individual who is working with the stone, and the radiance of Gaia, or what you term the Goddess of your Earth, or the Earth-consciousness, and all of those life streams—the Devic forces and Angelic kingdoms, who work with this energy. You will find that this is a supportive crystalline essence, or a supportive life force for that which allows a fuller dimensional creative flow for those upon your world. Are we clear?

ROBERT: Yes. I would like to ask . . .

AURILOITHA: You would of course have to understand that this should be a clear instruction which should be used in steps, where the individual would first work with this stone, and its property in the area of the sixth chakra, and then the seventh chakra, and then the third. It can also be used, as you continue in your understanding and your unfoldment, for the fourth chakra, and for healings. The reason why it can be used for healings is because it originates in the Source vibration of the creative flow—as we have spoken—the eight hertz and the C. Therefore, it provides a supportive environment for perfection to manifest in the etheric energies of the crystalline structures. This is of course most useful for those individuals who are actively working in building their Bodies of Light, or are working with the crystalline energies to bring forth the fuller frequencies which will be needed when the Earth and your planetary system moves into its fuller vibration.

ROBERT: What is the connection, if any, between Moldavite and the Stone of the Holy Grail?

AURILOITHA: The connection would be in the energies of the individuals who have been present through the cycles of enlightenment upon your planet. It is a Source vibration and a creative energy direct from the beings who are thus associated. The energies are intertwined, and the pool of Light that was sent into the energy of the Holy Grail, and is the same Source vibration from which forth was drawn the stone in question.

ROBERT: Thank you. In working with Moldavite, does the size of the stone matter in relation to energy?

AURILOITHA: It depends upon the individual and the function for which they seek to use. For individualized use, the individual should seek entry way psychically or telepathically into the center of the stone. You will find that the consciousness of the energy or entity which you term "stone" is in the central . . . swing . . . of the atomic flow, in the very exact center of the stone. Therefore, it is not really critical the size, since the source vibration is equal. It is that the atomic structure and flow within . . . is from a central core or source, and is implanted in each vibration. It depends more on the energies of the individuals, and their capabilities to work within the energies of the stone, than the quality of the stone itself. Those specimens of stone which were close to the core energy of the meteor, as it was sent through, would have a greater concentration than those which radiated out at the outer surface of this ball as it was sent. However, it is important here to remember that this project was designed in such a way to imbue all aspects of the meteor with the qualities which they desired to bring into fullness in your world. It is more important . . . the . . . you call—"shape" of the stone. A stone in its raw essence is perfect. It is the greater intensity when it is spherical in nature, where the energy of the center can emanate in all areas, or when it is designed in pyramidal shape which also allows a focusing of the energy to escape. These are the two most potent forms of use for this stone, and indeed for any stone, when you take it and plane it from its natural state. Understood?

ROBERT: Yes. Along that line, I wondered about such shapes as the tetrahedron, octahedron, icosahedrons, and duodecahedrons.

AURILOITHA: Those also are useful shapes, for they serve the same purpose of allowing a focal point, and then exits from the focal point that are specifically directed in the various directions.

ROBERT: Thank you. Was Moldavite known and used in any previous civilization?

AURILOITHA: It is a part of the Atlantean history, though not in the same format, but the source designs are the same. And, of course, similar uses for similar stones were also used in the lost civilizations throughout your world, which are extraterrestrial in origin, including those which you would find in your South American continent and in Egyptian flow as well.

ROBERT: Thank you. We have used Moldavite in conjunction with a stone called Sugilite, and we wondered what you would say about that combination.

AURILOITHA: Each holds its separate property, and though the energy flows out together, it does not meld in unison. The stone [Moldavite] was designed to meld with the crystalline energies of the Quartz of your world, and if you understood the matrix of your planet, that would be clear. In essence, when you bring this stone into the energies of the Quartz, the molecular structure shifts and allows a cohesion to take place between these two stones, which creates an amplified energy, or a harmony of creative thought patterns to take place. Do you understand?

ROBERT: Yes.

AURILOITHA: So, though it may be used with other stones, it does not create a cohesive flow, but holds separateness when used with these other stones.

ROBERT: We have created a crown, or headband, using Moldavite in conjunction with Herkimer Quartz. I wondered if you could comment on that as an effective use.

AURILOITHA: It is most useful, not only for expanding the third chakra, but also for allowing the telepathy to activate, for it allows a contact with cosmic bodies which are around your planetary system.

ROBERT: Does Moldavite need to be cleared or cleansed energetically?

AURILOITHA: Once it has been established, and is being used by an individual working with the Light, then no, it does not. However, if it falls into the hands of an individual of negativity, it creates a force field that turns the energy back inwards towards the

Source, and does not act as a radiating flow, and would need to have the barrier which it sets into motion removed, in order for it to be useful once again by individuals of the Light. And this could be done simply by placing the stone which has been injured by the negativity of others into direct sunlight in an area that is out of doors. Not in your building, but out of doors.

ROBERT: Can elixirs or gem essences be made from Moldavite which would also help people?

AURILOITHA: Yes, but you would find here that the effect of the elixir would be to open the flow of what in your world you call the Kundalini—the clarity to clear, and to strengthen the flow, more than working on the specific chakras, which it does when it is in solidified form.

ROBERT: Can you give us some guidance on how to access the information we need to channel in our book about Moldavite?

AURILOITHA: For you both to be channels or receivers, you need to alter your present life-day structure in your world, or your schedule. This is the greatest barrier to your opening of your gifts, and when you have removed this barrier of your schedule, you will find by sitting in meditation with these headbands on, you will be more in harmony with the flow of information that will reach you telepathically.

ROBERT: This is on a slightly different subject. Can you give us any information on . . .

AURILOITHA: Before we change the subject, we would like to recommend that for the elixir, you mix the Quartz with the stone [Moldavite], and also that you mix the various Quartzes individually, to bring more than one elixir into play. [We recommend] that you work with all the Quartzes and their properties mixed individually with the [Moldavite] Stone to form different vibrations.

ROBERT: I just thought of this question. Does Moldavite have another name on different planes?

AURILOITHA: Yes, and in Pleiadean language it is known as Kishu [pronounced: KEE-shoo].

ROBERT: In terms of making elixirs with Moldavite, is placing the stone outdoors in the water in moonlight a good way to begin?

AURILOITHA: This stone resonates more to the sunlight than to the Moon.

ROBERT: Yes. Is there anything else, before we change to a different subject, that you wish to tell us about Moldavite, or anything that we can offer our readers as a message from you in our book?

AURILOITHA: It is to understand that this stone has the ability to bring the macrocosm of the Universal flows into the microcosm of its own infinite spark. Here is why it needs the energy of the sun. It brings the universal flow down from its expandedness into a concentrated universal spark. Or here what you would understand as bringing a solar design or what you call your solar system down to atomic size within the center of its own energy. Here is why it is so important when you design these [polished Moldavites] that you allow it a focal point, because it allows the greater use and potency of the energies. And to re-energize them, simply wear them in the sunlight and give them full exposure. It re-energizes them every time you place them in sunlight. This stone should be recognized to be used in a conscious manner. It should not be bought or used by those who do not understand its properties, its purpose, and the function for which it was designed. It should be brought forth to those individuals only who are walking the full path of spiritual understanding, and who wish to have a greater expansion, a greater exchange of energy with the cosmic Source, the cosmic flow. And recognize that the individual has an obligation to the [Moldavite] stones, to the cells of their own body which shall become attuned to the stones, and to their spiritual pathway. The [Moldavite] stone should not be obtained lightly. It should be obtained in understanding in complete seriousness and in dedication to one's spiritual pathway.

ROBERT: I have one more Moldavite question that I've just realized I need to ask. Some people who have gotten Moldavite from us have found that, initially at least, they have reactions of nausea or other physical discomfort from the stone. I have felt that they were clearing something in that respect, but can you give us some guidance on that?

AURILOITHA: Of course. What is occurring is that each cell of your body, being its own cosmos, reacts to the stone. And when they are imperfections in the cellular system, it is crossed into by the energy of the Moldavite. And since it is of the potency that it is of the creative Source, it goes to the source of the imbalance or disease, seeking to re-establish the vibration of wholeness of perfection. Therefore, individuals who have disease or imbalance, be it of the physical or etheric—such as in your world you call blocks—they will respond. It is, if you would imagine, a vibration coming in and setting up a whirlpool within another energy. Since there is discordance, there is a response physically, but it will pass as the energy seeks to clear through and qualify that which is not of the eight hertz, or vibration of creativity.

ROBERT: Thank you. (The interview then turned again to personal matters.)

CHAPTER 14
MOLDAVITE MEDITATIONS

One of the most powerful ways to work with Moldavite is to meditate with it. In meditation, we can attend more closely to subtle energies, and we can learn to visualize, which gives our perceptions a more vivid means of expression.

In my worldview, consciousness is present everywhere, including all matter. In my experience, the consciousness I have encountered with stones is organized sufficiently for one to view each kind of stone (and even individual stones) as a Self. When I meditate with any stone, I try to connect with the Being of the stone. In this way, such meditations become vibrational "conversations." One may not use words, but there is a mutual exchange of energies and a feeling of friendly familiarity.

Consequently, in the meditations I am offering here, I encourage you to envision the Moldavite as having its own consciousness and set of qualities. In other words, I invite you to treat it as a Being with whom you can relate. As with people, when one views the stone as a Being rather than a "thing" that one can just use, there is much more potential for beneficial exchange. One can feel stone energies and get some benefits, even when one views the stones as mere objects that emit vibrations, but I prefer the richness that can come through regarding the stones as Beings.

Perhaps this has something to do with the fact that the universe seems to respond to our intentions and expectations. We know from quantum physics that if one sets up laboratory equipment to measure a light photon as if it were a particle, the photon behaves like a particle. If one sets up equipment to measure the photon as a wave, it behaves as a wave. Yet the materialistic mind boggles, because light is supposed to be one or the other, not both!

It appears that we are linked in an infinitely complex web of relationships with everything else in the universe. Our choices influence the way reality itself arises. Therefore, I prefer to view Moldavite and all the stones as Beings, as self-organized centers of intelligence. When I approach them in this way, what occurs tends to confirm my intention—I *experience* the stones as Beings. And, as I say, much more happens between us than might otherwise be possible.

I always make my first connection with a stone by holding it near my heart and inviting it into my heart. I use my breath to invoke a "feedback loop" between myself and the stone. I have found that this simple method works very well, and it plants the seeds of mutual exchange in which we offer something to the Being of the stone, as well as asking for its benefits.

I invite you to give it a try.

MEETING THE BEING OF MOLDAVITE IN THE HEART

In this practice, you can enter into relationship with the Being of Moldavite. You will also have the experience of perception through the heart.

1. Go to your collection of stones and crystals and choose a Moldavite. If you have more than one piece, take the time to allow one of the pieces to choose *you*.

2. Sit down and relax while holding the Moldavite. Put all of your sensory attention on the stone. Look at its color and shape in detail, feel its texture with your fingers, and touch it to your cheek. Smell it, touch it with your tongue, and even hold it up to your ear and listen. You may not taste, smell, or hear anything, but giving attention in this way helps to sensitize your awareness.

3. Bring your subjective attention to the center of your chest, at the level of the heart. Hold the Moldavite in your two cupped hands, a few inches in front of your mouth. As you inhale, drawing air over the stone and into your lungs, imagine that you are inviting the Moldavite Being into your heart. As you exhale, silently offer yourself to the Moldavite Being, letting it know that you are available for relationship.

4. Continue this breathing for a few breaths—at least three and probably not more than ten—but let your intuition guide you. When you feel ready, bring the Moldavite to your chest and hold it there, touching you. Let your eyes close and allow yourself to attend fully to your inner experience. Continue to affirm the invitation on the in-breath and the offer of yourself on the out-breath. Picture the Moldavite's image responding to your invitation by moving into your chest, finally settling into the center of your heart. Notice what that feels like, and attend to the presence of the Moldavite Being in your heart. Greet it from your heart and thank it for coming into you.

5. Let this meditation continue for several minutes. It is not necessary to do anything else, other than to maintain the visualization, and give yourself over to whatever feelings or images you experience. Don't hold back. Allow the heart to hold and cherish the Moldavite Being.

6. Notice everything that happens. Sometimes this sort of meditation will trigger a more complex visionary experience. If that happens, go with it. If the Moldavite Being starts to communicate with you, attend to it inwardly, and respond as your heart moves you to respond. Also, take note of your bodily sensations. You may feel the Moldavite energies moving into and through your body. You may find that the currents travel to one or more specific places. If so, pay attention to where the energy goes, and how it feels. Afterward, make notes about your experience in your journal. Don't be concerned about specific results. Just allow yourself to breathe and see and feel the stone in your heart. Continue to do this for at least ten minutes. When you feel ready to stop, or have the sense that the session is completed, you can gently open your eyes.

Discussion

This practice is the way I begin all of my intuitive work with stones. Following this ritual each time one sits down with a stone does several things.

First, it teaches you a simple way to quiet distracting thoughts and direct your attention, both outwardly to the physical Moldavite and inwardly to your inner experience of it. This is important because this sort of communication occurs in the subtle realm, and going there requires focused, sensitive attention.

Second, this practice helps you learn to make your heart the place you go for spiritual work with your Moldavite. Our hearts have their own intelligence, and they have long been viewed as the seat of the soul. The heart is the place where Wisdom dwells within us, and where spiritual beings can most readily meet us. By practicing visualizations in the heart, you will become familiar with how it feels to be heart-centered, and will come to recognize the heart's distinctive intelligence.

Third, this type of practice can help take one into the inner Silence, which is where the spiritual world exists. Most of us live with a constant stream of inner talk going on whenever we are awake. Using visualization and heart-centering can quiet that ongoing monologue. This is, in itself, one of the main goals of many meditation practices.

Fourth, this simple exercise, using breath and imagination, can take one to the threshold of profound spiritual experience. Once we have successfully visualized the Moldavite in the heart, we may find that more things happen spontaneously. All sorts of inner events can occur, ranging from flowing currents of energy to conversational dialogues to inner journeys, or even to physical events. Sometimes the heart will temporarily change its rhythm of beating when it feels the presence of the Moldavite Being. (I smilingly compare this to a dog wagging its tail.)

MUTUAL BLESSING MEDITATION:
Meeting The Being of Moldavite as an Inner Figure and Having a Conversation

In this practice, you'll be asking the Moldavite Being to come to you in human form, or as some sort of an inner figure. When the being appears, you'll engage in a conversation with each other—either verbal or non-verbal.

1. Select a piece of Moldavite to work with, or if you have more than one Moldavite, let a piece chose you. Follow that feeling. You can use an unfamiliar stone or a favorite stone. In this case, let intuition guide you.

2. Begin by looking at the Moldavite and sensing it with all your senses. Breathe over the stone, offering yourself with the out-breath and inviting the stone with the in-breath.

3. Close your eyes and pay attention to the interior of your body.

4. Hold the Moldavite against your chest, at the level of the heart. Breathe deeply and slowly, bringing attention to your heart.

5. Place within your heart feelings of love and appreciation, and invite the Being of the Moldavite into your heart.

6. As you breathe, offer your well-wishing and love to the Moldavite Being. Feel the circulation of the blessing energies between you. Allow the intensity of the feeling to increase, and pay attention to how that feels. Notice if there is a mutual reinforcement of the blessing energies. Continue the self-giving to the Moldavite Being, and the receiving of its energies, as you breathe out and in.

7. When you're ready, and can feel the stone energies resonating with yours, put your attention in your heart and say inwardly to the Moldavite Being: "Please show yourself to me in human form, or as an inner figure, and please tell me or show me what I most need to know. It can be about you, about me, or about whatever you wish to show me." If you prefer, you can ask this through a felt sense of intention and inquiry instead of words.

8. Pay attention to whatever you see or feel. Wait for the Moldavite Being to come to you. If nothing seems to happen, go back to breathing and the feelings of appreciation and ask again. When the figure of the Moldavite Being comes to you, it may be as a visual image, as energy, a felt presence, a voice, or in another way. We're asking to meet an imaginal inner figure—a living image—but the Being may have reasons to appear in its own way. Keep your contact with the stone and its currents as you breathe and ask for the inner figure to come. Then wait and be alert.

9. Stay with it until you see or feel the Moldavite Being arrive. Inwardly ask what it wants to tell or show you. If you don't understand what you are shown or told, don't worry, just try to remember it so you'll be able to write a description of what happens. (You can also ask the Moldavite Being for further information or clarification.)

10. Once the communication is established, you can ask questions. Do so with or without words, but keep yourself centered in your heart, and ask your questions from there. Stay alert, but in your heart, and try to remember everything that happens. You can even have a "conversation" if you can keep it going while staying in your heart. Allow yourself to go with whatever wants to happen.

11. You can also express your point of view to the Moldavite Being. Depending on the connection you are able to establish, this can become a real conversation, verbal or otherwise. Let the Moldavite Being know your ideas, needs, or wishes, and ask how you can work together. Or communicate whatever feels appropriate. Often, the fewer words you use, the better it works. Try expressing your thoughts as images or feelings, while continuing to breathe in the exchange of mutual blessings with the Moldavite Being.

12. It is often fascinating and illuminating to go on a journey with the Moldavite Being to its realm—its "world." Every Stone Being has its own world in the psychoid/imaginal realm. If it will take you there, you will understand the nature of the stone better, through observing the type of world it has. The Moldavite Being can often show you things in its world that are related to its capacities for working with you, so watch carefully what it does, and pay attention to anything it shows you. If and when the Moldavite Being takes you into its world, this is a great gift, and it deepens your relationship. Most likely, you will be able to return there again and again, as long as you are relating with the Moldavite Being on a regular basis. (If the Being is not ready to take you to its realm, it is likely that you are not ready to go there. Be content to develop your relationship in other ways, and ask again at a later time.)

13. When this experiences feels complete, you may begin to disengage. Before doing so, bring your attention back to the exchange of blessings through the breath, and focus on intensifying that feeling for a few moments. Then thank the Moldavite Being and gently withdraw yourself and begin to come back to your body and the physical world.

14. When you can feel yourself in your body and fully present in the room, put your attention in your feet and wiggle your toes. When you are ready, open your eyes, have a drink of water, or whatever you need to do to ground yourself. A stone such as Hematite, Black Tourmaline, Nuummite or Guardianite may be helpful for this. Then, before the experience fades, write some descriptive notes about what happened—the messages, conversations, etc.

Discussion

By inviting the spirit of a stone to display itself to us as an inner figure, we are opening ourselves to the natural activity of that Being's nature. We have begun by paying attention to it and offering our blessing and inviting it into our heart. Then we proceed by inviting it to use its creative ability to communicate with us. In my experience, as long as I am making a genuine invitation and giving my focused attention to my inner experience, the Stone Being will show itself and communicate in a very generous way.

The fact that we can often feel the energetic currents of the stone shows us that we are actually being met. The energies themselves have already come toward us from the realm of pure spirit and are meeting us in the in-between realm of the psychoid/imaginal domain—the realm of subtle bodies. By initiating energetic feedback with the Moldavite Being, we enhance and expand the potential for what can happen.

It is important to remember to offer and invite, but not to control. This is true, of course, in any relationship. If we offer ourselves to another person and invite them into relationship, love and spontaneity can exist between us. We can enjoy the other person, and even learn from him or her. And because we do not try to control the other person, there is no way to predict what he or she will do or say. This is part of the magic of love. If we tried to control things, we would destroy the spontaneity and there would be no real relationship.

With the Moldavite Being, or with any Stone Being, the same pattern holds. The richness and magic of what can happen depends on our light touch. We make ourselves available, offer ourselves and invite the other being to meet us. Then we wait, and we respond to whatever occurs. If we are honest, we know how it feels to force things, and we know when we are doing it. So, we avoid that and attend gently to the magic.

MOLDAVITE GRAIL MEDITATION

Moldavite has long been associated with the fabled Stone of the Holy Grail. In this meditation, you are invited to work with the image of the Grail, and to allow the Moldavite to play its role in the manifestation of the Grail within you. If it is helpful, you can play some appropriate spiritual music with this meditation.

1. Select a piece of Moldavite to work with, or if you have more than one Moldavite, let a piece choose you. Follow that feeling. You can use an unfamiliar stone or a favorite stone. In this case, let intuition guide you.
2. Begin by looking at the Moldavite and sensing it with all your senses. Breathe over the stone, offering yourself with the out-breath and inviting the stone with the in-breath.

3. Close your eyes and pay attention to the interior of your body.

4. Hold the Moldavite against your chest, at the level of the heart. Breathe deeply and slowly, bringing attention to your heart.

5. Place within your heart feelings of love and appreciation, and invite the Being of the Moldavite into your heart.

6. When you feel the connection and can sense the Moldavite's energies, begin the meditation by envisioning a golden chalice inside your chest at the level of your heart. Take the time to allow yourself to examine it in detail, noticing its color, its texture, the patterns of its design.

7. Bring your attention to the interior of the cup. Notice how it glows with golden Light. Now look inside the cup and notice that your Moldavite is there. It is emitting a pulsating golden glow.

8. Bring your perspective back to where you can view the whole chalice that is resting in your chest. The golden Light coming out of the cup becomes liquid, and it begins to overflow from the chalice. The energy of the Moldavite is blended with the golden Light. You feel it pouring out, filling your chest and beginning to spread through your whole body.

9. Notice the liquid golden Light filling your body and circulating through your veins. It is permeating your entire body now, and is going into every cell. And with the golden Light comes a feeling of Divine Presence and a great surge of joy. All of your cells are singing this joy.

10. While you are bathed in this golden Light energy, place your attention again on the Grail chalice at the level of your heart. Notice the way the energy radiates from it. It may appear in the form of a torus, with the rays of golden Light circulating all around the central channel of your chakra column, rising out of your crown chakra, circling outward, and re-entering at your root chakra.

11. Take time to dwell in this golden torus of Light, joy, and Divine presence. Let your attention move through your body, noticing the feeling of Light and grace in all of your parts. Emphasize the intensity of the circulating light. Notice that the chalice may become much larger, perhaps the size of your whole body, and the circulating Light extends further beyond your immediate environment.

(NOTE: It is possible to allow the chalice to become vast in size, with a corresponding embrace of a much larger space within the circulating Light. But your heart should always be at the very center. One can take this as far as one wishes, encompassing the whole Earth or even the entire universe in the golden torus of Light.)

12. When the intensity begins to diminish, spend a few minutes anchoring the intention in your body that this Light and joy has now become a permanent part of your being. Bring everything back into your physical body and into your heart. See the Grail chalice and Moldavite in your heart again, as you did in the beginning. (Give this part of the meditation as much time and attention as you feel is needed. Integrating the expansive aspect of the meditation into your body and your normal consciousness is important for creating lasting effects.)

13. If you wish, you can bring your attention back to the chalice and ask for guidance about your highest spiritual destiny, and what you can do to achieve it. Sometimes a voice will come to you from the chalice itself.

14. When you feel that the experience is complete, gently begin to bring your attention back into your physical embodiment. Wiggle your toes to ground yourself, open your eyes, and take a few deep cleansing breaths.

15. Write some notes in your journal about what you saw, felt, and learned in this meditation.

Discussion

In legend, the Holy Grail is viewed as a mystical object that had the effect of setting the knights who beheld it on their path of spiritual destiny. It guided them through life, not allowing them to make wrong choices (which they often attempted to do). The Grail especially guided its knights to their true love, and to their highest purpose. Moldavite has been observed to have similar effects on those who acquire it.

By calling in the Grail image and energy while holding a Moldavite and attending to its vibrations, one can readily connect with the Grail that exists in the subtle realm. (To invoke the Grail, we use the tangible Moldavite and the imagined chalice together. This is because the Grail has been described in two different ways—as a cup or chalice, and as an "Emerald that fell from the sky.") In my view, the Grail of the legend was always a sacred object in the realm of subtle matter/energy. The legend says that the unworthy cannot see the Grail, even when it sits before their eyes. But the pure knight Galahad immediately beheld the Grail. I view this as the story telling us that the Grail is not of the mundane world, and that one must be able to attune to the subtle realm in order to connect with it.

Many chroniclers of the Grail story contend that the true Grail is in the heart. The Grail is, more specifically, the heart transmuted by coming into union with the Divine. To achieve the Grail was to be transformed into a human window for the Divine to shine in this world. By inviting the Divine Light emanated by the Grail to permeate one's body, one is visualizing and actualizing this transformation. Moldavite's energies can bring great power to this meditative ritual.

Those who have a powerful experience in this meditation, and who feel called to the Grail quest, are invited to repeat this meditation multiple times. In esoteric circles, it is known that repetition is a key factor in vivifying images, objects, energies, and beings in the subtle realm. It is also true in the material world. Practice makes perfect!

MOLDAVITE JOURNEY TO THE GREAT CENTRAL SUN

My original meditative journey with Moldavite, which activated my latent capacity to feel stone energies and set me on an accelerated spiritual path, involved a spontaneous inner journey into the cosmos. It culminated with my arrival at the Great Central Sun, and with my being told (and realizing) that its Divine Light was the same as the Light of my own being. The meditation described below is meant to invoke a similar journey.

For this meditation, it may be helpful to use music that feels like one is flying toward the Divine. I like to use a rather old piece called "Lunamuse" by Kay Gardner. It is easy to find online. Sometimes I play it on "repeat" for a longer meditation. But choose the music that feels best to you.

1. Select a piece of Moldavite to work with, or if you have more than one Moldavite, let a piece choose you. Follow that feeling. You can use an unfamiliar stone or a favorite stone. In this case, let intuition guide you.

2. Begin by looking at the Moldavite and sensing it with all your senses. Breathe over the stone, offering yourself with the out-breath and inviting the stone with the in-breath.

3. Close your eyes and pay attention to the interior of your body.

4. Hold the Moldavite against your chest, at the level of the heart. Breathe deeply and slowly, bringing attention to your heart.

5. Place within your heart feelings of love and appreciation, and invite the Being of the Moldavite into your heart.

6. When you feel the energetic connection, center yourself in your heart, feeling the dynamic, uplifting currents of the Moldavite.

7. Gently allow your center of awareness to rise up from your heart, through the throat chakra, the third eye chakra, and out through the crown. Let yourself float up a few feet higher, and look down on your body from above.

8. Continue to float up, through the ceiling and roof (if one is inside). When you are up fifty feet or so, look around you at the landscape. Then continue to ascend.

9. Notice that you are moving upward faster now, much faster, yet there is no wind or friction. You are rising like a balloon, but much faster. As you look down, you can see a much wider landscape below you, and the sky above you shifts from blue to indigo. Now you are far above the clouds, high enough to see the curvature of the Earth.

10. Notice that you can now see the whole globe of the Earth, and perhaps the Moon as well. You are in space, and the stars shine sharply, like diamonds. Allow yourself to keep flying into space, leaving the Earth far behind.

11. When you are deep among the stars, look around and see if you can find a gold-white star that calls to you. If so, move toward it. You can now go at speeds faster than light. Perhaps the stars will disappear for a short time.

12. Notice that you are now near the golden star. It is huge in your vision. Allow yourself to fall into orbit around it. Look to see if any other objects or beings are orbiting that star.

13. Now look down at yourself, to the space of your heart where you began the journey. What do you see? How does it feel? Is there a golden globe of Light that echoes the shape of the star you are circling? What are you, who are you, in this place?

14. At this point, just follow the experience wherever it takes you. Feel everything to the fullest.

15. At some point, you will find yourself back in your physical body. Or perhaps you will still be among the stars and will know it is time to return. If this occurs, just allow it to happen. Your soul will know the way back.

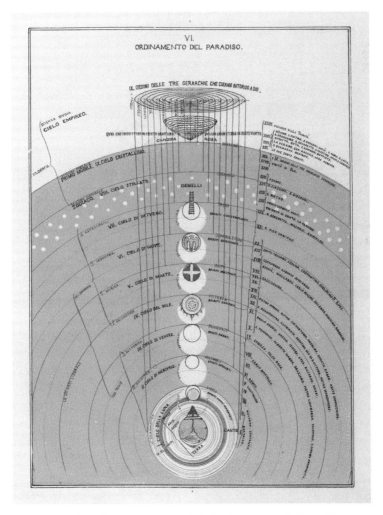

The Ordering of Paradise by Caetani, 1855. This drawing portrays the Seven Heavens described in Dante's *Divine Comedy*. I find it valuable to view "Heaven" and the Light Body as the same thing. The seven chakras echo the Seven Heavens, and vice versa. And since both of these exist in the subtle realm, where relative "size" is meaningless, why should the Body of Light be less than, or different from, Heaven? As William Blake wrote: *To see a World in a Grain of Sand / And a Heaven in a Wild Flower, / Hold Infinity in the palm of your hand / And Eternity in an hour.*

16. When you are ready, wiggle toes, drink water, walk on the grass—whatever you need to ground yourself.

17. Take some time to contemplate the experience and/or write in your journal.

Discussion

This meditation offers a journey to a higher realm of reality, a realm in which a golden Sun appears as the manifestation (and the Source) of Divine Light. The meditator is invited to get near this holy energy source, and to let it have its effect on one's entire being. Moldavite is a good partner for initiating such a journey, because it has its own connection to the stars, and it emanates high and powerful vibrations.

There is less to say about this meditation, because it is open-ended, and can take one beyond what can be adequately described in words. My advice is to visualize as vividly as possible in the beginning, and when the experience begins to take off on its own, let go of purposeful imagining and simply go with it. Have a good journey.

MOLDAVITE LIGHT BODY ACTIVATION MEDITATION

This meditation is intended to increase the activity of one's chakras, and one's ability to access them. At the same time, it is meant to activate the Light Body by bringing a great deal of energy into the entire chakra column or central channel.

1. Select a piece of Moldavite to work with, or if you have more than one Moldavite, let a piece choose you. Follow that feeling. You can use an unfamiliar stone or a favorite stone. In this case, let intuition guide you.

2. Begin by looking at the Moldavite and sensing it with all your senses. Breathe over the stone, offering yourself with the out-breath and inviting the stone with the in-breath.

3. Close your eyes and pay attention to the interior of your body.

4. Hold the Moldavite against your chest, at the level of the heart. Breathe deeply and slowly, bringing attention to your heart.

5. Place within your heart feelings of love and appreciation, and invite the Being of the Moldavite into your heart.

6. When you feel the energetic connection, center yourself in your heart, feeling the dynamic, uplifting currents of the Moldavite.

7. Once you feel the currents of the Moldavite, visualize a black tubular column about one to two inches in diameter, running through your core, up to the heavenly realm and down to the center of the Earth. Feel your heart, resonating with the Moldavite, at the midpoint of this infinite column.

8. Bring your attention to your root chakra, and feel the Moldavite energizing it. Notice in detail how this chakra feels. Notice color, warmth, or coolness. Dwell there in the energy for a few minutes.

9. Now switch your attention to your crown chakra. Feel its high frequency vibrations. Notice how they mingle with the currents of the Moldavite. Feel the texture of this chakra. Notice color, warmth, or coolness. Stay in the crown and enjoy the feeling for a few minutes. See if you can intensify it.

10. Now move your attention to the second chakra. Allow yourself to feel a thread of connection to the root and crown chakras, while emphasizing the sensations of the second chakra. Notice temperature, color, vibration. There can be a lot of energy here.

11. Shift your attention to your third eye chakra. Notice the connection with the crown, root, and second chakra. Feel the pulsations or other vibrations. What color is here? How intense are the energies?

12. Now move attention to the third chakra, at the solar plexus. Feel how the currents are vibrating in this area. What color or colors arise, what pattern or patterns? Allow yourself to notice the threads of energy linking this chakra to the root, second chakra, third eye, and crown. How does this chakra feel uniquely different from the others?

13. Switch your attention now to the throat chakra. Feel its vibration, and its resonance with the other chakras you have touched on so far. Notice any color or patterns that arise. Feel the vibrations here.

14. Now move to the heart chakra, where you are still holding the Moldavite. Notice its color, texture, patterns, and vibrational currents. Feel the heart's resonance with all of the other chakras, above and below.

15. Envision all seven chakras aligned within the tubular column that reaches infinitely above and below the body. See each chakra brightening, with its light and energy being activated, in resonance with all the others. See all seven chakras blazing like a vertical rainbow of light. Feel them vibrating in your body.

16. Now, from far down below your feet, see a red light or energy rising up from the depths. It is pouring upward like a volcano erupting. And at the same time there is pure white Light pouring down through the tube from far, far above. It is streaking down the tube, into your energy field, like a descending meteor.

17. Now, at the level of the heart, the red light with its intense heat and power meets the pure white light from above, with its deep coolness and brilliance. These two beams meet at your heart and there is a powerful merging, forming a globe of pure pink light, encompassing your body, with your heart at its center. There is a feeling of joy and glory as these lights merge and create the pink star that you stand within.

18. Feel the pink star, and know that this is your heart's star, in union with the Above and the Below. Explore the feeling of being in this globular Body of Light. Allow its energies to modulate and let the color become whatever fits you best. Feel the powerful currents of its energy and recognize that you are free to use them as you wish. Bask in the grandeur of your Glorified Body of Light.

19. Now, to integrate and incarnate the Light Body, bring your attention back to the central column and your aligned, activated chakras. See and feel the resonant power of your Light Body, and its infinite connection with the above and the below.

20. Finally, begin to focus individually on the chakras, moving slowly downward, pausing at each chakra to inwardly speak the following affirmations. Commit your full intention and energy to each statement. Envision your seven chakras as perfectly aligned and fully activated, situated midway between the highest Heaven and the deepest Earth:

CROWN: "Know the Truth."
THIRD EYE: "See the Truth."
THROAT: "Speak the Truth."
HEART: "Feel the Truth."
SOLAR PLEXUS: "Will the Truth."
SECOND CHAKRA: "Share the Truth."
ROOT: "Incarnate the Truth."

[NOTE: You can further emphasize this culminating point in the meditation by circulating through the chakras two more times and substituting the words "Light" and/or "Love" for "Truth." (They all point to the same thing anyway!)]

21. Inwardly claim your Light Body as the throne of your being. See and feel it again, as vividly as you can. Then begin to gently bring yourself back to your physical body.

22. As the intensity of the energies begins to subside, remember that this experience is real, and that it is always a part of you that you can access at any time.

23. When you are ready, allow your eyes to open and wiggle your toes, ground yourself, but allow yourself to play with the feeling of having your physical form and your Body of Light superimposed on each other.

Discussion

The number of different meditations one can do with Moldavite is literally unlimited. I encourage readers to use your imaginations and experiment. I must also say that my early trip to the Great Central Sun was not planned at all. I started visualizing floating out of my body because of a spontaneous urge, but after a few minutes, the process took off on its own, and I had no part in controlling it.

This is an important point in many kinds of meditation. Imagination takes one to the threshold of spiritual experience, but Divine Intelligence carries on from there. I advise you to begin with your intention, attention, and imagination fully engaged, but when the experience begins to take on a life of its own, by all means go with it!

MOLDAVITE ENERGY TOOLS & PRACTICES

W hat arc the optimal ways to work with Moldavite's exceptional energies? Are there things we can do to enhance, focus, or magnify Moldavite's effects? How can we integrate Moldavite's vibrations into our bodies? What can we do with Moldavite to share its energies with other people and the world?

These are the kinds of questions that have inspired my efforts, and the attempts of many others, to create Moldavite Energy Tools. The range of these endeavors is wide, and in this chapter we will touch on a number of them.

Perhaps the most obvious way to maximize the benefits of Moldavite is to wear or carry some. A great many people simply keep a raw Moldavite in a pocket or elsewhere on their person. But perhaps even more choose to wear a piece of Moldavite Jewelry.

People often ask whether it is better to wear Moldavite in raw or polished form. There is no blanket answer to this question. But, from my experience, raw Moldavites often seem to be more dramatically powerful, while polished pieces and faceted gems emanate a more refined and focused energy.

Another question is whether size matters, and what is the optimal amount of Moldavite to be worn. Again, this varies widely among people.

TOP: Moldavite "Ray Gun"; MIDDLE: Faceted Moldavite pendants in Sterling silver; BOTTOM: Half-raw, half-polished Moldavite pendant in 14k gold

But I like to say that a tiny Moldavite vibrates at the same frequencies that a large one does. It can be compared to music—all Moldavites play the same "song," but bigger pieces tend to play it louder. And something like a necklace made of 100 or more pieces of raw Moldavite can feel VERY "loud." But, once again, different people often resonate strongly with different specific pieces of Moldavite, regardless of size. All this is something one needs to approach intuitively.

Another frequent query I receive is where on the body is the best place to wear Moldavite. With pendants and necklaces, I feel Moldavite resonates best when worn at the level of the heart. With rings, one might wish to wear Moldavite on the index finger for manifesting, or on the third finger if the priority is a harmonious love relationship. The currents from the stones in a pair of Moldavite stud earrings often feel stronger than they might otherwise, because there are energy meridians in the ear lobes. Moldavite earrings also have a powerful effect because they are quite near the brain. In my view, one of the "strongest" ways to wear Moldavite is to combine a pendant with a pair of earrings. This creates a triangle of Moldavite energy that resonates in all of one's upper chakras.

Having said this, I must also say that having Moldavite anywhere in one's subtle energy field will affect that field. Listen to your inner voice and you'll make the right choices.

Sleeping with Moldavite

If one wants to find out whether Moldavite really affects one's consciousness, the surest way is to tape a piece on one's forehead and sleep with it there. I've tried this many times, and recommended it to thousands of people. Virtually everyone who does this, myself included, reports a major increase in dream activity, and often a deepening of the numinosity of one's dreams. In fact, for many of us, sleeping with Moldavite at the third eye stimulates such intense dreaming that we are forced to remove the stone during the night, in order to get some quieter sleep! Sleeping with Moldavite under one's pillow or on one's night table is usually less intense.

TOP: Necklace of Moldavite chips; BOTTOM: Moldavite stud earrings in Sterling silver

One can moderate or enhance the effects of sleeping with Moldavite by combining it with other stones. After offering various stone "recipes" over the years, we put together a number of harmonious combinations in what we call Dream Pouches.

The two pictured are called Chakra Power and Synergy 12. Both contain Moldavite. The Chakra Power Dream Pouch is intended to balance and strengthen all the chakras during sleep. It contains Moldavite, Herkimer (Quartz) Diamond, Auralite-23, Lapis Lazuli, Azumar, Aquamarine, Emerald, Ruby, Garnet, Himalaya Gold Azeztulite,

Chakra Power Dream Pouch

Synergy 12 Dream Pouch

Golden Healer Quartz, New Zealand Carnelian, Orange Kyanite, Black Tourmaline, and Magnifier Quartz.

The Synergy 12 pouch offers the most potent combinaton of stones for energizing and calling forth the fullness of the Self. It contains Moldavite, Phenacite, Tanzanite, Danburite, White Azeztulite, Petalite, Tibetan Tektite, Satyaloka Clear Azeztulite, Natrolite, Herderite, Scolecite, Brookite, and Magnifier Quartz.

The above are only two of endless possible combinations. Experimenting with them can yield your own ideal recipes—for lucid dreaming, peaceful sleep, self-healing, chakra activation or any number of enhancements of one's awareness and well-being. Moldavite is quite versatile, and can add energy to most combinations. Just remember that, if you feel so much energy that your sleep begins to suffer, you may want to put the Moldavite aside for awhile.

Moldavite Water

Making Moldavite water and elixirs is easy and fun. The simplest method is to place some Moldavite (as much as possible) into a water pitcher and place it in the sun for a couple of hours. (The sunlight energetically stimulates the Moldavite, and the water as well.) After that, pour yourself a glass and drink up! More sensitive people will feel the stimulating effects of the Moldavite right away. And, when I have experimented with doing this in groups—even friends and family around the dinner table—I have noticed an obvious elevation in the mood of the entire group within five to ten minutes. About nine out of ten people usually report being able to feel a positive shift in their consciousness.

Because we are talking about drinking this water, it is necessary to caution readers to make sure the Moldavite is clean and free of residue. Being a glass, the Moldavite itself will not leach into the water, but any material stuck to its surface might. And do not put the Moldavite into one's drinking glass. It might be possible to accidentally swallow or choke on the stone.

Crystal Canteen with Moldavite/Magnifier Quartz mixture

Making this kind of "stone water" provides opportunities to combine other stones (with or without Moldavite) to energize one's drinking water in ways that produce a whole range of interesting effects. Once again, a word of caution: You must be certain that any stones you immerse in water you plan to drink are inert and will not leach anything into the water. And, as with the Moldavite, they must be clean and free of residue.

I have also found that it is not necessary to immerse the Moldavite (or other stones) in the drinking water. If the stones are placed very near the drinking water, the charging works just as well. And this method eliminates all the concerns about leaching or other contamination. One way to do this is to place the Moldavite and/or other stones in a tightly sealed jar and immerse the jar in the drinking water, ideally in a sunny area.

This method has been incorporated into the design of the lovely glass drinking water bottles called Crystal Canteens. These consist of a glass cylinder for the water, and a jar for stones that screws on at the bottom of the cylinder. This puts the stones in close proximity to the water, without physically touching it. And it allows for continuous charging of the water throughout the day. Once again, there are an infinite variety of possible stone combinations one can use. The recipe I created to feature Moldavite's energy exclusively is called Moldavite Power. In this case, the charging jar contains six or seven small Moldavites and around eighty to ninety grams of Magnifier Quartz. (As its name implies, Magnifier Quartz is used to amplify the energies of stones with which it is combined, without otherwise changing them.)

Moldavite Gemstone Essences

A Moldavite essence is somewhat similar to Moldavite water, but the elixirs I make go through an intensified charging process, and they are also fixed with a small amount of alcohol, to keep them fresh. I find gemstone essences to be more potent, such that a few drops under my tongue, or a spray of essence mist over my head both have as strong an effect as a whole glass of Moldavite water.

To make the essence, I soak a good amount of Moldavite (at least ten grams) in about one liter of spring water, and put it out to sit in the sun for a few hours. Then I "potentize" the charged water by diluting it with ten liters of additional spring water. This second batch of water is also charged in the sun for a few hours.

[NOTE: Potentizing by dilution is a well know practice used in creating homeopathic remedies. Although it may feel counterintuitive, it is believed that the dilution increases the vibrational strength of the remedy by the amount of dilution. Thus, the Moldavite water would become ten times more powerful with one dilution. If I were to do a second round of dilution, the resulting elixir would theoretically be 100 times as powerful as the original Moldavite water. I have not done this yet, because I would end up with 100 liters of water! I admit that I am curious, and expect to try this sooner or later. But the essences I have made are already quite powerful as they are! Some homeopathic medicinal remedies go as high as 100 dilutions. The ones seen in health food stores are typically diluted six to thirty times.]

Once the water has been charged by the Moldavite and the sun, and then potentized, I subject it to an additional charging process. For this, I place the charged water in a large glass container, sitting on a small table within a six-foot copper pyramid. The copper pipes are filled with several kinds of Azeztulite, plus Rosophia. Also, there is a large Phenacite attached to the apex of the pyramid, and another one on the floor beneath the table. The whole assembly is surrounded by a grid of Azeztulite, Rosophia, and other high vibration stones. I leave the water under the pyramid overnight.

The next day, the water is "fixed" by adding ten percent 100 proof, high-quality vodka. Since the person is only using a few drops, or an external spray of the Moldavite essence, there is no concern about getting intoxicated. (However, I believe that people who are alcoholics should only use the essences externally.)

The gem essences we make using Moldavite, as well as a variety of combinations of other stones, are then bottled. (One of the most popular blends is the Synergy 12 group, which contains Moldavite

TOP: Moldavite Gemstone Essence; BOTTOM: Synergy 12 Gemstone Essence

and eleven other high-vibration stones.) After initially using dropper bottles, we have since gone exclusively to spray bottles. Spraying the Moldavite essence over the head provides a rush of refreshment and energy throughout one's auric field. It also works well when applied to specific chakra points.

Moldavite Power Wands

Wand shapes are frequently use when a directed flow of stone energy is desired. It is easy to discern this by placing the point of a Quartz crystal at the third eye, or over the hand. When one compares the energy felt in this way to what one senses when the

crystal is at a right angle to the chakra or hand, the verdict is usually that the flow from the point of the crystal is more focused and more powerful. Even stones that do not naturally form as crystals seem to exhibit this linear energy flow when they are formed into wand shapes.

With Moldavite, there are very few pieces large enough and thick enough to make anything larger than a very tiny wand. And in most cases, the owner would not want to cut up the raw Moldavite specimen. However, we have discovered several ways to work with Moldavite, while still getting the benefit of the additional power and focus the wand shape can provide.

Back in the 1980s, I made the Moldavite energy tool shown at the beginning of this chapter. I glued polished Moldavites all over a natural Quartz laser wand, to which I had attached several small laser wands. When I hold this over the palm of just about anyone—even those who claim stone energies are not real—they immediately get a tangible tingle wherever the main crystal is pointed. Often, they report sensations of heat, which indicate that the Moldavite currents are coming through. I have made many such Moldavite and Quartz power wands for people, though usually less ornate than this one! A quite powerful wand can be made by simply attaching some raw Moldavites to a Quartz point, using either putty or glue. Most energy-sensitive people will notice the intensity and focus of the currents coming through the termination of the Quartz.

Moldavite and Quartz energy wands

TOP: Selenite Wand with Moldavite, Magnifier Quartz, and Herkimer (Quartz) Diamonds; MIDDLE: Selenite Wand with Synergy 12 Stones; BOTTOM: Selenite ET Power Wand with Moldavite, Tibetan Tektite, Libyan Gold Tektite, and Prophecy Stone

Tube Wand with Moldavite chips

Tube Wand with Synergy 12 stones

Another type of Moldavite power wand can be created by attaching Moldavites to a Selenite wand. Selenite acts as a natural amplifier of the energies of whatever stones one combines with it, and it has the additional virtue of being able to harmoniously blend the currents of multiple stones, as it is magnifying them. At Heaven and Earth, we offer a wide variety of such wands, with many different stone recipes, with and without Moldavite. One of the most popular is the Synergy 12 combination.

The final type of power wand I want to describe is somewhat sleeker and more stylish, and it provides an excellent focused stream of stone energies. These are what I call "tube wands," and they consist of a glass or plastic tube with a polished Quartz point on one end, and a sphere or rounded cabochon on the other end. Small Moldavites and/or other stones are used to fill the tube. This is an excellent use for tiny chips that might otherwise go to waste. The energy that pours through the pointed end is powerful and highly focused. The currents coming from the rounded end are more diffuse, but still quite strong. The two photos shown are of an all-Moldavite tube wand and a Synergy 12 wand, which contains Moldavite and eleven other high-vibe stones.

Moldavite Templates

Gemstone "templates" are palm-size grids in which a pattern of small stones is attached to a larger stone that is usually flat or slightly domed. As with the wands described above, templates are meant to enhance the vibrations of stones which are not readily available (or are expensive) in large sizes. They provide a portable platform for the smaller stones, and offer the added magnification of the pattern's geometry, as well as the influence of the base stone itself. Templates are excellent to hold in

Large (6 inch diameter) Template with Amethyst base. Quartz and polished Moldavite are attached.

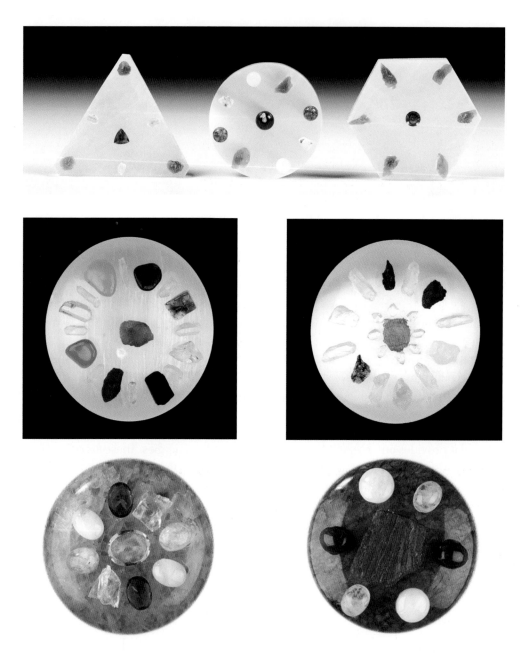

TOP: Three Selenite Templates with Moldavites; CENTER LEFT: Super Chakra Harmony Template with Moldavite center stone; CENTER RIGHT: Alchemical Transformation Template with Moldavite center stone; BOTTOM LEFT: Great Central Sun Template with Himalaya Gold Azeztulite base, Moldavite gems, Libyan Gold Tektite, plus three types of small Azeztulites; BOTTOM RIGHT: Philosophers' Stone Template with Rosophia base, Moldavite centerpiece, Master Shamanite, and Azeztulite

meditation. They also work well in body layouts, allowing one to place a harmonious vibrational "chord" of energy at any point along the chakra column.

Templates provide an ideal option for optimizing Moldavite's energy, and for combining it synergistically with other high vibration stones. The super-template shown at the beginning of this section was made in 1988, and is seven inches in diameter. It is combined with Lemurian Quartz, Amethyst, and Moldavite gems. Other base materials that I like to use include Selenite, Himalaya Gold Azeztulite, and Rosophia.

Moldavite Pyramid Templates

If one has access to a polished Quartz pyramid and a few small Moldavites, it is possible to make a very powerful little energy tool. One can simply glue (or attach with putty) four Moldavite pieces to the four sides of the Quartz pyramid. The finished piece can be held in the hand during meditation, or placed on any of the chakras in a body layout. The Quartz amplifies the Moldavite's energies, while the pyramid shape provides a resonating form for them, as well as focusing the currents through the apex.

Quartz pyramid with Moldavites attached

A Moldavite pyramid template can also be used to transmit a stream of energy in a treatment. If one points the pyramid at the third eye or heart chakra, one is likely to feel something like a "laser beam" of subtle energy. This tool can also be used on the body's meridians to perform a kind of subtle energy "acupuncture."

Moldavite in Grids

A stone energy grid is basically a larger version of what I called a template in the section above. The purpose of grids is similar—to create a beneficial field of energy by placing a harmonious array of stones in a symmetrical geometric pattern. A grid can be small enough to hold in your hand or as large as one wants to make it. Some people build crystal grids around their entire properties. The largest grid I have made is an Azeztulite labyrinth that was thirty-seven feet in diameter. However, as I wrote in an earlier chapter, in 2007 I planted Moldavites among the monoliths of Stonehenge, one of the world's largest and most ancient stone energy grids. Whatever the size of the grid, the energetic principles remain the same.

Wood Mandala Crystal Grids

Recently, laser-etched wood bases for gemstone templates became available. I like these very much, because the designs on the new bases are mandalas in their own right, and carry spiritual energies through the patterns they depict. They also provide a relatively inexpensive

TOP: Ascension Grid; BOTTOM: Cosmic Prophecy Grid

175

platform for the stones. I use Moldavite in a number of these pieces. They range from two to six inches in diameter. The smaller ones are ideal for placement on the chakras in body layouts. The large ones can be held or placed at the heart or crown chakra (or other chakras, if needed). And they can be used as a constant source of vibrational harmony in one's environment.

Glass-Base Mandala Crystal Grids

Going the next step up in size, we have the glass-base grids. I like to use square pieces of tempered glass. These are available from companies that supply display equipment to businesses. One of the advantages of glass is that it is composed mostly of fused Quartz, so it can provide a neutral but resonating base for the other stones. And, of course, glass is an excellent resonating material for a natural glass such as Moldavite.

Another benefit of using the tempered glass squares as bases for stone mandala grids comes from their shape. A definition of the word mandala from Vocabulary. com states, "As a symbol for the cosmos or universe, a traditional mandala is a square containing a circle, and the entire design is symmetrical and balanced." And Carl Jung stated: "In the products of the unconscious we discover mandala symbols, that is, circular and quaternity [square] figures which express wholeness, and whenever we wish to express wholeness, we employ just such figures." In alchemy, one of the metaphors for producing the Philosophers' Stone, the goal of alchemy, was known as "squaring the circle." So, if we begin a stone grid with a glass square as a base, and then create a circular array of stones on the base, we are evoking this archetypal pattern of wholeness through the mandala that we create. The two photographs in this section show two of these glass-base stone mandalas. One predominantly uses Moldavite, and the other uses the Synergy 12 stones.

Glass base grids like these are excellent for filling one's home or work space with beneficial energies. Another powerful way to work with these is to place the grid on one's lap during meditation. Or if one meditates while lying down, placing the grid at the crown chakra can initiate dramatic experiences of expanded awareness.

All Moldavite Glass Grid

Synergy 12 Glass Grid

Desk Grids combining Moldavite with various other stones

Perhaps the most efficacious way to utilize one of these glass-base mandala crystal grids is to position it above the head during sitting meditations. To do this, one can set up a wood framework to hold the mandala, so that it sits right over the meditator's head. This might require a bit of carpentry, but will be fairly simple to do. I have experimented with this positioning of the grid, standing beside the person and holding it over his or her head. This has produced powerful responses in over 90% of those who have tried it. I believe this kind of setup could be of great benefit in expanding awareness, healing, and in any number of other applications. With a Moldavite grid, I would expect dramatic shifts of consciousness.

Moldavite in Larger Stone Mandala Grids

One can create larger Stone Mandala Grids on a table top, floor, or other flat area. When I make grids such as these, they are usually temporary and are meant to enhance the energies of a meditation altar, healing room, or other area designated as sacred space. Sometimes I set them up to amplify a positive intention for the world. I always use Moldavite in these grids because of its dynamic transformative energy.

The primary benefits of these larger grids have to do with building a more powerful energy field by bringing in larger stones, a greater number of stones, and (if one chooses) a wider variety of stones than are typically included in smaller grids and templates.

When building a larger grid, it is ideal if one meditates before beginning, asking for the participation of the Stone Beings, and the all-pervading Wisdom of the world. Then, as much as possible, one should do the stone placement in silence and without outer distractions, keeping one's intention and attention linked to the guiding impulses one receives. When this is done, the effect can often be astonishing, as one recognizes that one is truly participating in co-creation with these beings.

On page 177 there are photos of a tabletop Stone Mandala Grid that I have made. Its purpose is to magnify the intention for worldwide awakening, healing, and well-being. (In the close-up photo it is easy to see the large Moldavites I placed near the center.) I invite you to take a few moments to contemplate these images, and receive their energies.

Moldavite Pendulums

Pendulums are used in a variety of practices—including divination of future events, finding lost objects, discerning which choice is best in a given moment, learning whether a stone, food, or relationship is good for you, etc. Pendulums can also be used as a spiritual practice, nourishing the relationship between one's everyday self and one's soul, or Deep Self. Most readers of this book are likely to be familiar with consulting pendulums. For those who are not, there are numerous good online resources, such as askyourpendulum.com.

Pendulums made from crystals and other stones are in widespread use. Moldavite pendulums are seen more rarely. If I were to try to describe the

Moldavite Pendulum

subtle difference between a Moldavite pendulum and a Quartz crystal pendulum, I would say that the Moldavite pendulum can be easier to use, because its action tends to be more forceful and dramatic. Also, its answers are powerfully oriented towards the evolutionary growth and highest good of the user. A Moldavite pendulum may tend to encourage more adventurous choices, but I completely trust the guidance it offers.

One can simply use a drilled raw Moldavite or a Moldavite pendant for a pendulum. But for those who like to go for elegance and precision, the hollow, cone-shaped pendulums pictured with this section are, in my view, the best.

And for those who enjoy combining stone energies, as I do, the hollow pendulums offer endless opportunities. The second image, next to the all-Moldavite hollow pendulum, contains the Synergy 12 stones—a remarkably powerful combination.

Synergy 12 Pendulum

Moldavite in Orgonite Devices

Among the newer developments in stone energy tools is a class of items grouped under the name "orgonite." These contrivances, inspired by the "orgone accumulators" of the controversial scientist/inventor Wilhelm Reich, are typically composed of cast polymer resin in which substances such as metal shavings, spirals and/or tiny spheres of copper, as well as crystals and stones, have been embedded. They are cast in a multiplicity of forms, but the most popular shape for orgonite is the pyramid. Like other crystal tools such as templates and wands that combine the currents of chosen groups of stones, orgonites are intended to engender an energetic synergy among their components.

According to Reich, orgone is the life force energy that permeates the universe. He believed that, by combining certain inorganic and organic materials in the proper way, one could enhance and magnify this life force. In modern times, the energies we feel from stones are quite possibly the same energy Reich believed he had discovered. People who, like myself, enjoy experimenting with enhancing and focusing stone energies, began embedding crystals in their homemade orgonite creations. When I noticed that some of these emanated energies that I could feel, I decided to try using the highest vibration stones, within the focusing form of the pyramid, to build the most powerful and beneficial orgonite pieces possible. Of course, Moldavite was

TOP: Orgonite Super Power Pyramid;
MIDDLE: Orgonite Shamanic Journey Pyramid;
BOTTOM: Orgonite Synergy 12 Pyramid

at the top of my list of stone choices. The orgonite pyramids pictured here all contain Moldavite, combined with other stones, to foster different effects.

Drawing Moldavite Mandalas

A fascinating way to deepen one's connection with Moldavite and its spiritual qualities is to meditate with a piece of Moldavite and, afterwards, draw its essential energy signature as a mandala.

The basic technique for this is quite simple, and it begins with a meditation. Before beginning, set out a set of colored pencils or crayons. It is important to have a good assortment of colors at hand. (If you are an artist, feel free to use oil paints or acrylics.) Then take a piece of paper and trace a large circle on it. (A plate or pan can be useful for this.) When these materials are gathered and ready to be used, you can start the meditation.

Begin the meditation by bringing the Moldavite to your heart chakra. Hold it there for at least the first few minutes of the meditation. Take a deep, relaxing breath. Center your attention in your heart.

When you are calm and centered, go to your heart, and invite the Moldavite to join you there. Visualize the piece in your heart. As you breathe in, repeat your invitation to the Moldavite. As you exhale, offer your friendship and gratitude to the Moldavite.

When you can see and feel the presence of the Moldavite in your heart, ask it to show its qualities to you in mandala form. You may inwardly see an image, or perhaps you will simply feel the stone and its qualities. Either way is correct. When you have the connection, stay with it and enjoy the feeling. Watch and see if anything changes, or if something new appears.

When you sense that this part of the process is complete, thank the Moldavite Being, take a deep breath, and open your eyes. Now go to your art materials and start drawing the feeling and/or image of Moldavite that you received. For some, this will be easy. Others may think that the idea of drawing Moldavite's energies is impossible.

If you have difficulty conceptualizing this, imagine how you might draw something to express a specific sound, such as a bird song, or a teacup hitting the floor and shattering. It is easy to imagine images for these that are not literal drawings of the event, but which depict the *feeling* of the event. This is what I am suggesting you do with the Moldavite energies.

 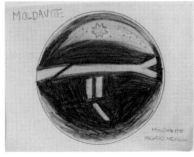 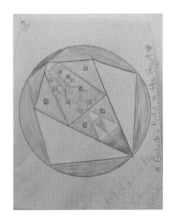

Mandalas made by workshop participants, representing the energies and presence of Moldavite

I have led a number of workshop groups in doing this practice, with an array of different stones. There are three drawings adjoining this text which show Moldavite mandalas made in these workshop settings. Participants are often surprised that they can express stone energies visually in this way. One thing I notice is that, although each mandala is different, there are common qualities to be discerned when different people make a mandala of the same type of stone.

I hope readers will look at the three drawings and observe themselves inwardly, noticing the way the drawings reveal that they all depict Moldavite. To me, they all resonate with one another, and if I allow my focus to soften and go inward, they conjure up some of the sensations of Moldavite itself!

Ultimately, the purpose for doing such mandala drawings with Moldavite is to enrich one's link with its energies so that one can call upon them at will, even when no physical Moldavite is present. This is a more advanced practice than most other stone meditations, but it is quite simple to do, and the results are often amazing. When one can view the mandala in a receptive way, one can actually connect with the spiritual energies behind Moldavite, of which the stone is merely a physical expression.

Working with a Moldavite Altar

Once you have co-created a mandala of the Moldavite Being, the next stage is to begin working with it meditatively. As with the Hindu mandalas which represent various deities, a primary purpose of making a stone mandala is to co-create an image that enhances communication and the exchange of blessing energies between yourself and the Stone Being. It is a little like installing a window between two rooms—now that it is there, it is important to look through it! And in this case, it is important to love through it, bless through it, dialog through it, and build relationship through it. To help you get started with this, I will describe two suggested exercises. [NOTE: The photo on the next page shows the Moldavite altar I have in my own sacred space.]

EXERCISE ONE: Set Up the Altar: After you have completed a mandala of Moldavite (or any other Stone Being), find a table or shelf that you can designate as sacred space. Clear the space and do not let things clutter it up. Maintain the sacred space.

Place the mandala onto the table or shelf. I suggest that you also put a piece of the actual stone on or near the mandala. Create a ritual in which you affirm your appreciation to the Moldavite Being, and reiterate your wish to deepen your relationship with that Being.

From this point, there are many ways to go. I suggest that you come to the altar several times a week and bring a little offering. The best offerings are often things you go out and find in the natural world—twigs, feathers, little rocks, whatever calls to you. Each time you make an offering, spend a couple of minutes gazing at the mandala and the Moldavite.

Imagine that you are looking at a fuzzy image of the Moldavite Being's essence, soul, and/or its subtle body—as if you were seeing it through a mist, or through wavy glass. Look *through* the mandala and try to see and feel the Being.

If you are able to feel a link with the Moldavite Being, the next step is to try engaging in a dialog with it. Ask the Being questions about its qualities and about the kind of

Robert's Moldavite Altar

work you might do together. Let the Moldavite Being know what you would like to ask of it, or to co-create with it. You might want to work with it in self-healing or healing someone else. Or perhaps you may wish to enhance your psychic abilities and intuitive perception. Let the Moldavite Being know this, sending your wish or intention through the mandala and listening inwardly for what comes back. Feel free to ask the Moldavite Being if it is willing and able to help you. Also, ask the Moldavite Being what it wants or needs from you.

When you feel you have completed this stage and that you have a solid connection with the Moldavite Being, you may disassemble the altar and take the offerings back to where you found them (more or less). If they are bits and pieces from the outdoors, take them out into nature and let them go.

EXERCISE TWO: Journey into the Mandala: The primary purpose of the first exercise was to establish and strengthen your relationship with the Moldavite Being, who is represented by the mandala you co-created with it. To take this further, I suggest using the mandala drawing as a window into the world of this Moldavite Being.

For a process such as this, I suggest sitting down in a comfortable chair with the mandala in your hands. You may also hold or wear a piece of the Moldavite, but this is not the main focus. We want to work through the mandala.

Gaze into the mandala with your eyes soft-focused. Hold your intention to visit the Moldavite Being in its world. Relax and allow your attention to flow into the center of the mandala, as if you were descending down into a mine shaft or a well. (If meditation music—or even shamanic drumming—aids in this process, feel free to utilize it.) When you reach the bottom of the well or shaft, look for a light somewhere around you. Follow an inner passageway towards the light until you emerge. When you come through, look around and see what this world is like. Perhaps the Moldavite Being will be waiting there for you, or you may have to go on a search.

When your journey into the world of the Moldavite Being feels complete, offer your thanks, say your farewells, and retrace your path, emerging back up through the mandala and into this world.

You may go into such journeys with any intent you wish—healing, learning, etc.— or with no agenda other than to explore and deepen your relationship with this Moldavite Being. How deep you go can depend on practice, focus, imaginative ability, and sometimes on pure Divine grace.

In some cases, you may feel drawn to try this same type of journey with the mandalas of various different Stone Beings. I think this is a very good idea. There are many stones to meet and many worlds to travel.

Body Layouts with Moldavite

Among the most popular and powerful ways of working with all energetically active stones, including Moldavite, is utilizing them in stone body layouts. The basic idea involved in this type of work is that, because both stones and people have subtle energy vibrational fields, one can affect the state of a person's field—and ultimately their health and consciousness—through bringing together the individual's field with the fields of appropriate beneficial stones. Since the human energy field is closely linked with the physical body, it seems to make sense to try to bring about the desired changes and benefits through placing stones on or near the body. Most of us find it easier to feel stone energies when we are holding or touching the stone. Placing stones at various points on the body is a way to orchestrate a coordinated overall "chord" of vibrational energy that can benefit the recipient.

Stone body layouts are easy to do. Hundreds of thousands (or millions) of people have experienced them. When I offer my intensive workshops, we always include body layout sessions where participants pair off with partners to do the work. These sessions often prove to be among the high points of the event for many attendees. Because I believe my readers will almost all have heard of stone body layouts before, or have read about them in other books, I will touch only lightly on explanations, and will offer some examples of layout "recipes" in which Moldavite is included.

To prepare to do a stone body layout, one should set an intention. It is best to do this together with the person who will either receive the layout, or who will place the stones on you. Having set the intention for the session, one can then choose stones that will energetically support that intention. Two of them are illustrated in this section of the chapter. In my book *The Alchemy of Stones,* there are many other body layout recipes to try, or you can tune in and create your own.

Before placing the stones, both the receiver and the giver should do a short meditation to get centered and relaxed. Both should then affirm the intention for the session. Next, both people should invite the Stone Beings to participate and help to manifest

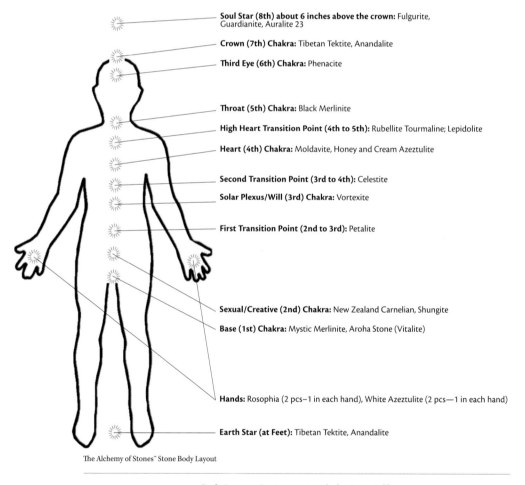

Soul Star (8th) about 6 inches above the crown: Fulgurite, Guardianite, Auralite 23

Crown (7th) Chakra: Tibetan Tektite, Anandalite

Third Eye (6th) Chakra: Phenacite

Throat (5th) Chakra: Black Merlinite

High Heart Transition Point (4th to 5th): Rubellite Tourmaline; Lepidolite

Heart (4th) Chakra: Moldavite, Honey and Cream Azeztulite

Second Transition Point (3rd to 4th): Celestite

Solar Plexus/Will (3rd) Chakra: Vortexite

First Transition Point (2nd to 3rd): Petalite

Sexual/Creative (2nd) Chakra: New Zealand Carnelian, Shungite

Base (1st) Chakra: Mystic Merlinite, Aroha Stone (Vitalite)

Hands: Rosophia (2 pcs–1 in each hand), White Azeztulite (2 pcs—1 in each hand)

Earth Star (at Feet): Tibetan Tektite, Anandalite

The Alchemy of Stones™ Stone Body Layout

Body Layout: Conjunction with the Deep Self

the intention. After that, the layout can begin. Often, I use music in the background, and try to choose it to fit the intention.

During the session, it is important to pay attention to the energies in one's body, as well as any images or inner guidance that comes. This is true for both the giver and the receiver of the layout. The session can last from fifteen minutes to two hours, depending on the available time and one's intuition about the appropriate time period. Afterwards, it is good to make notes of one's experience and then have some discussion between both persons. All of this helps to integrate the energies and manifest the intention.

I like to use Moldavite in any body layout in which the intention is to bring in dynamic energy for transformation or expansion of consciousness. Because Moldavite acts as an accelerator of one's spiritual evolution, it can enhance any layout in which one wishes to bring about beneficial change.

Most often, a single Moldavite piece is placed at the heart. The heart is Moldavite's most naturally resonant chakra. However, if one has additional pieces of Moldavite available, one can place Moldavite at the third eye, crown chakra, solar plexus, or

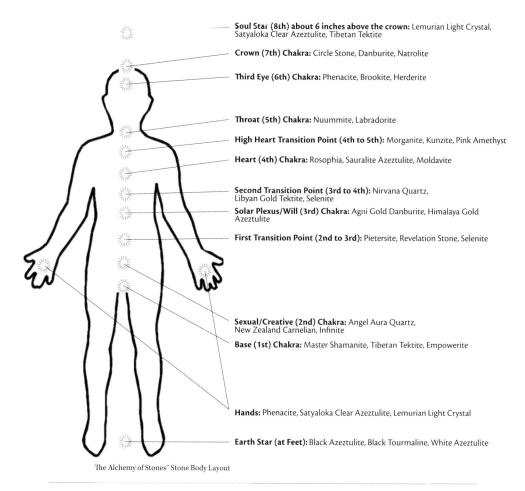

Soul Star (8th) about 6 inches above the crown: Lemurian Light Crystal, Satyaloka Clear Azeztulite, Tibetan Tektite

Crown (7th) Chakra: Circle Stone, Danburite, Natrolite

Third Eye (6th) Chakra: Phenacite, Brookite, Herderite

Throat (5th) Chakra: Nuummite, Labradorite

High Heart Transition Point (4th to 5th): Morganite, Kunzite, Pink Amethyst

Heart (4th) Chakra: Rosophia, Sauralite Azeztulite, Moldavite

Second Transition Point (3rd to 4th): Nirvana Quartz, Libyan Gold Tektite, Selenite

Solar Plexus/Will (3rd) Chakra: Agni Gold Danburite, Himalaya Gold Azeztulite

First Transition Point (2nd to 3rd): Pietersite, Revelation Stone, Selenite

Sexual/Creative (2nd) Chakra: Angel Aura Quartz, New Zealand Carnelian, Infinite

Base (1st) Chakra: Master Shamanite, Tibetan Tektite, Empowerite

Hands: Phenacite, Satyaloka Clear Azeztulite, Lemurian Light Crystal

Earth Star (at Feet): Black Azeztulite, Black Tourmaline, White Azeztulite

The Alchemy of Stones™ Stone Body Layout

Body Layout: Spiritual Enlightenment

anywhere a powerful source of energy is needed. Another good place for Moldavite in layouts is in the hands. People are often highly sensitive in their hands, and the hands contain many energy meridians.

Mandala Body Layouts

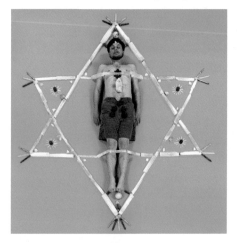

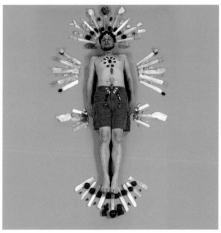

TOP: Merkaba Stone Mandala;
BOTTOM: Ascension Stone Mandala

The only limit to what we can do with Moldavite and other stones is the limit of what we are able to imagine. The images in this section show some very powerful layouts that combined the synergistic energies of Moldavite and other powerful stones with the magnifying power of geometric symmetries. The large white rods that were used for the overall forms are Selenite crystals. Moldavite was used at the heart, and at other spots, in both layouts. My friend Justin, who received the layouts, reported very powerful high-energy experiences from each of them.

The Star of David shaped layout is called the Merkaba Mandala Grid Layout. It contains Moldavite, Merkabite Calcite, Selenite wands, Mystic Merlinite, White Azeztulite, Cryolite, Petalite, Phenacite, Spanish Aragonite, Datolite, Tibetan Tektite, Darwinite, Libyan Gold Tektite, Sanda Rosa Azeztulite, Natrolite, and Circle Stone.

The second layout is called the Full Ascension Mandala Grid Layout. It contains Moldavite, Moldau Quartz, White Azeztulite, Golden Azeztulite Crystals, Pink Azeztulite, Himalaya Gold Azeztulite, Sanda Rosa Azeztulite, Satyaloka Azeztulite, Selenite Wands, Nirvana Quartz, Petalite, Creedite, Cinnabar Quartz, Crimson Cuprite, White Danburite, Agni Gold Danburite, Mystic Merlinite, Tibetan Black Quartz, Circle Stone, Phenacite, Prophecy Stone, Fulgurite, Spanish Aragonite, Satya Mani Quartz.

Photonic Layouts with Moldavite

Stone energies (and all subtle energies) are not bound by limitations of space and time. I have learned this through leading online stone meditations with groups. Even when I am the only one holding a stone, almost all members of the group can feel the stone's energies. (This is true of people who have learned to discern subtle energies, but may not be the case for others.) This principle on non-local influence in the subtle energy realm also underlies the effectiveness of the practice I have named Photonic Body Layouts.

A Photonic Layout is basically a stone body layout in which the stones are placed on a photograph of a person instead of the person's body. It makes use of the principles of *radionics,* originally discovered in the early 20th century. In essence, it is believed that by treating a photograph of a person (or an animal, a piece of land, a body of water, etc.) the effect of the treatment will go to the person, place, or thing represented in the photograph.

The concept behind radionics originated with two books published by American physician Albert Abrams in 1909 and 1910. His work was later taken up and expanded by Andrew Knuth and George DeLaWarr. Knuth originated the practice of using photographs as focal points for radionic energy treatments, which we now use in Photonic Body Layouts with stones. (For a more in-depth discussion of radionics, see *The Alchemy of Stones*, chapter 23.)

I was intrigued by the ideas suggested by the story of radionics, but I didn't know whether they would work or not until I tried them out. In 2016, I led an Alchemy of Stones four-day workshop in Vermont, USA. I asked all the participants to bring a large, full-length photo of themselves, but did not say why. Then, in one of the afternoon sessions, we passed out sets of tiny stones and asked everyone to pair off to do photonic layouts with one another.

The receivers of the treatments were to lie down on mats with eyes closed, and tune in to their bodies as the treatments proceeded. Their partners were to lay out the tiny stones on their partner's photographs. They were given general instructions on where to place the stones, and they were also given some flexibility about that.

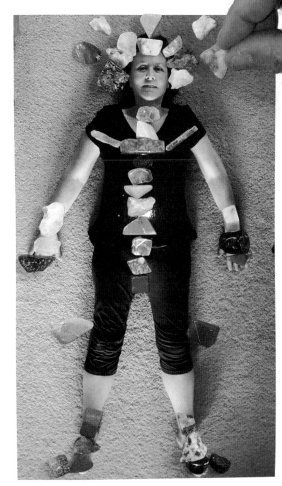

After the treatments, I asked the group to raise hands if they had felt the energies of the stones when they were laid out on their photographs. Over 90% raised their hands! And I got the same result three years later when I tried the same experiment with two groups in Japan.

I was interested in whether it would make a difference if the person was far away from where the Photonic Layout was being done. So, with the permission of my friend Keryn here in New Zealand, I did a layout on her photograph at my home, while she was at her home. In this case, I kept the layout in place for a week.

When I asked Keryn about it, she not only felt the stone energies while I was doing the layout, but she also felt them for the whole week! To me, this is very exciting information. It suggests that we can treat other people anywhere in the world (with their permission), and that we can also work to improve the energies of cities, countries, landscapes, polluted waters, and the entire Earth.

Of course, there is a major role for Moldavite in such work. Not only can Photonic treatments

Keryn's Photonic Layout for spiritual activation

potentially trigger beneficial transformation in one's friends, relatives, or clients anywhere in the world, but also the world itself can receive these treatments. If one chooses to do so, one can place Moldavite and other harmonious stones on a photo of our planet, holding the intention for the rapid, positive spiritual evolution of our world and all beings here. Because everything is connected, these intentions and energies will go everywhere. And, in my view, the combination of one's focused intent with Moldavite's transformational power can influence things far more than we might imagine.

For this book, I asked my friend Amber to help me perform a special experiment. We agreed that I would do a Photonic layout of pure Moldavite on her photograph. I would not tell her the exact time I would be doing the layout, and her job would be to tell me if and when she felt anything, what she felt, and whether it continued over the following two days while I kept the layout in place.

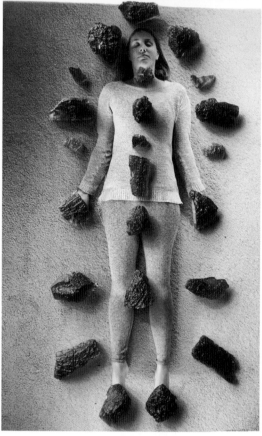

This is what Amber wrote the day after I placed the Photonic Moldavite layout on her photo: "I was about to start a meditation when Robert let me know he had put Moldavite on my photo. I closed my eyes and my awareness opened instantly. I felt connected to everything. I could feel my whole body tingling, energy dancing over my skin. The energy condensed in different areas and moved around my body. After awhile I noticed that the cells of my body were shifting, changing and evolving to fit better with each other—like pieces of honeycomb slotting into place. There would be a shock of energy like electricity rippling through my body and at the point it stopped a new group of cells would start to shift. It was electric.

TOP: Photonic Layout for Earth Ascension; BOTTOM: Amber's Moldavite Photonic Layout

"This continued until I felt a bright beam of light. But when I put my attention on the light all I could see was sludge. The light was still there but it seemed to be in disguise. I think it was protecting itself and me by not letting its full power be seen. At the end of the meditation, I felt super-charged—energy coursing through my body. Throughout the day when I closed my eyes or took a moment, I noticed the tingling sensations over my whole body. Joyous, dancing energy."

After getting the report from Amber, I called her to discuss it. I could understand everything she mentioned, including the tingling energy, the cellular harmonization, the rippling electricity, and the bright beam of light. But what about the "sludge?"

Amber explained that the feeling she got was that the Moldavite was, by nature, such a powerful source of light that it could call undue attention to itself and to the person who is linked with it. The "sludge" was like an energetic camouflage that allows the light to have its effects without being so obviously noticeable. She told me that the feeling she has is that it is not yet time for the fullness of what Moldavite emanates to be out in the open. In a note the next day, she wrote, "The Moldavite appeared not to reveal itself in order to go unnoticed by anyone who would wish to manipulate its power. At the same time, it was also protecting me by keeping me 'under the radar.'"

In our conversation, Amber also mentioned that the Moldavite energy (which was miles away from her) kept her awake much of the first night that the photonic layout was in place. She did not feel sleep-deprived the next day, and was actually full of energy and vitality.

On the next day, I was inspired to see whether something could be done to enhance the effects even further. With Amber's permission, I placed the Moldavite glass grid discussed earlier in this chapter slightly above her photonic layout, using books to hold it up on opposite edges. I received feedback from her the next day. Once again, her sleep had been affected, but apparently without any unpleasant consequences: "For the second experiment with the Moldavite glass grid, I felt immensely energized, with much more energy than normal. I was able to achieve more during the day and felt vibrant. When I closed my eyes and tried to sleep the rush of energy coursing through me made it impossible to go to sleep even though I felt tired. It is an exhilarating energy!"

Two days later, Amber's photonic layout and the glass Moldavite grid above it were still in place. I had spoken to her the day before, and she was willing to continue the experiment. I wasn't expecting any more feedback from her, but I got this email: "Wow!

Moldavite Glass Grid overlaid on Amber's Moldavite Photonic Layout

No wonder I am feeling amazing! Keep that on as long as you can. My energy level is skyrocketing. I can do so much more in a day, and I have much more resilience."

This message interested me very much, because Amber had been dealing with chronic fatigue and other debilitating problems caused by long term exposure to black mold. To learn that her energy level had improved this much during the time of her Moldavite Photonic Layout made me feel happy for her, and more eager than ever to pursue this work.

After another two days, Amber reported in again: "There continue to be amazing changes. As I've said, I am experiencing a big boost in energy, increased resilience (no need for naps anymore), and am able to accomplish more in a day. When I close my eyes, focus on myself, or meditate, I can feel vibrations all through my body. I have increased mental clarity and capacity. And I didn't get cramps with my period. (Normally they last for a day but this time there was only a very slight bloating for maybe thirty minutes.) My overall wellbeing has improved a lot. I'm not sure what else is happening but I am having massive progress and it is helping me through this really busy time where I was uncertain how I was going to cope."

We'll leave Amber's story now, and move on to other things, but I hope this will have adequately shown that there is much to explore in this arena. I encourage readers to experiment with Photonic Layouts. I hope those of you who do so will write me with your stories: (heavenandearth@earthlink.net).

This chapter has been a survey of the kinds of Moldavite tools I have designed and made, and of some of the practices I have tried. From my perspective, these could be seen as just the beginning. The possibilities of what can be done in working with the energies of Moldavite (and other stones) are endless. As Amber's story above tells us, Moldavite can be a powerful catalyst for profound inner experiences.

CHAPTER 16
THE MOLDAVITE TIKTOK SURGE

Moldavite's saga in the modern world began in 1986. That's when Kathy and I opened our business, Heaven and Earth, as has been described in earlier chapters. Over the ensuing thirty-six years, Moldavite has steadily grown in popularity. This is unlike the patterns I've observed with many other stones, which are often in vogue for year or two, and then fade back.

In the first several years, Moldavite was most eagerly sought by customers in the USA. Then the word got out around the world, and soon we were selling Moldavite to buyers in Europe, Japan, Great Britain, and Australia. In the past decade, Moldavite became highly popular in China, and this led to higher prices and increasing scarcity of the raw stones.

In the 1990s, the Home Shopping Network and QVC were selling jewelry like there was no tomorrow, and Moldavite soon found its way onto those cable TV platforms. During one of our years exhibiting at the Tucson Gem and Mineral show, a buyer approached us, asking whether we could fill an order for 1500 faceted Moldavite gems in six weeks. Having just met the owner of a gem cutting factory in Sri Lanka, we said that we could, and we managed to fill the order. We later learned that when the Moldavite rings with our stones were put on the air, all 1500 pieces sold in ten minutes. That began a period of about five years, during which we sold over 100,000 Moldavite gems through the home shopping venues. (And in my view, it has been affecting the lives of all those purchasers, whether they know it or not!)

As time went on, Moldavite found its way into the hands of people in all walks of life. It was no longer just for New Age spiritual types. In a 2017 New York Post article entitled "Wall Street Bros Get infected by Flakey L.A. Fad," journalist Doree Lewak wrote about wealthy "alpha males" who swear by the positive effects of a variety of crystals and stones, especially Moldavite:

Anthony C., a 37-year-old who works in luxury commercial real estate and lives in exclusive Sands Point, Long Island, spent two months to find exactly the right Moldavite, a rare stone said to be from a meteor that crashed into Earth nearly fifteen million years ago . . . Anthony . . . eventually found a European dealer to sell him a 46 gram Moldavite set in 22-karat gold for a cool $10,000 . . . Anthony, who declined to give his last name for professional reasons, and who lives in a 15,000-square-foot waterfront home, thought nothing of dropping that kind of cash on a rock. "I'm not thinking about the money—I'm thinking about what I need," he says. "I'm doing it for all [kinds of] reasons—finance, making things happen in business."

It has been interesting to have a front-row seat, watching and participating in Moldavite's emergence, and seeing its energies become known by people all over the world. From my perspective, this is an important thread in the story of the Earth and its human inhabitants. But nothing in my first thirty-five years with Moldavite compared with the surge that occurred in late 2020 and the first half of 2021.

And it was all (or mostly) because of TikTok.

At first, we didn't understand what was going on. Around December of 2020, Heaven and Earth experienced a steady, rapid rise in Moldavite sales. By January of 2021, the surge was huge. Dozens of Moldavite orders were coming in every day, and most were from new customers. In March and April, the flood of orders became a tidal wave, and our Moldavite stock was severely depleted.

When I contacted our suppliers to order more Moldavites, I was stunned to discover that none of them had any Moldavite to sell. Apparently, everyone with a business that sold Moldavite was experiencing the same thing. And because of the sudden overwhelming demand, the prices for whatever Moldavite one could find had risen astronomically. Our own costs quadrupled.

Finally one supplier said to me, "Don't you know what's happening? Moldavite is a fad on TikTok." I had only the vaguest idea what TikTok was, but it soon became clear that my supplier was right.

There were other problems with the Moldavite supply. The demand in China was continuing to increase, and the amount of Moldavite being found by free-lance diggers and official miners was diminishing. After thirty-five years of production, the Moldavite supply was beginning to run out.

Because we loved Moldavite, and because it had always been a centerpiece of our business, Kathy and I made a special effort to procure more stock, paying the new, more expensive prices. We realized that they were not likely to go back down, because literally millions more people were hearing about Moldavite, and the mining production was dropping.

During the rage on Tiktok, numerous articles were written about Moldavite. It has been interesting to read interpretations about its energetic effects that resonate with those we described in the first Moldavite book, way back in 1988.

In an online publication called "Her Campus" (geared toward female college students) Ashley Aviles wrote this in May of 2021:

Moldavite is a rare and expensive healing crystal that can be found all over Tik Tok . . . What makes it so special? Moldavite is intended to cleanse all the negative energy present in someone's life. It gets rid of any obstacles faced and brings you to be your highest self. Sounds great right? Well, for some, this has not been the case. If you were to search Moldavite on Tik Tok, videos of girls crying will appear. Many have claimed bad things happened to them because of the stone, such as losing their job, or even a loved one . . . But, when I take the time to think about it, this stone has truly changed various aspects of my life since having it. There were several people in my life who I knew were not good for me, but I could never muster up the courage to get rid of my relationships with them. It was not until getting the Moldavite stone that something happened where my relationships with these people ended without having to do anything myself.

In the March 7, 2021 Issue of "Her Campus," Sierra Moore wrote:

Moldavite is known for fast-tracking your life to reach your higher self. It does this by removing any and all negative parts of your life now, rather than allowing you to naturally do it. When looking at people's experiences, it can sound scary at first. People get out of long-term relationships, lose opportunities they thought they wanted, change majors, quit their jobs, and overall seem to be having a really negative experience. But, as time passes it becomes clear as to why these changes were needed and the outcomes are far better than what was left behind. The journey with

Moldavite is hard, and it seems sudden and emotionally draining. Deciding to get Moldavite on a whim is not the best idea. You may not be ready for the specifics, but before getting your own piece, think if you're ready to potentially change every aspect of your life in order to see your manifestations and dreams come true.

The sentiments expressed by these young writers echo those of my own introduction to Moldavite. There were rapid-fire changes in my life and relationships, all of which worked to my benefit. But in the midst of the changes, one can sometimes feel like one is on a bit of a roller coaster. Still, I have learned to completely trust Moldavite's influence, and to recommend it without any reservations.

In the TikTok heyday of 2021, even mainstream publications were talking about Moldavite. Below is an excerpt from the April 30, 2021, issue of Cosmopolitan.com. In an article entitled "WitchTok is Obsessed with This Life-Changing Piece of Glass," Rebekah Harding writes:

The moss green, glassy mineral is HUGE on spiritual TikTok, or WitchTok. Since the trend first gained traction last September, #moldavite has racked up more than 280 million views, with new TikToks still being posted every week. Looking through the top results, you'll find users recounting the dramatic, sometimes even traumatic, experiences that followed after Moldavite came into their lives—from layoffs to breakups to unexpected cross-country moves . . . But while voluntarily signing up to have your life flipped upside down (in the middle of a pandemic, no less) doesn't sound like anyone's idea of a good time, there's a neat reason this tektite has become one of WitchTok's biggest and most long-lived trends. Moldavite removes blockages and obstacles on your path toward becoming your highest self—often in the most chaotic way possible. Basically, whether you like it or not, Moldavite is going to take out the trash.

In preparing to write this chapter, I did some research on TikTok itself, and indeed there is a lot of focus on the dramatic transformative changes Moldavite can usher in. Some of this is, in my opinion, completely valid. Yet, at the same time, it's good to bear in mind that life in general tends to feel rather dramatic to people in TikTok's age demographic, and there is probably a tendency to put more attention on the big upheavals—the sometimes-upsetting changes that may not have been what people were expecting. But even on TikTok, there were many videos that reassured potential Moldavite users that they could trust Moldavite.

As I watch Moldavite work its way around the planet, connecting with thousands of new people every year (and probably hundreds of thousands or more in the TikTok surge), I marvel at the way this once-obscure stone has become world famous. And I believe that all of this is part of the unfolding of Moldavite's purpose—to facilitate the spiritual evolution of humanity. In regard to what happened with TikTok, I'm pleased to see Moldavite getting into the hands of large numbers of young people. With so many lives being redirected in the early years, I sense great potential for positive and long-lasting transformational effects in the world.

And the last time I checked, in July of 2022, there were over 540 MILLION views of Moldavite videos on TikTok.

Rock on!

An impossibly large counterfeit Moldavite photographed in a jewelry shop, Hanoi, Vietnam

CHAPTER 14
COUNTERFEIT MOLDAVITE

Moldavite's special qualities and distinctively beautiful color and contours have made it an object of value to people for at least 25,000 years. Given that fact, it is not a big surprise that people have created counterfeit Moldavites. This has been happening, on a fairly small scale, since the middle of the nineteenth century. However, Moldavite's huge current popularity, and especially the recent TikTok surge, have inspired the greed of many more unscrupulous individuals. As a result, there are far more fake Moldavites on the market today than at any other time in history. In this chapter, I'll discuss the counterfeits and how to tell them apart from genuine Moldavites, and I'll provide some photos of the fakes.

Moldavite imitations have been around for over 150 years. During the last half of the nineteenth century, faceted Moldavites were quite popular in Czech jewelry, and were often combined with Czech garnets or river pearls. This popularity begat some of the early fakes. In an article in the GIA (Gemological Institute of America) online journal, the author mentions that when he examined four 19th century Moldavite sets from the Museum of Decorative Arts in Prague, only one set contained real Moldavites.

By the early twentieth century the awareness of the imitations made people suspicious, and this diminished the popularity of the real Moldavites. They remained in relative obscurity until the 1980s, when the story told in this book began.

For a gemologist, it is easy to distinguish a genuine faceted Moldavite from a counterfeit. Real Moldavites contain numerous "flow lines" and bubbles, which are usually not seen in the imitations. Also, real Moldavites contain "wires" of lechatelierite, which is a high-temperature form of silica. If one knows what to look for, it is easy to see these differences under the magnification of a jewelers' loupe.

Other differences between genuine Moldavites and imitations are more subtle, but are discernable if one has the necessary scientific equipment. The RI (refractive index) of Moldavite varies from 1.480 to 1.510, while the RI of Chinese imitations was measured as 1.520. The density of real Moldavite is 2.27 to 2.46, compared to 2.52 to 2.53 for a Chinese glass imitation. Regarding fluorescence, Moldavite is inert in UV light, while the Chinese glass appeared chalky in short-wave UV.

Until recently, it has been very easy to visually identify counterfeits of raw Moldavite. Most of the imitations were crude globs of melted glass, and usually the color was more like a beer bottle than a Moldavite. Many of the early fakes had visible lines along their edges showing where they had been molded. A friend in the crystal business told me about seeing an unethical vendor at a trade show who had a whole tray of identically shaped "Moldavites." When my friend challenged him, the vendor quickly put the tray under the table and refused to discuss the matter.

These days, the spectrum of fake Moldavites ranges from very convincing to completely ridiculous. On the convincing side, the fakers have started to make molds from genuine Moldavite pieces, and to produce a large variety of different pieces. Some have also learned the art of acid etching their imitations to mimic natural Moldavite's wrinkly surfaces.

On the ridiculous end of the scale, online sellers are pushing multiple colors of "Moldavite," including yellow, white, blue, red, and bright green. Even when the color is correct, the clumsier fakes can be picked out because their surfaces are much too shiny.

Of course, one can sometimes tell a fake by price. The old adage that, "If it seems too good to be true, it is," applies here. Nobody is selling a genuine Moldavite pendant for $10 or less, or a large raw piece for under $100. But a high price is no guarantee. I have seen obvious counterfeits for sale online for thousands of dollars. At least some of the grifters have learned that a high price may lend credibility to their deception.

The proliferation of phony "Moldavites" has fortunately generated a number of good articles online, warning people and giving advice on how to avoid buying a fake. In one of them, I noticed this flattering comment from Harusami of Soul2Soul Treasures:

> *I felt a strong need to educate the public on how to spot fake or suspicious Moldavite. Here at Soul2Soul Treasures I only purchase my Moldavite pieces from two trusted vendors/designers who get their Moldavite directly from the Czech Republic. Robert Simmons is one of them, and he wrote the book* Moldavite: Starborn Stone of Transformation *that introduced this amazing gem to the general public back in 1988. . . . The best information I've found about the metaphysical and historic references to Moldavite can be found in* The Book of Stones *by Robert Simmons & Naisha Ahsian.*

Harusami's comment brings up the most important safeguard for people who want to be sure they purchase a genuine Moldavite: Deal with a company that has a long track record, and that will stand behind its products with a money back guarantee. Unfortunately, it's no longer enough to request a certificate of authenticity. Plenty of the fakers are offering those, because it's difficult or impossible to hold them accountable for their deception. Many of them are based in Asia, and even the unscrupulous online sellers in the USA are hard to find when one has a complaint.

Here are a few more rules of thumb for discerning if you are buying a genuine Moldavite:

1. Avoid pieces with very shiny surfaces. Most real Moldavites have a somewhat dull or frosted outer surface.

2. Look for flaws and inclusions, especially internal bubbles and "flow lines." Sometimes there are bits of tan colored sand stuck in crevices, which usually indicate a real Moldavite.

3. Be skeptical of pieces with a too-bright green color. Most Moldavites are forest green to olive green.

4. Beware if the price is too low! As of 2022, it would be unusual to find a genuine raw Moldavite selling for less than $50 per gram, and prices of up to $100 per gram are not uncommon for the finer pieces. If a piece is under $20 per gram, it's phony 99% of the time.

5. Don't buy Moldavite online, unless you know the vendors and have 100% confidence in them. There are, of course, a number of reputable Moldavite sellers online (including my company, Heaven and Earth), but the great majority of the scammers are there as well.

6. Whatever you do, don't buy a "Moldavite" that is not green! Some of the counterfeiters are offering multiple colors of etched glass and calling it Moldavite. Also, there is a real stone, an elestial Calcite, that some sellers are calling "White Moldavite." It's not glass, but it sure isn't Moldavite!

7. Don't buy a "Moldavite" that is represented to come from anywhere besides the Czech Republic. None of these are genuine. I have seen something called "African Moldavite" that is nothing more than bottle glass. There is no such thing as Moldavite from anywhere besides the Czech Republic.

8. Don't buy a "lab grown" or "man-made Moldavite" unless what you want is a piece of common colored glass. Some of the online sellers are admitting that their products are not from nature, but are still trying to capitalize on the Moldavite name.

As I was writing this chapter, I went online to look for fake Moldavites. They were certainly easy to find! They were present on all the major platforms plus any number of more obscure venues. The site where I found the most fakes (and some of the most ridiculous ones) was a company based in San Francisco, but which ships a large percentage of its goods from China, where much of the Moldavite counterfeiting is alleged to occur.

Below you will see photos I took of what appeared on my computer screen as I did my quick research.

I wish I hadn't needed to write this chapter. It's rather discouraging to see that many people who want the experience Moldavite offers are being deceived by counterfeits. To me, the fakers are stealing more than money — they are cheating people out of the opportunity to connect with the spiritual energies Moldavite conveys, and which might have benefitted their lives. I hope this chapter, and this book, are helpful in steering readers to find and enjoy connecting with the real, wonderful, amazing Moldavite.

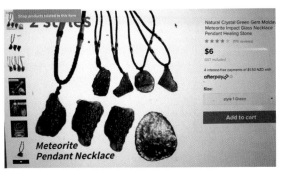

A handful of fine Moldavites from my personal collection

THE MOLDAVITE STORIES

Since the first years of Moldavite's emergence as a spiritual talisman, we have received hundreds of letters from people who were moved by their Moldavite experiences, and who wanted to share them with us. I have treasured these letters, because they reflect the spontaneous, genuine episodes of connection that people felt, and they made the effort to write them down and communicate them. In many ways, I view this as the most important chapter in the book, because these stories demonstrate that Moldavite's spiritual qualities are genuine. They also show that Moldavite has a unique magic that can bring dramatic benefits to those who choose it.

It is said that politicians use the rule of thumb that, for every letter they receive, there are a hundred other voters who feel the same way. Based on thousands of conversations, I believe that the ratio for Moldavite experiences may be even higher.

In this chapter I am presenting a mixture of letters received in the 1980s and the 2020s, with one or two from the times in between. I want to point out that similar themes run through many of these letters, even though each person's experiences are unique.

I'm still collecting Moldavite stories, so if you have one that you would like to share, please use the subject line Moldavite Story, and email it to me here: heavenandearth@earthlink.net

The letters below are from real people. Some have been willing to share their names. In cases where I was not sure about that, I have used initials. I have included the year in which we received the letter at the bottom of each entry. (Some letters have been edited for brevity.)

Dear Heaven and Earth,

I read about Moldavite in the *"Boston Globe"* nearly a year, I think, before I visited Heaven and Earth. I was not interested in the use of crystals at the time, although there we some incidents in my life that had opened my mind to the unseen possibilities of the world. When I was four years old, I had fallen off a dock and drowned. My grandfather had used mouth-to-mouth resuscitation to restart my breathing, and I remember clearly what it was like to die. When I was seven, my pediatrician taught me to meditate, and meditation has been an important part of my life for nearly thirty years. I was not then, however, nor am I now, part of any movement.

My search is very personal, and it is based on the belief that what each of us needs will be given to us, and that we are free to accept or reject any aspects of the ideas that come our way. I am suspicious of movements. They all too easily become bearers of a recipe for enlightenment. Enough with the disclaimers, already, right? Anyway . . . I remembered the tiny article in the *"Globe"* for twelve months, and always intended to have a look at what became in my mind a piece of a star. (It is a humbling thought to realize, as I have just now understood that hearing Perry Como crooning from my mother's radio about, "take a falling star and put it in your pocket, save it for a rainy day," may have had an enormous effect on my life. We never know, do we?) So, there I was, driving down the street with half an hour between appointments, and there Heaven and Earth was, just sitting there, so I stopped.

I didn't like most of the Moldavite, but one piece I not only liked, I loved. So I bought it, and the owner of the shop said my life was going to change drastically, and I said, "Uh-huh," and he said, "You don't believe me, but I want you to come back in a year and tell me what has happened to you." Then he gave me a sheet of paper that had the supposed properties of Moldavite listed on it, and when I got home I read it, and I thought, "riiiiight," and I threw the paper away. But I wore the Moldavite, which was shaped and veined like a leaf, finished on one side and raw on the other.

The next day I met someone who loves me in a way that has given me wings, who I love with a depth and freedom I would not have believed possible. I have ended an eight year personal and professional interchange with someone who was literally making me crazy. My marriage has ended, but has become a wonderful friendship. People with whom I had associated daily have become much less important in my life. I have become very close to others with whom I have previously unrecognized ties that extend back to my childhood and, in one instance, for several generations. I have changed careers; my income is 1/10 what it was but I am doing something that is deeply fulfilling. It has been a year filled with almost unbearable pain, and with unthought of delight.

None of this has come easily. It had been grinding, soul-scraping work. What has come easily is knowing what was waiting to be accomplished, and confidence that I have the strength to accomplish it.

S.L. MASSACHUSETTS 6/21/88

My Experience with Moldavite

In late August 1987, I visited Heaven and Earth. I purchased a pendant consisting of a small amethyst with a cut and polished Moldavite. Before I left the shop, I put the pendant on my gold chain on which I was wearing a small diamond pendant.

Within hours, powerful deep issues which I had been working on since 1982 (i.e., using various forms of therapy—polarity, Ro-hun) came to the surface. I was working on my root chakra, and [awareness of] first and second chakra blockages came to the surface.

The issues came forth like a blocked dam exploding. I was challenged almost immediately to deal with them, and within the next few days people who I had never met before, but who were working on similar problems, were surrounding me. A scenario unfolded where all of us had to face a very difficult situation. Since I am an astrologer, I immediately felt the power of Pluto and the issues that Pluto represented at that time—transformation.

Upon arriving back in Florida, I continued wearing the Moldavite. Situations from the past, which I had ignored but which needed immediate attention, kept cropping up. They were not all pleasant, but I realized I was going through an accelerated cleansing. It got to the point that at night when I was "asleep" (ha ha), information from the past, present, and future was coming in. I couldn't sleep, I was highly energized, and had to remove the Moldavite.

I gave another pendant to a friend, which she returned to me soon after, due to the powerful energies. My husband, who is a high energy Sagittarius and has absolutely *no interest* in metaphysics, wore the pendant for two to three weeks and found absolutely no change in his energy level.

I started to wear the Moldavite again after two or three months, and I found that the initial experience I had was not repeated. However, during those months, my creative self, after years of blockage, *flowed.* I am more self-confident. My channeling sessions and especially my writing have had a powerful impact on others.

Since I received my latest order [of Moldavite] I am experimenting by wearing the raw pendant, and I have found a feeling of high energy, but it is something I am capable of handling. It's almost as if I have adjusted to the energy level. It has been a year since I first touched the Moldavite, and I can honestly say it has helped me be in touch with myself more, encouraged growth, and given me a freedom to be who I am.

Thank you for sharing this wonderful stone with me. I intend to spread the world of my experience to others. We have a growing Light center in Florida which is very much needed.

P.S. Today I meditated with my Moldavite and I felt a calm feeling of womblike warmth envelop me—even though daily circumstances have been hectic. It's almost as if the Universe is saying: "It's okay—you're doing fine."

Love and Light,

RACHAEL BAT MEIR
BOCA RATON, FLORIDA 9/9/88

Hi Robert Simmons,

My experience with Moldavite is tingling and heat, mainly in the heart chakra area and third eye. Also, when I hold it in my hands it feels like it pulsates and has waves of energy. I feel energy in the heart chakra and third eye which has the feeling of waves in the third eye and heat in the heart chakra and solar plexus.

A significant meditation I had with Moldavite was when I had it on my solar plexus and I saw a strange cave that had plants with a type of leaf that was unusual. It was as if it was on another planet. The leaf was shaped like a violin snowflake (that is the only way I could describe it) and it was green. I thought after my meditation, "Where in the Universe are there plants that can grow in caves?"

I have slept with Moldavite, and I feel it makes me sleep soundly and deeply. I can't recall any dreams that came from sleeping with Moldavite, as it just makes me sleep very deeply. But my husband does not like it when I sleep with it, as he states that it causes pressure in his head and disturbs his sleep.

When I first found out about Moldavite I went online and there was a particular site that said it was not selling Moldavite anymore, as they felt it was "evil." (I do not remember the site; it was a small crystal seller.) After that, it was about two years later when Moldavite literally followed me around a Sound Therapy Conference. There was a man at this conference, and we got chatting about crystals, and the topic of Moldavite came up. I instantly said, "No way, I am not wearing that!" He convinced me to hold his Moldavite necklace and I thought. "Ok this is all right. Nothing 'evil' happened." I sat behind him at the conference, and I felt this warm feeling in my heart area, I thought, "What it this?" So, I spoke to him when we had a break. He told me I was experiencing Moldavite. During that whole weekend, when I looked at my phone there was something about Moldavite. People I had met were wearing Moldavite. It was like it was following me, so I had to get one. I went to a crystal shop in Atlanta and purchased one (it was a Heaven and Earth one). Now that was my first Moldavite.

I do feel Moldavite has accelerated my spiritual growth, and it pushes me to do things I need to do in order to better myself. Even something like going to the gym—it will not let me procrastinate. I have to go. As far as relationships are concerned, I feel when I worked in a toxic corporate work environment, [the Moldavite] protected me. I think people don't realize that it is a protective stone. Also, it is great for meditation; it helps me stay focused. I have noticed that if someone sees a small piece of Moldavite I am wearing, they ask about it, and they sometimes feel the energy without touching it. I feel Moldavite finds the people who need the energy from it.

I have worked with Moldavite for self-healing more on a spiritual level. I notice the energy of Moldavite encourages me to go forward, not to procrastinate, and to be assertive when I need to be. I wear Moldavite every day and I notice that it almost feels like a part of myself/skin.

Moldavite has opened me up spiritually. I feel connection to everything when I work with it, it's like a piece of the Universe and Earth plus communication to other energies.

I hope this information is helpful.

Kind regards,

STEPHANIE GIBBS
JUNE 2022

Dear Robert,
Here is my story of meditation with Moldavite. (Lee Nelson and I were meditating via Zoom.) We meditated only with Moldavite and dedicated this meditation for World peace.

At the beginning of the meditation, the Moldavite energy strongly activated the third eye and the crown chakra. I felt the bright light energy was flowing to planet Earth. After that, I began to feel that my heart is one with the heart of planet Earth. I felt it beating in one rhythm. I saw how Moldavite embraced our planet with his strong energy and sent light. At that moment, I felt hope and faith in peace on Earth. My consciousness began to rise strongly and expand. I flew and felt myself and everything around in the golden bright light. There was no separation, just love, bliss and trust. Also, in the second part of meditation when I was flying. I saw my past lives. The setting was in some old beautiful buildings and museums. Pictures from those lives crossed my consciousness so fast and then disappeared. The main focus of all this meditation was that Moldavite energy flowed very strongly through us to planet Earth. It was a light energy transmission. I notice when I meditate with Moldavite that his energy is very powerful, transforming, expanding and has high frequency vibrations.

With love.

RASA
LITHUANIA, APRIL, 2022

First Moldavite Report

Rasa and I meditated on Zoom today, using only Moldavite, but with the intention of permeating the World with healing Love. It was a VERY powerful session! I could feel the currents of Love emanating from the Heart. Focusing on Ukraine, it seemed to encounter an interference with the flow. Then the hum, the sound of Love, increased in volume and shattered the resistance with steadfast determination, and all was Bliss.

Near the end of the meditation, I saw a very clear image of an indigenous man with grey hair. He was saying something. His lips were moving, but unfortunately, I had pressed the "Mute" button on my inner hearing! Would have loved to have heard what he had to say.

This was a very powerful meditation! To put it into words, realising the inherent inadequacy of so doing, "Love conquers all!"

LEE NELSON
MOTUEKA, NEW ZEALAND, MARCH, 2022

My first Moldavite experience was about one and a half years ago. I am an associate member of the Aquarian Fellowship Foundation in Upton, MA. It was there that I was first introduced to Moldavite. Our Executive Director and founder, Mary Louise Knox, brought some back from a buying trip to Heaven and Earth. I held a rough piece (approximately 1½ grams) in my left hand and immediately felt a warm, pulsating energy in my hand. This energy travelled up my arm and into my heart chakra. My heart began to beat with extreme force. I knew I had to experiment more with this stone.

I began meditating with it, placing the Moldavite on various chakras in conjunction with various crystals and healing stones. I discovered that Moldavite had the most profound effect when placed on the heart or the third eye. It was also very effective for activation of *all* the chakras if held in my left hand. I found the Moldavite energy would "force" its way through them and open them wide. This was manifest by my physical reactions of a dizziness in the third eye or strong, accentuated heartbeat from my heart chakra. I also found that sodalite would ease my dizziness and Rose Quartz would quiet my heart if used in conjunction with the Moldavite. These offsetting stones were no longer necessary after the first few times. The blockages had been overcome. Since that time, in any of my meditations in which I have used Moldavite,

I have found that I can tune into the "God-force" much easier and quicker because of the energy that the Moldavite radiates.

My most profound meditations with Moldavite have been absolutely inspirational. The first one occurred about six months after I began to use Moldavite. I placed my 1½ gram rough piece on my third eye and held a Purple Fluorite octahedron in my left hand. I went under very quickly and found myself leaving my body and floating up. In my mind's eye, I saw a long spinning tunnel of clouds. I willed myself to go into the tunnel. At the other end was not the bright light that one might expect.

Instead, I found myself in a total darkness, a void. I still felt myself moving upward. All of a sudden, the entire area filled with hundreds of tiny pinpoints of light, similar to the night sky on a clear night. I also noticed that these lights moved. I was overcome by the powerful feeling of pure love, unconditional love. The lights began to "talk" to me about my life's work on the Earth plane. I understood that these lights were entities and that I had entered into a different level of reality. After some personal conversations and counseling, I was told to open my physical eyes. I did this and saw that I was back in my bedroom but that I was floating about two feet above my body, which was still filled with the same unconditional, pure love. I was told to remember the feeling and to reproduce it often. I was told I would have a very difficult choice to make. I was told that the entity which I communicated with the most was named Horus, and that he was my spiritual guide. With that, the meditation ended and I floated gently back to my body. As I came out of the meditative state I was crying. These were not tears of sorrow, but of Love and understanding. I knew that I was now on the path totally. I can still reproduce that feeling at will.

The second meditation of real importance happened about a week ago. I placed a piece of raw Moldavite on my third eye, my heart, and my solar plexus. Along with each, I placed a piece of triangular shaped ulexite on each of those chakras. I *immediately* left my body and passed through a shimmering veil of lights. Then that same spinning tunnel descended over me. This time it had a bright light. Soon I sensed another object going by me and I willed myself to stop time (in this state, this is easy). I looked over to the object and saw that it was a man dressed in a brown plaid shirt with brown corduroys and work boots. He was in a "free-fall" position, similar to a sky diver, and he was looking at the Light with a look of sheer joy. I knew in my heart that what I was seeing was the soul of someone just departed. When I realized this, he was gone, through the Light. Then the tunnel disappeared and I saw clouds against a dark sky. Soon a *black* cloud came towards me and opened up to reveal a drawing in brilliant white lines. I couldn't recognize the drawing so I asked for an explanation. The first cloud disappeared and another came. This revealed a gridwork in the same white lines, in *reverse perspective*. I still didn't understand so I asked for more. Another larger cloud came out and revealed another white line drawing which I immediately recognized from my own past life regression. It was the view of the courtyard from the school where I taught in Atlantis. I was beginning to understand. Then the first drawing came back in greater detail. Shortly after this I came out of my meditation and discussed the experience with my wife. After a lot of conversation, as well as drawing for her what I saw, I looked over at a thirteen-pound clear Quartz crystal point that I have. Inside it was a 3-D rendition of the first drawing I saw, in every detail. (This crystal is a record keeper.) I quickly went back into meditation to contact my guides and was told through an extremely personal story that what was provided to me was the map and the code to the information held within the record keeper crystal. I know that one day this information will help others as it is helping me.

The energy of Moldavite, to me, is in no way comparable to the energy of other stones. Moldavite has an energy of its own, whereas other stones and crystals seem to depend on and enhance the energy of other things, such as people.

Moldavite has definitely accelerated my progression on the path. I have been working with crystals for the past sixteen years, and I have learned more in the past one and one half years, since Moldavite opened my energy centers, to completely allow for this acceleration. It also "turbo-charges" my meditations.

In answer to your question about whether Moldavite facilitates communication with extraterrestrial or higher dimensional beings, yes. I have been using Moldavite with a channeling crystal and a Fluorite octahedron, and I have found this to be the best combination for me in contacting interdimensionals.

It has been my experience that for meditations raw Moldavite is the best. Jewel cut is best for every day wearing—the energy is more focused.

I don't think the size of a Moldavite is particularly proportional to its energy, but I would not use less than a 1½ gram piece.

In regards to spiritual protection, Moldavite opens you to the truth. You are limitless, one with the God-force. What more protection could you need than that knowledge?

I feel that Moldavite was sent here. The channelled information on this rings true for me. This has also been confirmed by my spirit guides.

Does Moldavite help people awaken to their spiritual path? Yes, absolutely.

My energy level has definitely increased. Consistent use of Moldavite helps it stay "up" when some of the traps of this world try to bring it down.

In terms of cautions, if you have a heart condition or high blood pressure, I suggest you use a counter balancing stone such as Rose Quartz or Sodalite, as I described earlier.

I used Moldavite both every day and at special times. I wear a Moldavite ring on the middle finger of my left hand to energize my heart chakra, as well as a pendent with Moldavite on a double terminated tabular clear Quartz. These are jewel cuts. I keep four different shaped and sized raw pieces for meditation.

Yes, I do feel Moldavite has applications in regard to spiritual healing. I do crystal healing and in the beginning of the session I have the client hold a piece of Moldavite in their left hand. Based upon the physical manifestations created and described by the client, I know where to concentrate my work. If the client is basically healthy in both body and spirit, I will use Moldavite to open the entire system and balance it.

JAMES ALBRIDGE
MASSACHUSETTS 9/14/88

Hello, here I'm sending my contribution:

My first ever experience with Moldavite was when I borrowed a six-gram piece from my friend who introduced me to it. I was wearing it on my chest and felt a lot of heat from it, and a lot of intensity—so much that my mind was quite consumed by it. I wasn't wearing it for long periods because I felt that it was too much, and I was losing touch with myself.

What happened the next day was my first experience of what this stone can do. I'd had some long-standing troubles with some of my roommates, as I was living as part of a migrating workforce in a house shared by several people. There are usually all sorts of people in these situations, including some asocial individuals who can disturb other tenants. A band of young adults were also there, living a miserable lifestyle, partially as homeless and partially residing in this place, doing parties and regularly consuming drugs. I was strongly bothered by this issue, which went on for several months. They were unsanitary, behaved noisily and stole food. As this was against the rules of the accommodation, I and others attempted several times to solve this issue with the landlord, who was really reluctant to do anything. This was partially because he was too lazy to look into the matter properly, and also because the troubles weren't happening at the time when he was visiting the house. Needless to say, informing the police about this was fruitless.

The morning after I began wearing Moldavite, there was a test of the fire alarm in the house, with the landlord present. When there was no response from their room, the landlord entered and found several young adults and juveniles so high on drugs that they were unconscious. The room was practically demolished on the inside, in a way that drug addicts often do. The breach of the rules and damage to the property was so significant that the landlord ordered immediate removal of these problematic tenants.

I've had several experiences of Moldavite solving troublesome situations. (I mean solved in the time frame close to wearing Moldavite.) None of them as illustrative as the aforementioned one, but what I see in all of them is a great deftness with which all the events, situations, and interactions play out in an advantageous way for me. And if not advantageous, they at least provide a valuable learning experience or an insight.

My regular way of wearing Moldavite these days is to take about forty Moldavite chips and wear them on my way to work. I often get up early, and mornings are cold. I keep Moldavite in my pocket and it gives me a feeling of heat. It isn't exactly physical heat, but it warms me up inside nonetheless. It helps me to start functioning, as a coffee would do, and I can feel it all over my energetic system, including my chest and head. But what is more important to me is that I feel the energy in my lower chakras. These I need to feel and activate in the mornings so I can be in touch with ordinary reality and with the situation of being a physical body in a physical world.

If I didn't do this, plunging into a setting which is mentally and physically exhausting, as my work is, would give me a lot of inner pain and unpleasant feelings.

Kind Regards

JIRI M.
DORSET, ENGLAND, MAY, 2022

I cannot recall my first encounter with Moldavite, although I know it was through you, Robert and Kathy, and it impressed me by how much intensity I felt in such a tiny piece.

In holding Moldavite, I have experienced pulsing sensations, especially in my upper body, and flushing. In meditation, I have found Moldavite to facilitate depths of level, speed of relaxation and focus, and perceptions of expansive oneness.

It is difficult to discern specific instances, but I have experienced acceleration along my path since accepting the companionship of Moldavite. Concurrently, I have slept with, meditated with, worn, studied and played with many other crystals and stones in a several-year period of rapid acquisition and intense involvement. And this past fall brought the beginning of the cycle of planetary influence called the Harmonic Convergence, which seems to be working synergistically with all evolutionary tools and processes. (i.e. crystals and stones)

Yes, I do think that the use of Moldavite can help people connect with extraterrestrial or higher dimensional intelligences. Yes, I do think that Moldavite would be useful to those wishing to develop their clairvoyance or "channeling" ability. Moldavite has a powerful effect on my third eye.

I am attracted to various forms of Moldavite, most strongly to selected museum quality raw pieces and to spheres. I do feel that the size of a piece of Moldavite is somewhat related to its energy, as with most stones. And, as with most stones, I feel that different individual pieces of Moldavite have somewhat different energy qualities. I look for pieces of Moldavite (and other stones as well) that resonate most closely with my own vibrational level.

I feel that Moldavite provides spiritual protection, at least in part by fostering increased spiritual awareness in one's daily life. In terms of whether Moldavite was somehow sent to Earth or came here by accident, I find it difficult to believe that anything occurs by accident, although I have only guesses on how Moldavite came to Earth. It seems inevitable to me that we and/or our guides were involved in the co-creation process which brought Moldavite to Earth. For me, Moldavite serves to reaffirm and clarify my spiritual path, and I suspect it does so for others.

Since my initial connection with Moldavite, I would say that the vibration of my whole being has been raised and that my physical responses to pieces I spend time with decreases, probably as we synchronize. I still experience physical sensations when handling unfamiliar pieces.

I would suggest that those as yet unacquainted with Moldavite, and any others who are experiencing struggle or discomfort from working with this stone, might appreciate learning and practicing methods of grounding themselves in their bodies and on the planet, for both stability and safe release. The rootedness is advantageous with all stones that work primarily on the upper chakras, especially with a stone whose origins are far from this planet, and for people who need to remember that they have chosen to manifest spirit in matter rather than transcend into the ethers. Also, as with any stone that prompts transformation, in making space for the new, the old automatically comes to the surface for acceptance and discharge. Being anchored to a large, receptive, neutralizing and compassionate therapist like the Earth can help us retain a sane center while confronting our own insanities. Grounding can be accomplished through some forms of breathwork, through dance, through visualization, through physical labor, through direct contact with the Earth and trees, through the assistance of black and brown-colored stones, through bathing, etc.

I use many other stones in conjunction with Moldavite as intuition directs, but I do love the connection of Moldavite and Phenacite for meditations. I wear and/or sleep with Moldavite most of the time, with "time outs:" to enable sharpened awareness of guidance and to ensure ongoing growth and healing.

To answer whether Moldavite has any applications in regard to spiritual healing—it would seem that this is its mission—to encourage the flow and consciousness of this process.

In terms of describing my most interesting Moldavite experience—at a mundane level, I was intrigued by how giddy and silly and speedy I felt upon first wearing a ring with Moldavite on my left hand.

LESLIE DEVAS TAWNAMAIA,
DORCHESTER, MASSACHUSETTS 6/13/88

When I was 16 my father went to the light. Following his passing my mother gifted me with some of his belongings so I would have a few mementos. Among the pocket knives and pins was a wire-wrapped pendant that looked like a textured piece of green glass. I didn't know anything about the pendant or even what it was called, except that it was something of spiritual significance to my father, and that he bought it when he got sick. I wanted to wear it, but my intuition was telling me that it might hold the negative imprints of my father's battle to live. So I put the pendant in a cigar box and placed the box in the bottom drawer of my nightstand.

Roughly five years passed. I was cleaning my room one day and going through things I wanted to get rid of. The cigar box resurfaced and there inside was my father's mysterious green pendant. I decided it was time to wear it, so I put it around my neck and continued cleaning my room. In a matter of moments, I felt a strange vibration emanating from the area around the pendant. My chest and face started to feel warm and I was beginning to see everything around me as vibrating energy. I sat down and became hypnotized by the look of my physical environment. It was as if I was seeing the invisible structure of reality. The more I focused on what I was seeing the more everything looked immaterial. There was something strange going on with me and I knew it had to be the pendant. I became concerned that if I kept the pendant on me, I was going to be visited by beings from the spirit world. So, I took the pendant off and, much to my surprise, it took quite a few minutes for my senses to normalize.

I began experimenting with wearing the pendant for a few hours a day over a period of two weeks. With the necklace on, all of my fears in life were coming to an unbearable head. It was as if the little green glass was a living being that consciously had it out for me. On some level, I believed that the pendant was bringing healing to my psyche, but it was very difficult work that the two of us were doing. The experience was so tangible that I decided I had to share the pendant with a friend to see what his experience would be. I gave my friend the pendant, and a few days later he called me on the phone, saying the pendant was also bringing him to emotional places he didn't want to go. During our conversation I told him that, with some research I had done while he had the pendant, I discovered that it was something called Moldavite. He gave me back the pendant and said he wanted nothing to do with it.

Later in life, my friend ended up working in a crystal shop and he still will not handle Moldavite after his experience. I, on the other hand, have been wearing Moldavite and working with stones now for nearly two decades. Over time, I have become more sensitive to stone energies but less sensitive to Moldavite. I believe this is because, in a way, I am an initiate of what Moldavite has to offer, and we don't have as much heavy work to storm through together. My blind experience of my father's Moldavite made me a believer in the spiritual value of stones, and I think it is a story that proves stone energies are more than just a placebo.

DEVIN SHOEMAKER
WINDSOR LOCKS, CT, SEPTEMBER 6, 2022

My Moldavite Breakthrough

For me, Moldavite is a dramatic and extraordinary topic, because it led me into the entire experience of working with crystals and teaching people about them. Back in 1987, I was invited by a friend to go visit the legendary Heaven and Earth crystal shop, which was run by Robert Simmons and his wife Kathy in Gloucester, Massachusetts.

When we arrived at the shop I looked around, but nothing really caught my eye. I wasn't even really interested in crystals yet. Robert and Kathy were both there, and as my friend milled about the tumbled stones, Robert regaled me with the tale of Moldavite and how it had fallen to Earth 15 million years ago. He talked about the history, and how unique it is because of its green color (unlike the black color of the other tektites in the rest of the world), and the fact that it can be faceted (which is very cool). But what's most amazing about Moldavite is that when you shine a light through it, you get an incredible other-worldly green color that ranges from a dull, almost brown shade to a rich green to a vivid, bright neon green.

After my friend made her modest purchase and we were ready to leave, Robert gifted me with a piece of Moldavite, which had to be worth $50 or more. I was surprised but grateful. My friend and I left, and as we were driving home on the highway, I suddenly felt an enormous vortex of energy coming from above, and the universe sucking the life out of me, right though my body and into my pocket where the stone was. It felt horribly wrong, so I took the stone out of my pocket and put it on the floor of the vehicle for the rest of the ride home.

That night when I went to bed, I placed the Moldavite up on the mantlepiece, not far from where I was sleeping. I began to dream. In the dream, I was at the food store where I was a produce clerk, arranging vegetables at the front window. A middle-aged woman, barely five feet tall with short, curly blonde hair, came up outside the window and looked at me. She opened her mouth and let out a sound, the likes of which I'd never heard before. It was harrowing! I looked around to see if anyone else had heard it, but nobody did. It was unlike anything I had ever heard. And then after a pause, and to my utter amazement, I responded using the same language.

I've since come to recognize that sound as harmonic singing—a wordless vocalization in which a chord is created with two or more simultaneous overtones. The Tuvan throat singers from the Himalayas do it. Back during the Harmonic Convergence of 1987, practitioners offered harmonic singing for healing purposes, through what they called "toning."

Between what she said and what I replied, the intensity of the experience so rocked my world that I woke up and sat bolt upright and looked directly at the piece of Moldavite on the mantelpiece. It was clear to me that the stone had brought about this entire interaction. I immediately became aware of what our two-phrase conversation included. She had said, "The mother ship is over us; now would be a good time to come home." I responded to her: "No, I'm not going. I refuse. I've been here too long."

Within days, I had more visions in my sleep, during which this drama played out further. I was asked by a strange (unknown to me) and well-dressed man to show up for a job interview somewhere, but I was instructed not to tell anyone where I was going. I took this to mean I was being set up for an abduction. Needless to say, I didn't comply.

Then I had a dream where a different woman and I were in a large cathedral. Although she was unknown to me, I knew she was a friend. All the organs began to play in concert, delivering a cacophonous, deafening version of the type of expression I'd heard first from the woman outside my store window. I grabbed her hand because I knew we had to get out of the building immediately. I assured her—not knowing specifically what was being said by those great organs, but comprehending the import of their sounds—that if we didn't get out of there quickly, the entire building was going to dematerialize with us in it.

This was all very traumatic at the time and it took thirty years for me to retell these experiences without getting goosebumps. I eschewed Moldavite for twenty of those years, because it felt anathema to my existence here on Earth. As someone who'd chosen a terrestrial life, it felt unnatural to connect with something so otherworldly.

I'd had cancer twice, when I was twelve and eighteen years old, so I knew what it felt like to be pushed up against the veil, near death and expulsion from this mortal coil. It took some doing, but I had decided—and acted accordingly—not to cross over to the other side. Even after I was almost killed in a robbery and when one of my children was nearly carried away by a rushing river, I managed to hold onto life with a steady stream of good luck and perseverance.

But that is not the end of my Moldavite story. Within two weeks of my various transformative waking and sleeping experiences, I discovered that I suddenly knew all kinds of things about crystals! I had miraculously become what I call geo-sentient. By that, I mean I had become sensitive to the energies of stones in a very specific way. I suddenly knew intuitively how to feel and focus crystal energies. I had gone from considering rocks inanimate and irrelevant to a deep knowledge that they can be quite impactful. They are rife with positive energies, capable of imparting benefits to our lives that are far beyond our expectations, or even comprehension.

I once named Moldavite the alien messenger because it brought me key information from extraterrestrial civilizations. While that might sound completely out of this world, I'm a very grounded and logical person. Apart from that experience, I've had a pretty down-to-Earth existence here on the planet. Moldavite is here to let you know about specific high-level information. However, I will caution you that a tray of Moldavite is like a tray of cell phones. One might connect you to the leader of a galaxy or planet far, far away, but another might take you to the local pizzeria. It's not guaranteed that every Moldavite stone you pick up is going to connect you to extraordinary sources of information. I'm very selective about the Moldavites that I pick. I prefer ones that have a harmonious and balanced physical appearance, and I do like large pieces of Moldavite. But each Moldavite is different from every other one. There is really nothing else like it.

KYLE RUSSELL
AUGUST, 2021

I was working as a real estate agent and driving a white Mercedes Benz. I was forty pounds overweight and concerned mostly with material gains. A friend who was looking at expensive property had invited me to spend the weekend at her ski condo in New Hampshire and I wanted to bring a bread and butter gift. I had a cut glass crystal ball that hung in a bay window at home and refracted rainbows around the room. I was looking to buy a similar item when I noticed the sign in front of Heaven and Earth which said crystals and meteorites. I entered the store and asked Kathy, the owner, if she had any cut glass crystals. She said, "No, but we have natural crystals." I stopped and looked around, smelled the incense, heard the pretty music, and felt transported to an earlier time in my life when I was less intrigued with the material and virtually had a different set of values. This was back in my early twenties when I had spent time living in a commune, bumming around Europe, and going to art school.

Standing there in the store, I stopped dead in my tracks and a grand curiosity overcame me. I purchased a pair of amethyst earrings for my friend at a very good price, and left the store a changed person.

I continued to sell real estate, but dropped into Heaven and Earth often to savor the atmosphere, listen to people talking, and buy gemstones. Eventually, I purchased some Moldavite because I heard a story that it helped prosperity. I started meditating and continued reading and studying. I quit my job and devoted more time to my children and household. I didn't seem to have anything in common with old friends, as my values had changed, and new friends came into my life.

I became interested in the Course in Miracles and went to a group meeting. I met a woman there who was teaching psychic development classes and I went to her class. Meanwhile, each time I purchased Moldavite, new and different areas in my life would come to a head, and I examined them and discarded the things about myself I didn't need. I became interested in healing myself as well as others. I meditated daily and sought a quieter life doing the Course in Miracles, and reading any metaphysical material I could get my hands on. I became interested in channeling and listening to my Higher Self for guidance. I lost forty-five pounds. People didn't recognize me. The spiritual changes had brought forth an inner beauty and peace. I became aware of guidance in meditation, meanwhile working more and more with healing others as I had healed myself. I became involved with aura reading and I was acutely aware of people's etheric fields. I started a Course in Miracles group in my home and—with my group—healing, channeling, meditation, crystals, and tarot. I had been reading tarot cards on and off since I was a teenager, but I now infused a more psychic and spiritual dimension to my readings through help from my guidance. I became interested in crystal healings and started doing them in my home. I took more classes and met more people. All this time I wore Moldavite and crystals on my body daily. I took the Randall Baer crystal seminar and became more aware of the influence that crystals and Moldavite were having on me. I was creating with the Moldavite a matrix of spiritual change all around my body. I studied world religions and all the saints. I became aware of ascended Masters such as Jesus, Buddha, Mother Mary, Mohammed, Saint Germain, and Saint Augustine.

I became aware of the nature of God in everything around me. I stopped listening to my ego and started listening to and relying heavily on spiritual guidance. About this time, I became aware of two off-planet guides that I call Emma and Ivan. They told me they had been with me for a long time and I remembered dreams from years ago when they were in them. They started telling me about my past incarnations and how they were here in my present incarnation as my teachers. They transported me in my dreams and meditations to a place where they taught me with crystals and Moldavite. I started calling them my Moldavite guides. I came to realize that a lot of the things I had done and experienced in this lifetime had occurred with their help. I came to realize that I had not always lived on the planet Earth, but had been trapped for many incarnations in the Earth's astral field, because of discoveries and misuse of my discoveries during an incarnation in Atlantis. I learned that my greatest soul desire is to learn how to raise the vibrational force of myself and the Earth by helping other people to discover their spiritual selves. I became aware of prayer and the power of intention and spoken word. I started praying every day. I often ask Mother Mary to help me and help the world. I became aware of forgiveness, trust, and the reality of speeded-up miracle events with right-minded awareness and thinking. I became aware of rising above the four lower bodies and seeing the highest light and good in everyone and everything around me. I became aware of the element beings in my garden and the forces of nature. I started working with them and produced an incredible garden with their help.

Meanwhile, my guides Ivan and Emma suggested I go and work at Heaven and Earth once a week to be around the Moldavite and people who came to buy it. I suggested this to Robert and Kathy, and since that time have enjoyed working at Heaven and Earth on Saturdays.

To sum it up:

Moldavite seems to have brought up karmic patterns that needed to be worked on by me. I realize that it is a gift to people who are ready for it. Its off-planet properties are essential to awakening the deeper soul values we may have forgotten in our materialistic incarnations on Earth. Moldavite brings about a deep cosmic connection to the universe and our creative communion with the universe. Ego values fall away and we become aware of the divinity of ourselves and in everything else. I also realize that there is off-planet guidance readily available. Beings from different dimensions, planets, or solar systems are here now! They want to help the Earth awaken spiritually before we blow ourselves up.

I always wanted to see a UFO or meet people from outer space. I expected them to land on the front lawn one day and say hello. My meeting with them was much more subtle, as I was contacted on the inner planes.

I continue to grow and expand my awareness every day. My hope is to heal others and the Earth. Moldavite is a great tool for awakening yourself to the grand cosmic scheme of things.

MELISSA LUCAS
GLOUCESTER, MASSACHUSETTS 8/9/88

In 2007, my adult daughter and I participated in a weeklong choral residency at Ely Cathedral in the U.K., where we served in singing choral evensongs each evening at 4:00 pm. The choral music of the Psalms and cathedral repertoire is among the highest frequency music the Church has ever created. And when singing in the sacred space of the English cathedrals, a transformative space is created that reaches beyond the words coming from any homily. We were engaged in creating very powerful musical energetics.

My daughter and I lodged in Cambridge, a few miles south of Ely. One day, we walked down an old street past a curiosity shop, filled with many interesting objects, and I felt my "shopping antennas" activate. (This sometimes happened when some object called to me from inside a shop as I walked past.) We stepped inside to take a brief look around. The shop held the musty weight of long-lost items, and was filled with very old collectibles, under a very low beamed ceiling. We made our way to a counter in the rear where a frail-looking woman offered assistance. We browsed only a moment before she unlocked a rickety old cabinet door. She removed a small precious Moldavite shard, nestled into cotton batting and encased in a small box with a glass lid and placed it on the counter before gently saying, "You might like this!"

The clerk proceeded to tell us about the rarity of meteor glass and where it was found. I had never heard of meteor glass before. Yet, even before I touched it, its signature current flowed through my body, and I felt immediate affinity with this little darling. The expansive resonance reminded me of the Hermetic Emerald Tablet for some reason. Later on, I would recognize it as *The Presence,* but in that moment, I just knew I loved it. When I asked if she had any more pieces of this stone, she pulled out a much larger Moldavite/Amethyst pendant.

Gob-smacked, my daughter and I were stunned and instantly in love with these green treasures. Our questions began, since we had not heard of such a stone, and had no inkling of its nature. We were simply mesmerized. I was as yet unfamiliar with resonance of a stone; this was my initiation into such companionship. But by the time we purchased both pieces, we were hooked.

We hurried back to our room and stashed the pieces on my bedside table before dashing to catch the train to Ely Cathedral choir rehearsal and Evensong. I felt uplifted and energized! But that night, I could not sleep, and did not know why. By 3:00am, it dawned on me that the Moldavite was very near my head, and it might be the source of my insomnia. I moved both pieces to the other side of the room and all was well again. In fact, this was the beginning of many sleepless nights, as my system attuned itself to higher frequencies. My theory is that my companionship with Moldavite has been instrumental in raising my frequency. Especially during that week, the higher frequencies of harmonics in the singing added to the Moldavite and really amped my system.

For the next two years, I wore my Moldavite pendant, resting over my heart, when working with the choral harmonics. Eventually, I left the choral organization, feeling I had received all I could from that experience. Perhaps Moldavite facilitated the graduation from that developmental stage. (I was ready for quite some time, but did not wish to leave the music.) In the coming years, I purchased Moldavite companion jewelry pieces that I wear as power "armor," as well as for pure comfort. But now all it takes is mere touch to switch on the power between us (me and my Moldavite friends!).

To give credit where credit is due, Moldavite stones have also been instrumental in my writing, helping focus the flow of imagination to pen. My books, *The Häling and the Scottish Templars* and *Voyage of the Templar Guardians,* were brought into manifestation, with book three in the works. Other stones have joined my writing "team," such as Azeztulite, Phenacite, Charoite, and Danburite. But the one who brought me to the dance was Moldavite. Now I sleep easily with it and carry it regularly, and my toddler grandchildren just love to hold them!

After all these years, I feel that these exquisite, wavy green jewels are my portal to Earth's creative abundance, to ancient Hermetics, and to my starry origins. They help soothe my restless desire to connect in some way with my celestial home-star. Their resonance bridges time and space, dimensionalities, kingdoms, while connecting hearts in unexpected ways.

L.S. BERTHELSEN
MAY, 2022

I first began my experience with crystal healing at the very start of the year 2021. I had a long time chronic struggle with anorexia from ages thirteen to thirty-eight. I was at a breaking point of just wanting to release my struggles and transform into my highest high, without the baggage of the eating disorder. I had been interested in crystals since I was a child and I was intuitively enraptured when a friend gifted me Robert Simmons' *Book of Stones.* I wanted every stone in the book!!! After having experiences with other crystals and doing a crystal healing immersion I became curious about Moldavite and desired to further my crystal healing experiences and felt ready for something greater. Moldavite always stood out to me because it is only found in the area of Czech Republic where my grandmother's ancestry originated and I had several visions and messages from her with other crystals.

I am very sensitive to the energies of crystals and knew Moldavite would have an effect on me, so when my piece arrived I waited a couple days until I had time and space to handle its effects. When I first meditated with the Moldavite I received from Heaven and Earth I felt a warmth in my hands and became flushed. Then I gazed at it intently and I am certain it began changing different shades of green. It shifted to being a bright green and then back to extremely dark green, almost black. In addition the lights in the room began to grow very bright, more like white lights.

Then the next day I wore the piece of Moldavite near my heart. In the morning I experienced extremely loose bowels. This was very unusual for me. I have had continual solar plexus energy blockage in past Reiki sessions and believe the Moldavite could have been unblocking this chakra, resulting in physical releases. Midday I experienced a high degree of light-headedness and dizziness. At the moment I did not connect this with Moldavite, however a couple hours later I took it off for my yoga practice and the dizziness stopped!

I had experiences in the past with crystals that have led me to believe they assist me in accessing my Akashic records. Before sleeping with it under my pillow one night I connected with the crystal and asked it to show me what I needed to know from my past lives. I saw a girl about thirteen years old in the mountains in Europe. She looked very sad and there was a sense that she was crying and feeling alone because she was being hurt/abused by someone very close to her.

My experiences with Moldavite soon became more transformative. I was doing a Yin Yoga and crystal singing bowl sound healing session for myself one night with Moldavite and a carnelian in front of me. I gazed at the stones while doing the yoga poses and supressed memories of childhood surfaced. They were memories of OCD and eating disorder behavior that I had spent thirty years denying and pushing away. I felt a sense of compassion for myself and not a feeling of anger. I then put the Moldavite in the heart chakra bowl and the Carnelian in the sacral chakra bowl as I played them. A mixture of sadness and peace came over me. I felt I finally admitted to myself what I was really recovering from, and that I could move forward with my life.

Since that experience I have been able to cross the barrier of loving and accepting myself. Instead of being stuck I have moved forward with my life. I did a human design reader training, and got back to teaching in yoga studios. I will do a crystal therapy certification because I want to combine all the things I love and believe helped me into something that can help others. It is all about giving back. Since my relationship with myself has changed so has my relationships with others. I feel I am lighter and life is brighter. I have moved on to a brighter phase after decades of being stuck. I recently wore it every day for about two weeks. Spontaneous opportunities came my way. I started a new business to help others heal without being overwhelmed and breaking down, was asked to do a sound bath meditation class, won a sound healing contest, and was asked to do a demonstration for International Day of Yoga. Things have organically been falling into place. No doubt the energy of Moldavite showed me what I needed to acknowledge to myself in order to transform to my highest self!

COURTNEY A. DUNN, MA, LPC, YOGA THERAPIST 500HR.-CYT
HOUSTON, TX 77006, APRIL, 2022

In March 1988 I visited Heaven and Earth and was given a very small piece of Moldavite, the size of a flattened pea.

In mid-April I visited the store again. I was examining the merchandise in the case when I felt a pulling sensation in my abdomen. At first I thought it was indigestion. As I moved away from the counter, the feeling left me and I dismissed it. Again, I found myself in front of the same counter and experienced the same pulling sensation, and this time with a feeling of my insides being turned around (like when you just get frightened, mixed with butterflies). My first thought again was, "I'm getting sick." I felt flushed, and a lot of heat in my hands, shoulders, neck and head, plus nausea. My eyes began to water. As I moved away from the counter, the sensation eased. Robert Simmons was not sure whether it was the Moldavite or Sugilite or a combination of both. (The display case had this sort of assortment.)

NOTE: My marriage in March was on shaky grounds but neither of us would address the situation, hoping it would improve.

As I moved to the next case (which I thought contained no Moldavite or Sugilite) the feeling became stronger, and I became somewhat frightened. What I did not see on three previous inspections of that case then appeared. A necklace with a large piece of raw Moldavite and polished crystals and Amethyst seemed to raise itself, and I could see nothing else in the case. It had called to me, and I purchased her on layaway. I did buy Sugilite that day, and had a piece of polished Moldavite glued onto it. The piece of Sugilite is about ⅓ of palm size. As I looked at it, it seemed to take different shapes (bear, seal, rabbit, African woman with a headdress).

First Dream: with my first small piece of Moldavite—floating alone on the white cloud over a bottomless hole. No fear of falling in. Through the cloud I see a large tan snake with black markings. No fear of the snake; I felt he was no threat. I was quite puzzled by the dream.

Second Dream: had the Sugilite with the Moldavite piece, my "bear"—entering my mother–in–law's basement apartment, which transformed itself into an old abandoned dusty store. It had ribbons and ballet shoes I needed for my two daughters. There was a shallow wooden display case. It contained small beaded bags. I became excited and thought, "No, this isn't what I think it is . . ." As I looked up, an Indian woman appeared, middle aged, with striking features. I asked if this was what I thought it was. She asked, "What do you think it is?" I said, "A medicine bag." She said, "Yes." I asked if she would be my teacher: She told me no, that I would learn from someone else, for hers were the old ways and they would kill me. Then there appeared five young Indian maidens next to her.

She said she had something to show me and I would have to trust her. My thoughts were that if I was going to die, this time was okay too—what a way to go! She came close to me and blew her breath into my mouth and told me I would feel something in my abdomen. I was looking at my stomach thinking, "I don't feel anything." I started to look up when I saw a large black mass rapidly approaching me. I knew it was evil and wanted to destroy me. Just as it got really close, a large brown grizzly bear caught it in its mouth and started to shake it violently until the mass got smaller and smaller and vanished. As the bear looked up, I realized it was me looking up! I was the bear. Then the bear appeared before me, standing on hind legs with its front paws at its sides. Then it reappeared with the serpent. I felt I had met my power animals—my protection.

Third Dream: deep in the woods, a large waterfall. At the bottom of the falls, a large tree with huge roots. Some above the ground in the water and some above the water, like an island. At the trunk of the tree was a man I had thought about and cared for, but never knew his feelings toward me. He was leaning with his hands stretched out to me, motioning for me to come to him. I was near the bank of the water but in the water. I hesitated a moment and said I could not, I was married, my husband would see. He said, "He already knows." I went to him and we embraced. Upon doing that I turned and saw my husband turn and disappear. I knew then that my marriage was over. A month later, my friend called and he expressed his feeling about me, to my joy.

Meditation (with my bear piece): A cracking sensation in my head. Seeing a honeycombed, egg-shaped sphere, with a small hole in it. Upon looking out of it "like a window," I saw black space. Looking past black space I saw stars. Looking into stars I saw Earth and life being born of the stars.

Wearing or holding my piece makes me very sensitive at times to what is happening. I know who is calling before I pick up the phone. I get an image of that person. Sometimes I get two [premonitions] and get one phone call after another. Other times I can relay feelings of impressions to other people. I have on occasion felt presences that are not visible but not evil.

I have been separated since July and in the process of a divorce. However, I am dealing with this and not falling apart. I feel stronger and even happy at times and at *peace*. I get a strength from my stomach now. Effortlessly, I'm losing unwanted excess weight and people tell me I am radiating!

Moldavite *causes* rapid changes. Once the ball rolls there is no stopping it! You're on a cyclone, so hold on and brace yourself. Time to grow. Do not purchase this if you are not ready for these changes. I know at the end of my coaster ride the warmth of the Sun waits for me.

I keep my stone on or with me always.

L.C.

MASSACHUSETTS, 10/3/88

[AUTHOR'S NOTE: We received this letter from the sister of our friend Medley, who died in 2019.]

I am Marion, Medley's sister.

You gave me a Moldavite necklace one day when I was with Medley visiting you in your home. I loved that necklace, I often lost it and it appeared again in a few places. The wire eventually broke so I keep it as a stone now. When I first started wearing it, it was quite strong, but I slowly got used to the energy. I started getting more interested in crystals from our meeting and reading your book which Medley gave me.

I bought another Moldavite necklace which I wear regularly. It is in the shape of a four-leaf clover so it looks really special and I get quite a lot of comments about it. I had a ring but I found that the heat made my hands uncomfortable, so don't wear Moldavite in a ring.

The necklace makes me feel balanced, centred, and strong, and it conveys the feeling that I am expanding in life. I have many crystals, but Moldavite is my favourite. Other crystals are more for the look.

I feel I am growing most when I wear Moldavite. I choose it when I want to feel uplifted and truly centred and protected, and am open for transformation. I feel it vibrating more than other sensations. When I am wearing Moldavite, I often get synchronicities by meeting the right people or experiencing events which seem familiar.

I have been sleeping with it and often have very vivid dreams, and remember them, which is rare for me. I will keep monitoring those dreams.

MARION
NEW ZEALAND, OCTOBER, 2020

I felt a strong need to buy a piece of Moldavite and had no idea why—I was unable to wear it. I didn't feel that it opened any doors or opportunities to channel. However, a year after my purchase, someone mentioned that Moldavite protected the inner child. Suddenly I knew that was why I purchased it. I knew that the Moldavite had protected me enough so that I could accept the fact that I had suffered from emotion and sexual abuse, identify the perpetrators, AND let it go.

I felt no guilt, only relief. Moldavite has helped my understanding of myself and aided my path of forgiveness. My inner child feels very safe and happy. This has changed my life—I am living now.

I am now able to wear my Moldavite with my crystal, whose point is up, fairly often. The combination of the two give me great energy and I feel light.

NAME AND ADDRESS WITHHELD 7/1/88

Dear Robert,
Thank you for the opportunity to share my life-transforming Moldavite experiences.

I learned about the Most Powerful green crystal that transforms thousands of people's lives from Saratoga Ocean (Youtube on July 4, 2021) and she mentioned the book *Moldavite: Startborn Stone of Transformation* and *The Book of Stones* by Robert Simmons. I then watched your stories with Moldavite on your Youtube channel. I bought my first Moldavite as a pendant on July 6, 2021 and received it on July 9 which was a New Moon in Cancer, my Ascendent Sign in my Natal Chart. It seemed like Moldavite called on me and the first contact with Moldavite changed my life forever, like a phoenix rising from the ashes. The first time I wore it, I felt the heart sensation, so I had to put on a Rose Quartz pendant with Moldavite to calm the energy down. I could not sleep well with the Moldavite at the beginning of my experience, so I only wore it during the daytime.

On July 15, 2021, I went to do my Morning Ritual Sun Meditation in the park. I was standing and closing my eyes in a deep meditative state. Then I felt something on my right knee. So I swept it off with my hand while closing my eyes and it turned out to be a bee. The bee stung me right there and I pushed my finger and felt the pain. I had a severe allergic reaction with heat and rashes all over my body. I took sick leave for seven days to recover. I did not go to see a doctor as I wanted to heal naturally. That day, I bought the Moldavite book by Kathy & Robert, and *The Book of Stones*. I resonated with the Moldavite experiences that people shared.

I acquired Moldavite earrings on July 16, 2021 and I could only wear them for a few seconds, as they heated up my ears, which turned red and felt hot. The bee sting allergy started to spread more, so I had to take the earrings off right away. I still continued wearing the Moldavite pendant with Rose Quartz during my recovery period. This bee allergic event triggered my past memories as a child with a series of allergies. The Moldavites significantly transformed my life at a rapid pace and totally healed my heart and childhood wounds, so I could move on my spiritual ascension to my highest destiny.

There are some recent exciting Moldavite experiences, such as on March 31, 2022, a New Moon in Aries, my Moon sign.

My first Moldavite pendant broke a bit as it wanted to shape itself to be a point at the end like a pyramid shape in order to be a transmitter to connect with Benevolent Galactic Beings of Light. Later that day after the sunset of my meditative walk, I saw five UFOs with the Glorious Green Beam of Light on the Sky from Mothership which was hiding under a Cloud near the Kennedy Center Parking Entrance, in Washington DC, on Thursday March 31, 2022 around 8:00pm. They were beaming so much Love and Light. Blessed HEART. I waved to them and said "Glory in the Light of the Radiant One," and "May Peace be on your Way." Then I showed my Moldavites and my Phenacite. I read the book *Alcheringa: When the First Ancestors Were Created,* by Valerie Barrow. She mentioned that the Mothership was hit by an Asteroid. The Asteroid plunged to the Earth as Uluru in Australia and the Mothership fell and the Green crystals were known as Moldavites in Czech Republic.

I also used the Decree that evening: "I decree and I command Physical First Contact with Benevolent Galactic Being Now. I decree Divine Intervention Now." (3 times) "And So Be it, So it is. It is Done."

Then I visualized the Contact and I walked home. Here I was . . . Real Physical First Contact with UFOs. I AM Deeply GRATEFUL and Feel like HOME with Moldavites as a Starborn Child.

Best regards,

KATHY WARAPORN
APRIL, 2022

Dear Kathy and Robert,
My first impression of Moldavite was that it was a lovely and different kind of a stone and my first experience was that I could not wear it all night long.

The first physical sensation I experienced was the heat it generated. I would feel the warmth after wearing the stone, and my face would turn red.

The dream experiences were immediate. On the nights that I tried wearing the Moldavite, I would awaken and recall parts of the dream, only to fall asleep and dream again. I did not wear it at bedtime until I gradually got accustomed to it.

I have numerous dreams, and the most profound happened a few weeks ago. I dreamed of a voice telling me to call Bill. I had forgotten the dream until the following day when I received the sad news about my nephew Phil being in a fatal accident. The dream was as real as the reality. In my dream I recalled trying to call but the line was busy. In reality I tried to call several of our relatives and found the line busy. The only difference was my nephew's name. Perhaps it was my deceased husband Bill helping my nephew along the way.

The only comparison I can make between Moldavite and crystals is that recently I have acquired a Record Keeper and it seems that together with the Moldavite my dreams are so much more in detail.

The changes in my life are happening so fast that even my friends and relatives have noticed. I have returned to school after being away 30 years. Never in my dreams could I have had the courage to think I could go back, but I have, even working part time in the office.

I feel so connected to a force that is leading me in the right direction.

Moldavite will help others develop abilities that they may not have been aware of, or may have forgotten they possessed.

I have Moldavite in raw form and wear it in a pendant. I do not think that size matters. I believe the person seeking Moldavite will choose the size that is meant for them.

Yes, Moldavite does provide spiritual protection. No, it did not come to Earth by accident. Yes, it has awakened my spiritual path and it will help others.

Yes, my *spiritual*, mental, and physical energy has increased since my exposure to Moldavite, and yes, I have become accustomed to the Moldavite energies. Except for the time it had disturbed my sleep, I have had no negative reactions.

I always wear my Moldavite, and I immediately put it back on if I take it off to clean the chain.

I believe it will help in spiritual healings.

The knowledge I now have and the way it has changed my life are my most important Moldavite experiences. I can only write you of my own experience with Moldavite, but I am sure it will help all who are willing to learn and follow the light. God Bless you for introducing me to this precious gift.

With Love and Light,

T.V.
TRENTON, MICHIGAN 9/26/88

Here is my Moldavite story:
I decided to purchase Moldavite after reading about how it could possibly awaken/activate my kundalini energy. I became obsessed with kundalini energy after learning that it would balance both sides of the brain and basically make one capable of doing marvelous things. I am a singer and musician and was interested in seeing how kundalini energy could assist me in these areas. I went to a local crystal shop and found a nice, round piece of authentic Moldavite. The moment I held it, I felt its heat and pulsation. I purchased a small metal jewelry cage to put the stone in and hung it around my neck.

What I noticed was that I began to feel tired and outside my head a lot. I continued reading about Moldavite and learned that it was sometimes a good idea to pair it up with a grounding stone, which I did. Once I did that, I felt that my body was better able to handle the energy of the stone. I did attempt to sleep with the Moldavite once, securing it on my forehead. I experienced a lot of activity in my third eye and very vivid dreams.

After about a month or so, I decided to purchase two more pieces of Moldavite. I was interested in seeing if using more Moldavite would accelerate things. Indeed, they did, but not in the right direction. My life was literally falling apart right in front of my eyes. I decided it was because I was allowing myself to dwell on the negative aspects of my life and the Moldavite was magnifying the things I was focused on. So, I decided to stop wearing the Moldavite until I had worked on my thinking.

After a few months and much discipline, I decided it was time to start wearing the Moldavite again. Now, things began to move in the right direction and my whole life underwent a complete transformation. I did undergo a gentle kundalini awakening which opened up my heart and allowed me to start living my own life, unapologetically and fearlessly. I wore the Moldavite for about two years and then decided to stop wearing it for a while, as I had begun feeling that it was no longer working for me.

After about a year, though, my heart was feeling somewhat blocked and vulnerable, so I decided to start wearing my Moldavite again. After cleansing it, charging it, and pairing it up with some grounding crystals as well as Quartz crystals, I immediately felt my heart open up and began feeling calmer and more protected. I am looking to obtain more Moldavite, as I am truly in love with this wonderful stone, and I know that they are becoming harder and harder to come by. Moldavite came into my life at just the right time and I am forever grateful for it.

DANALYN ASH
PILLOW, PA., MAY, 2022

Dear Robert,

I knew when we spoke on the phone (prior to my Moldavite order) that we would be in touch again. I have not forgotten your request for me to document my experiences with Moldavite for your upcoming book on the E.T. gem. Well, here goes:

My first experience occurred before I even knew that Moldavite existed. When I dream, I usually dream in vague, etheric visions; my dreams are not very clear. Also, science fiction, extra-terrestrials, and other space subjects are not my usual "genre." I don't usually read about them, have great interest in them, and definitely *never* dream about them. About four months ago, I had the most vivid dream I ever had in this lifetime. In the dream, I was walking on a beach near a boardwalk (I could see a Ferris wheel and rides in the distance). I was walking along when suddenly I looked up and the sky was filled with millions of things that looked like this: [AUTHOR'S NOTE: Included was a drawing of a meteorite-like object with a spiral swirling tail.] They were spinning in clockwise circles, darker at the head, and had very sparkly tails.

I pointed at them and said to myself, "Look, meteorites!" When I said that, they all turned *green*. When I awoke I remembered every detail of this dream and I felt as if I needed to find something. I felt as if I should own and work with a meteorite. I purchased one (the metallic type) that was found in Odessa, Texas, but it wasn't what

I felt that I was looking for. When I saw your ad in *Lapidary Journal,* I became very excited because it was then that I discovered that there was a *green* meteorite called Moldavite, and that is when I called you.

I want to share what happened when I received my first order. First I would like to thank you for your excellent selection for me. I loved all the pieces and felt very in tune with them. The shapes and sizes were just what I wanted! Thank you again.

When I took the Moldavite out of the package and held it to my third eye, I immediately felt myself filled with and surrounded by beautiful, shimmering white light. I felt my body lifting and soaring into the white light and felt perfectly in balance with all dimensions. I felt that the Moldavite was very powerful so I did not want to continue my impromptu meditation for too long. I removed the Moldavite from my third eye and held it in my hand for approximately another fifteen minutes. To be perfectly honest, I then put the Moldavite down because I did not feel very well—I felt very nauseated and all my joints began to ache. I then placed the three pieces of Moldavite under a pyramid which I keep in my bedroom, because I wanted the Moldavite to be near me. During the next two weeks, I continued to keep the Moldavite near me most of the time (under the pyramid) but I only worked with it about fifteen to thirty minutes per day. As I continued to meditate with it I could again see and feel the WHITE LIGHT surrounding and protecting me and carrying me into other dimensions. Also, I could feel "electric" energy very intensely in the palms of my hands and running up my spine and out the top of my head. I felt this energy was lifting me up and taking me to other dimensions. During my meditations, I received clear information for personal and world healing. After approximately two weeks, I no longer felt the nausea and joint pain and I felt very in tune with the vibrations of the Moldavite. I still continue my Moldavite meditations and still feel very good and excited about them. Most recently I have begun to use my Moldavite for personal healing (physical). I have found that if I place the Moldavite on or near an area that "hurts" for forty-five to ninety seconds, the pain goes away. This has worked on low back pain, foot pain (I'm an R.N. who is on her feet for eight hours per day), and pain in my ankle from an old fracture. Sometimes when I use the Moldavite for personal healing, I also use one single-terminated clear Quartz to direct the healing energy. I have also used Herkimer Diamonds on top of the Moldavite to enhance its effects. I plan to use Moldavite in future healings, both personal and in client-related healing layouts. I also plan to work with other stones in combination with Moldavite to find out what healing effects I may obtain.

I hope this "little story" will be helpful to you in your effort to tell the world about Moldavite. It is a very powerful stone and I appreciate your helping me to bring it into my life. Thank you so much!

SINCERELY
NAME WITHHELD, MAY 27, 1988

I experience Moldavite as a pulsing warmth. It feels a bit like a warm wind stirring and ruffling my energy field. It's pleasant and like a Las Vegas summer it is something I can only comfortably enjoy for so long.

I use Moldavite for the steady energy flush it gives my system. It goes where it is needed. I don't wear Moldavite every day. I enjoy the energy and only use small pieces—mostly two rings I have. The other small chips I have are generally reserved for when I'm requesting a boost of energy to my crystal grids.

My primary use of Moldavite in my energy field is to break up dense energy and let my energy freely circulate. For instance, I spent a little over two years devoted to caring for a dear elderly cat as she moved through the end of body process. It was a significant commitment and I consciously chose it as part of my personal spiritual practice. I cared for her with unconditional love, without exception. It was demanding on all levels. When she crossed, it was a perfect and beautiful experience. I would not change a thing, regardless of how much it challenged me. One of the greatest challenges was physically getting enough sleep. For some reason she seemed dead set against me getting a full night's sleep. At the time I just kept digging deeper to care for and love her.

After she crossed and I could focus on renewing my energy, it was not an easy process. I bought two Moldavite rings, and when I need to get something done or I'm kind of lethargic or burnt out and would like to break up that density, I wear Moldavite on each hand. It helps me get through what I simply must accomplish. I feel light and capable all day and refreshed at the end of the day. It's been a tremendous boon in this regard.

My Moldavite rings stay in my bedroom but I've never slept with them on my body. Over the last few years, it's rare to have a dream. Having Moldavite in my bedroom seems to have no discernible effect on my sleep.

I have had an increase in synchronicities, such that I can think of something and have confidence it will unfold. I will think of something, visualize it and it seems to go out on an energy vine and bring back to me at least an acknowledgment in my life. An example of what has changed from working with Moldavite is that I rarely do the vigorous intellectual brain-rattling searches through known sources to find information. Instead, I visualize my question and then I will perhaps get a readjustment of language and then a never-before-seen resource or response materializes. It is quite satisfying to ditch the frustration and have fruitful information sources be brought to my awareness. Moldavite for me is an accelerator, so in this instance it also provides me more rapid and effortless feedback.

Moldavite has been one of those lovely tools in my life that fit certain needs. I only use it when I feel divinely led to do so. Consequently, for me it is simply one of many helpful tools in the tool shed. I've overdone many healing practices in my life as I was learning and growing. Moldavite has come along when I'm a little bit wiser and I make use of it for sure, but I don't rely on it or hold it above any other tools I am using. It is one of many helpful things but doesn't stand out in my life. I'm grateful I have some and for what it does. I'm grateful for how it helps others as well.

KELLY
MARCH 8, 2022

Dear Robert and Kathy,

I first experienced Moldavite by accident. I dropped into Heaven and Earth with a beau and we were just looking. I remember being fascinated by the green stones on display, and the case that held them kept drawing me to them. I had little experience with crystals at the time and didn't understand the body sensations.

We kept looking and one ring kept coming up for me. It didn't fit at first, until I decided it was the one I wanted, and the woman said "Try it on now." And all of a sudden it fit perfectly.

On the way home that day I felt hot all over, especially in my face. I also had sweaty palms and upper lip and like that, an out-of-ordinary occurrence for me. I'm not a "sweater." Life had a funny sound that day on the way home too, like a low hum, the sound of quiet before a storm pops out of the sky. And the smell of the air shifted too, like it was clean after a storm. All that added up to a deep, pensive peace for me, a peace and knowingness which has continued.

When I put Moldavite on my third eye and shut my eyes, I feel as if my eyes cross and look inward to the extent that a whole new focal point occurs. The images in my mind are clear, and distinctly different from the ones without the Moldavite. Also, I have experienced trances and being able to "see" friends who are not nearby (like knowing what's going on with a friend in Europe).

I have had experiences with pink Quartz before, and with some other stones, but since purchasing Moldavite, I find that no other stone holds any interest for me. I have given away all my other crystals. Also, I have given Moldavite to others and great things have happened to them as well.

Almost as soon as I got Moldavite, my life seemed to click, to take off on its appropriate course. Magic started to occur.

I think Moldavite provides a means of communications. Everyone remarks on my stones and asks what kind they are. People are often confused by the color, and it's even been called black by some. Interestingly, no one with any knowledge of crystals has called it black. I really think the stone talks to me and to others. It seems to house messages. My memory has increased—memory in every meaning of the word. I am clearer in my thinking and my recall. I am confident in my thoughts. I don't get lost on the road these days, and I call on my Moldavite for assistance often. It "grounds me" by putting me in touch with more intuitive paths of thought.

For me, discovering Moldavite was no accident. I assume there are others like me who are experiencing making a difference to the planet, profoundly, since getting Moldavite. I think it was put here as a tuning fork to call us forth to be what we came here to be, to get on track and produce whatever we promised to produce in this lifetime. At least that's how I feel since getting my Moldavite. I feel like a beacon of white light now.

My spiritual energy has definitely increased with Moldavite. I feel a bit unprotected when I don't have my necklace or ring on. I did have an earring also, and have a triangle of Moldavite on my body, and when I gave my earring to a friend I felt a break in the aura, the circle. At first, I wore my ring on my left hand, and during that time the universe poured knowledge into me. I moved it to my right hand, for no reason really, and others are gathering around me and getting empowered by me. It's amazing. I'm less settled without my Moldavite on and notice it is missing.

I feel Moldavite has brought the distinction of harmony to my life. I know if I have a headache and place Moldavite on it, it will go away. Or if I hold the Moldavite in my hand and concentrate, it will erase pain in me and sometimes in others.

I guess my most interesting observation about Moldavite is that it has a sound to it—that it communicates somehow. It seems like something alive to me, with an energy. My life is so clearly on its path of fulfillment right now it's amazing. Ever since getting Moldavite, that day in the car, when the world seemed to all of a sudden occur in a tunnel straight before me, with certain sounds and smells—my life has worked magically ever since. And I feel protected and comforted by Moldavite, like it's an old friend. It has a "smell" I like, and I always expect it to taste refreshing like a stream. I think it is possibly my most favorite possession. And I feel towards it like a best friend, an old best friend who has returned.

The only thing I'd like to add, just a P.S., and I don't know if it means anything, but in the last two months or so I have seen craft like flying saucers when I close my eyes. This especially occurs when I am feeling lost or sad or alone. I feel like someone is there loving me, coming. I don't know that it means anything, but I offer it.

I love my Moldavite and want it all around me. It feels cooling and warming at the same time. If I put it to my forehead, I always find the answer. And I trust its messages. And I trust people who choose it. I think they are chosen and have surrendered to serving the planet.

I wish you the best with your writing. Your assistance to me and to those who are touched through you through me is very appreciated. Thank you for being open to your purpose and committed to fulfilling life.

With much love and appreciation,

R. V.

7/18/88

I have received your email today about your new project. I do share your appreciation of Moldavite in the world and my life . . . I am a clinical social worker and am deeply into spiritually guiding dream interpretation so I find working with Moldavite in dream work interesting to consider.

Here is my story:

My spiritual path has been a challenging but often inspirational journey with many dramatic events, twists, turns and redirections. Many of these have been deep challenges that I embrace and appreciate for the depth of spiritual growth they brought to me.

In my early forties, after a spontaneous kundalini experience, and as spiritual gifts quickly opened, I was drawn to crystals and stones for their spiritual guidance, support and healing. Clairsentient and clairaudient, I experience the energy, messages and metaphysical properties of the Earth's gifts regularly. Walking through a shop with crystals and stones on display is a little bit of heaven to me. Over time, I gathered a number of helpful stones and crystals that have supported me on my spiritual path, and have gained much knowledge and wisdom of many pieces on the way.

But the strongest and most memorable energetic and spiritual experience of a stone was in placing a Moldavite pendant from Heaven and Earth around my neck to sit in meditation (purchased through a metaphysical storefront that works with Heaven and Earth). I expected a subtle or moderate energetic experience but received quite a bit more. I don't recall if the length of the chain rested on the heart chakra or higher heart but the powerful vibrational response in my entire chest was instantaneous.

I immediately felt destabilized in orientation, almost spinning but certainly dizzy. It was not a vague sensation but quite powerful—definitely a "Whoa!" moment. I moved to quickly sit down. It lasted some time and I enjoyed every moment of it. As the room/my orientation gradually stabilized, the powerful energy of the Moldavite remained with me. I had felt a powerful shift in my energy that became a defining moment of my spiritual development.

Throughout that meditation, I was keenly aware of the powerful positive effect on my heart chakra and crown chakra, though all of my chakras spontaneously and powerfully activated. It was one of the strongest massaging flows of high vibration divine light/universal energy I have ever felt streaming into my crown chakra and coursing through my central light channel, and below to ground me. It was, and is every time I reintroduce it into my energy field, like a tonic—a super shot of energy, strength and vitality.

Over the years since I first wore Moldavite I have had to remove it from my person/ energy field for varying lengths of time. Early on I noticed with appreciation that it had the effect of supercharging and accelerating my spiritual path, but, if worn too long, it at times felt too fast, too overwhelming. I intuitively knew when it was time to take it off for a period of time to catch my breath. And, I always felt intuitively when to place it back into my energy, or noticed when it was being called to my attention again.

Just last week I "felt" the call of its energy to be reintroduced back into my energy, and it was then brought into my line of sight, where it is stored when I am not wearing it. I made a mental note to place it on a chain and wear it, but delayed in acting. Your email today about your new project was the unmistakable "reminder" that it was time again to place it in my energy. I am wearing it as I write this.

Though I have not had the exact same unique experience as the first time, every time I place the Moldavite back into my field, I feel an immediate rush of powerful positive energy flowing through my crown chakra and into my central channel, then powerfully strengthening my entire pillar of light. My chakras activate, and are still most strongly experienced in my heart and crown chakras. There is a pulsing vibration outward from my core as though my aura is being strengthened or reinforced. And, the movement on my path quickens. What a divine gift!

MARYELLEN COUGHLIN
MEDFORD, MA., AUGUST, 2022

First, I wish to express my gratitude for having this opportunity to verbalize, for the first time, my experiences with Moldavite. Having given much thought to the subject, I find it a mammoth task to keep the information succinct, because it incorporates a year of my spiritual education, a year of remarkable accelerated learning and personal transformations. I'm learning to release all self-imposed limitations and attitudes based on past conditionings, which until recently had made my existence on Earth very difficult. My spiritual presence has resulted from a perseverance to accept all Reality, balancing the spiritual overview with the Will's Reality. I can now open up my heart to change and forgiveness.

My intuition suggests that Moldavite can be accredited to most of the following experiences:

1. My immediate response upon discovering "Moldy" in a New Age shop was one of finding a friend, and a distinct feeling that "Moldy" is not of this world.

2. When I picked her up, a very strong tingling vibration zoomed through my body and I became light-headed. Time seemed to stand still, and my bearings and orientation were distorted. I felt like a shift or change in consciousness. I was different.

3. My sleeping patterns began to change. I'd often wake with a suspicion that I had spent the whole night traveling to many places, healing the sick, and communicating with higher intelligences. I still can't actually give details of what happened or of the knowledge I acquired during sleep. Often, I'd be flooded with a "laser beam" of pure light, pouring down from the sky (in a tunneled or spiral form). The light would concentrate mainly around my head, before I fell asleep.

4. Quartz crystals have assisted my personal evolution on all levels (physically, emotionally, mentally, and spiritually). However, Moldavite has opened up for me a more powerful awareness of self and my relationship with the whole Infinite Scheme of Things. It feels as though it has helped me transcend my earthly "limitations".

5. I have experienced unbelievable changes and opportunities since "Moldy" appeared. The "right" books have just landed in my lap, amazing people have entered my life, showering me with knowledge, faith and love. My relationships with self, family and friends have become more loving and open. Many powerful mirrors (beautiful human beings) appeared, who have coerced me to confront my unrealized self. I chose the understanding that I created all of my reality.

For several months, I seemed to be bombarded with whirlwinds of "traumatic" and ecstatic encounters. Many past life visions surfaced and several past-life souls reappeared this lifetime, to either "pay back" a few "debts" or give me a few very difficult learning experiences. Several times, I suspect that I lost touch with reality — caught up on the melodrama of past life patterns. I found myself often rehearsing "acts" from a play that confused me. At times, I was emotionally and spiritually dull. Many feelings would flare up in me that did appear to be mine—feelings of alienations from self.

6. I believe that "Moldy" has assisted in connecting myself with higher intelligences. In the last six months an incredible chain of events has occurred which coincides with my work with "Moldy." The following events are in chronological order: (1) a realization of having been on another planet. (2) The names Lazeris and Etherine come to mind as names of entities or planets. (3) A sighting of four UFO's over my home (Sydney, Australia). They appeared as large bright lights that played together, weaving in and out of each other joining up into a formation, then separating. It was a brilliant display of aerial acrobatics, and I sensed they were being deliberately entertaining. (4) A meditation where I had a clear vision of being above planet Earth in another dimension. This continued to be a regular phenomenon. (5) On a

separate occasion, I received a vision of myself and another being leaving a planet of rich red desert soil, lush brightest of green vegetation, and transparent, possibly crystalline, buildings. We were embarking on a journey to another planet. I can't describe our appearance very clearly; it was like having an ethereal form. (6B) A heightened interest in dolphins and whales and a strong belief that they are connected to higher intelligences. (7) Being drawn to a holiday house owned by a friend at Kangaroo Valley at least four times in four months. (8) A New Age book shop becomes available for purchasing just fifteen minutes from this holiday house. (9) My friend and I pack up everything we own, buy the shop and move all our gear over a hundred and fifty kilometers to the holiday house at Kangaroo Valley. (10) Several bright lights flash through the sky, and the mountains have a pulsating aura around them. (11) I get a strong urge to write as many UFO organizations as possible overseas. (12) A compulsion to start up a UFO information center attached to the bookshop. (13) The locals tell me that the area is notorious for UFO sightings, unbeknownst to me beforehand.

The three of us who share the house have heightened telepathic gifts, and physically our bodies have spurts of excess energy or strength. I'm surprised at my stamina at times. Weights which would ordinarily tire me can be carried long distances.

Having lived in this "Garden of Eden" at Kangaroo Valley for one month now, I can confidently say that I feel very safe, loved and immensely guided. A strong sense of purpose is evident here. However, I seem to be only following instructions "from above" as to how I can be an active and fully functioning assistant of planetary consciousness raising.

The piece of Moldavite I have is raw, and about one inch by one half inch. For the first six months, "Moldy" had a very noticeable black spot inside. Somehow, the black spot has vanished, leaving me with a sense that all lessons and purposed have been completed. (I have not had any experience with other forms of Moldavite.)

"Moldy" has heightened my mental capacity—I have found it much easier to grasp concepts of time, multidimensional "beingness", the power of manifestation and the oneness of all.

There appears to be a very strong connection between the use of Moldavite and the awakening of one's own spiritual path. I have experienced brief channeling sessions, more clarity of purpose, automatic writing occasionally, a greater love for my fellow humans, and an inner peace, since working with "Moldy." When I wear "Moldy" (which is not often these days), my body feels warm and light. My encounters with others are invariably more intuitive, loving and enriching. People often pour out their emotions and fears, and somehow I manage to console and nurture them.

Since "Moldy" has come into my life, I've undergone an endless "discussion" inside my head, which differentiates between my genuine actions and my ego actions. My Higher Self always seems to correct me if I'm coming from a selfish or unloving space. Basically, I can't get away from anything that is regarded as untrue to self. I've finally allowed my "Christness" within more expression, after thirty-three years of resisting Divine Will.

NAME WITHHELD,
AUSTRALIA, 1988

About 1½ years ago I picked up an uncut piece [of Moldavite] at a health expo. My immediate impression was of agitation and a sense of chaotic, searing heat. I felt disturbed in my entire body, which is rare because usually, when I pick up a stone, I am sensitive to the specific body part and/or emotion for which it has an affinity. I literally could not hold it for more than a minute. A year ago, I picked up another uncut piece, and this time it felt fine! I bought it and took it home for my medicine pouch. Needless to say, I have been through a lot of changes in the intervening year.

A short time later, a very bizarre incident occurred with a Citrine Quartz ring I have worn for 8 years. I had bought it as a present for myself after my divorce.

I was plugging in a toaster and my ring finger brushed against the light socket. The ring blew up! Literally, the gold sparked and melted and my finger turned black. My initial reaction was fear and disappointment—then a voice from somewhere inside me seemed to say that it was okay, it was just time for a new ring.

A week later my new lover presented me with a small velvet box. Inside was a large, beautiful faceted Moldavite ring. I have worn it ever since and it feels wonderful. I get a peaceful soothing feeling from it. It looks and feels like pine forest green.

In the last year and a half, I have grown as a leader of rituals and ceremonies in my area. The stone coming into my life has been wonderful confirmation of my ease with the role of priestess. I find that my intuitive/psychic nature is moving more and more into conscious focus. While I used to focus on healing our beloved Earth Mother, I now seem to be thinking in galactic terms, and I *know* that prayers and visions can move creation. Thank you, beloved sister stones.

ELLEN EVERT
AMHERST, MA. 7/2/88

My love of crystals started back in my early twenties, I bought some online and received a little card that states the names and properties of stones. Moldavite was on there and I remember reading about it and it piqued my curiosity. Flash forward ten years and I had bought a Merlinite stone, and boy that was magical! I came across your *Book of Stones* and was told that Moldavite is a must and goes with Merlinite, so I got a ring and a heart pendant and it burned brightly and it transformed me from an unaware person to a Reiki Master in the space of ten years. Moldavite is a must-have if you are stuck. It took me from a muggle life to one of wizardry and magic. It helps to awaken and inspire all of us. For some of us it reminds us of our star origins, and in others it clears the karmic debris so we can truly become who we were meant to be. The fact that years ago Moldavite suddenly sparked in humanity was a sign that the Golden Age of humanity was truly upon us.

Thank you

SANDY STATEN
MEDFORD, OR., AUG 15, 2022

Hello Robert,

Joe and I are absolutely thrilled that you are beginning a follow-up Moldavite book! You have been a vital part of our Moldavite journey and we trust that our story will, if nothing else, validate and illuminate the gratitude we have for how much you have helped us and so many in the process of awakening to levels that we had never even imagined!

Our Moldavite story begins with Joe. He had received his Transcendental Meditation Initiation in 1990 and was always interested in spirituality and energy. However, he says he was never able to feel anything from crystals or stones, as many others he knew claimed to experience. As fate would have it, Joe happened to watch a one-hour YouTube video that you had done in 2018, explaining in great detail the story of Moldavite. It stirred his curiosity and sent him on a mission to find it. He called the only crystal store that he knew of, about an hour south of the town we live in. (Joe and I didn't know each other at that time.)

Joe recalls that the friendly young woman on the phone told him they did not have any Moldavite in their store, but she was hoping that a local vendor might bring some in later that day. She offered to call him when the vendor arrived. Joe thanked her and noted to himself that she seemed over-eager to help him in his quest, but didn't think too much about it, and went about his day. Early that afternoon, she called to report that the vendor did not have any Moldavite. But they had unexpectedly received some in an order that had just arrived, and she had saved a piece behind the counter for him. Joe told her he would be there in about an hour, as he wanted to give this unusal stone as a Christmas gift. As he parked at the shopping mall, his cell phone rang and he was surprised to hear the voice of a dear friend whom he hadn't talked to in quite some time.

Upon learning why Joe was out shopping, his friend exclaimed, "I didn't know that you're into crystals! My daughter works at the store that you called for the Moldavite!" That marked Joe's first awareness of the sychronicities that began unfolding in his life because of Moldavite, and he hadn't even seen it yet! His friend directed him to the store, and he was greeted by the friend's daughter with a warmth that solidified his feelings of being in the presence of magic.

Catching up with his friend's daughter, purchasing the Moldavite, and checking out the beautiful wares in the store took about 30 minutes. Joe had placed the beautiful piece of raw Moldavite in his pants pocket, still in the plastic bag. He proceeded to drive home, or at least that was the direction he thought he was going. After driving for about 20 minutes, Joe realized that he was feeling confused, nauseated, and flushed, and that he was headed in the exact opposite direction of home! It must be the rain and probably the fact that he was tired and hungry that caused all this mess, Joe thought to himself as he righted his direction and headed for home. It wasn't until he meditated with the Moldavite in his hand the next day and experienced the same feelings (and more) that he had no doubt about the Power of Moldavite. He was actually feeling that piece of Moldavite in his pocket as he was driving home, and again sitting in meditation, just as Robert had described it in the YouTube video!

Since that day, Joe has meditated with Moldavite at least once a day. He is a dedicated Moldavite collector, always wearing at least one. And he is eager to share his amazing Moldavite experiences with anyone who will listen. He loves to grab the back of his shirt at the nape of the neck to demonstrate how once Moldavite got ahold of him, it dragged him forward to clear away everything in his life that was weighing him down—including properties, vehicles, relationships and more. Joe also shares how his Moldavite experiences have opened his chakras, meridians, and energy centers, so that he can now feel the energy, vibrations and the Spirit of the Beings in all genuine crystals and stones!

As for me, I love the fact that his unending love of and quest for Moldavite guided him to walk into my crystal store last year, just as I was reading your first book, *Moldavite: Starborn Stone of Transformation,* and learning about the power of Moldavite. Joe encouraged me to let the Moldavite have its way with me instead of resisting the power that I was feeling. I began sleeping with the necklace on and would actually wake up in the middle of the night in a meditative state, holding it! Our lives since then have levelled-up in every way, with enough stories of synchronicity and magic to fill many notebooks. I am a Reiki Master and have seen many beautiful transformations happen for myself, my clients, and my customers through the power of Moldavite. The most profound transformation for me thus far happened as we were preparing to meditate on Bell Rock during our recent vacation to Sedona. That's when Joe proposed! Our wedding date is October 22nd 2022!

Thank you for keeping your appointment with the healer and heeding the advice of your screaming guide to hold nothing back in your first book, Robert! Please feel the gratitude that we all hold so deeply in our hearts for your willingness to speak the truth!

Wishing You Blessings, Love and Continued Transformation,

Sincerely,

JOE HAZARD AND PAM MALIK
AUGUST, 2022

My Moldavite Journey

Because of my grandmother, I have been an avid collector of crystals and gemstones all my life. I consider myself to be a student, as they have all taught me something valuable about myself in their own unique way. A few years ago, I was overtaken by a very severe depression that almost cost me my life. The world at large was going through changes no one had foreseen, and that no one could have fully prepared for. I knew many people who were struggling in all aspects—financially, emotionally, spiritually—myself included. Funny enough, I had never even heard of Moldavite before the pandemic. There seemed to be a trend running, which I discovered while doing my own research into the meteorite crystal, and the claims everyone had been making online about what it had done for them. I learned that it was an increasingly popular crystal that was both running out of supply and rising in price and value. So I did what I always do and contacted my grandma, "Amom," as my sisters and I call her.

My Amom told me that Moldavite was a coveted one, that it could be hard to get the real thing, and to be careful from where I purchased it. She also told me about the intense healing properties the stone was known for, and said that Moldavite was not just some pretty rock to collect. She explained that, if I were to find a genuine piece of it, and if I was meant to have it, it could be potentially life-changing. Thanks to my Amom, this was how I found out about the Heaven and Earth catalogue!

Up to this point, the stories I had seen online were about how this crystal could uproot the very foundation of your life, both spiritually but also literally, in order to rearrange things in such a way that would better allow positive flow in one's life. This crystal sounded like it meant business, and at this point in my life, I was in a very fragile place, so I hesitated for almost another year.

That entire year was an abysmal fog. I don't remember much, due to substance abuse, resurgences of past traumas, binge eating, binge sleeping . . . the very passage of time was becoming too much to cope with. I enrolled in group therapy that turned out to be almost detrimental to my mental well-being. There were a number of reasons. It just wasn't a good fit for me at that time. I was eventually forced into taking FMLA [Family and Medical Leave Act] disability leave from my job for that entire year, because I simply couldn't grind through the work day any more. I was falling apart, and the people around me were also suffering because of it.

One day my younger sister demanded I get out of bed and get dressed because, "We're going to the rock shop!" There is a little locally owned rock and crystal shop that we used to frequent, up until my depression took over. I was reluctant, but we went. At this particular rock shop, they tend to keep the higher-value, fancy, more expensive and rare stones and crystals behind the counter, under lock and key. I had a little extra birthday money on me that day and I felt that natural pull to indulge myself for the first time in a long time. So I walked straight up to the counter and looked to see if anything called to me. My Amom has always taught my sisters and me not to just look at the crystals and gems, but to feel what they have to offer. Because of this practice, my personal collection of crystals isn't made up of the most sparkling or radiant gems, but of a healthy mixture of specimens that are attuned specifically to myself and my needs.

I gazed around at what was available behind the glass, and to my surprise, there was one (no larger than two grams) green blob that looked like it had crash-landed on Earth from an alien planet. I looked at the label, and there it was—a real fragment of Moldavite.

I whole-heartedly believe that things have only as much power as we give them. I am not about to make any claims to the contrary. I purchased the Moldavite, but I felt like I was following the trend, after everything I had been exposed to online. I was skeptical. I cleansed the piece when I got home, as I always do, and kept it lying about for quite some time, with no significant or remarkable occurrences. At first, I felt silly about the whole thing. Usually, I create crystal grids, or use my smaller crystals in my body mapping meditations, but I felt like there was too much stigma around this tiny fragment of green glass.

My Amom laughed and explained that she has a few gems in her own collection that made her feel the same way—as if miracles should be happening all around her now that she has the "sorcerer's stone" or the "holy grail" of crystals. She said, "These expectations are only going to block the powers the crystal holds. You can't expect a new house, a pay raise, a tall handsome someone to sweep you off your feet. You can't expect anything, because then the crystal can't give you what you actually need from it." I hadn't even realized that I was coming at the whole thing all wrong. I was setting expectations. I was also avoiding the crystal by leaving it out and not attuning it to myself better.

I got myself a locket, and per my Amom's advice, only wore it when I felt the urge to do so. I wore it for a few days straight, sleeping with it on, only taking it off for showers. Then I gave it a break to let it recharge without my energy for a day or so before I felt emboldened to wear it again. After a while, I forgot all about it being the "all powerful, mystical, magical stone that creates miracles, so says the internet." I treated it with the same respect as I do with all of my crystals. It was funny, because when the changes in my life started appearing, as detrimental as some of those changes seemed, it felt like I was bringing the magic into my life. The Moldavite was right there around my neck, a powerful, intelligent tool that helped me open doors for myself that I had never even known were there before.

My Moldavite worked quietly, behind the scenes. I finished out my time in my group therapy, feeling disgusted for wasting so much time and money on a treatment program that didn't feel like it had helped at all. I was angry. I felt helpless, almost even worse off than I had before I started that treatment program. I felt like no one listened to me in that group, that those people didn't care to get better, and that we were all crammed in there against our wills. I returned to work after having stepped down from my original role as a phlebotomist, now working as the new receptionist. I felt weak. I felt frail. I felt like a failure. I had no idea at the time, but this was only the beginning for me.

I spent almost all my breaks throughout my work day crying my eyes out, feeling like I was wasting everyone's time, including my own, at this job. I was making less money than I had been before. I had let my fellow phlebotomists down who were relying on me, but without me, were left short-handed for the workload. These were people I had been working with for the last five or so years, we had been through a lot together. Now they worked in the background while I sat there, at this desk, answering phone calls and doodling sad things in a notebook. I ended up taking another short-term disability leave from work, after being rejected for a higher-up, higher-paying position. The rejection hurt at the time, but I know now that it was the best path for me to not have been chosen for that role. It was more money, but a much larger work-load with longer hours than my receptionist position.

I returned to individual, one-on-one therapy with a psychologist who specialized in PTSD and sexual trauma. With her, I discovered how little I had ever actually worked on healing myself. I also discovered how traumatized I still was from my heavily religious upbringing. I finally felt like I could see through the fog. There was so much work left to be done, but at least now, I knew what I should be working on with myself. I had zero self-respect, absolutely zero self-worth. I hated myself because, through my entire life, I was told that the love I might feel for myself would be more valuable if I gave that love to God. I had left the church years prior to this, but had never examined exactly why I felt compelled to get away from it. Now I could finally pinpoint the issues. The religious sect my family and I had been involved in for all my life turned out to be a cult that we had escaped. It was an abusive, highly demanding, manipulative cult that squeezed every last ounce of light from the congregation. For the first time in my life, I felt a weight being lifted off my soul. To come to this realization—I simply could not have done it on my own.

This was my life-changing moment. Looking back at it all now, I can say for certainty that this realization was the most spiritual of an awakening I had ever experienced, but it wouldn't be the last time I felt that way.

I finally found the courage to leave my job. I had absolutely no prospects for employment. I simply never returned after my disability leave was all used up. I came to realize how toxic that work environment had been, but I had always been fine with that because, in my mind, that was just how work was. I left, and not even a week later, I found a brand new company in my area hiring experienced phlebotomists. Not only was this a fresh start for me, it was literally a brand new company. It was a completely fresh start for anyone who applied. My younger sister applied as well, and we were both sent out of state for our training. I had never flown before, but that's a story for another time. I had never travelled so far away from home on my own before. (My sister and I went separately for a number of unrelated reasons.) It was terrifying. I was so outside of my comfort zone, especially after having spent the past year going from sobbing in my bedroom to sobbing in therapy sessions. I was stressed, but determined.

I had not felt determination like that since I graduated high school and got my first job. This experience showed me a strong, capable side of myself I had never seen before. It uprooted the very foundation of my life.

After our out of state training was concluded, both my parents found out they had COVID-19, and my Dad was being monitored for low oxygen levels. He was having an extremely difficult time, though my Mom was in better health and was able to recover more quickly, though never completely. My sisters and I came together and made the decision to bring Dad to the emergency room. He had been monitoring his vitals and oxygen levels from home, but we weren't sure if he was taking his predicament seriously enough. We got him there, only to find out we had done so just in time. His oxygen levels had dropped significantly by the time we arrived, and he was in horrible shape. He struggled to breathe, he couldn't even speak, and his inhaler for his asthma wasn't helping him at all.

They kept him there for a few days, and by some miracle it was never necessary to put him on a ventilator. He received the treatment he needed, we were finally able to bring him home, and he was able to make a full, albeit scarred, recovery. I don't believe in miracles, as I am not a particularly religious or spiritual person, but I do feel some of these "just in time" decisions my family and I had to make were not merely coincidences. My father is what some might call a "determined" and "steadfast" man, and to make a decision for his health on his behalf was not easy. Telling him to get dressed because we were going to the hospital . . . he wasn't exactly skipping out the door. Had we not had the strength to stand up to him, for him, I don't know where we'd be right now. Had I not had the strength within myself to be a little bit bossy that day, and instead, buckled under the weight of what was happening to my family . . . the timing was right, I don't know how else to put that.

After the health scare with my parents died down, my younger sister and I returned to work at our new jobs in a brand new facility. A whole world of opportunities opened up before us. We were offered responsibilities that came with pay increases, we were given promotions to leadership positions, and we became the trainers for our facility. We trained or had a hand in training everyone who's applied to work there from that moment forward. We believed this was an opportunity to build and cultivate a work environment in whatever way we thought was best, and we did it. We rose to the occasion. We were thriving so well in this new workplace that another one of our sisters decided to come work with us too!

I haven't had a relapse in substance abuse in over a year. My sister and I have been with our new job for a full year as I'm writing this. There have, of course, been a multitude of challenges and obstacles we've had to overcome, and by no means are our lives perfect. There is a lot of healing from the past that we have yet to do.

What Moldavite has done for me is this: it's allowed me to change the things I can, and to accept the things I cannot change. It has helped me realize my self-worth. It has shown me that life is not a Hollywood movie. It guides me along my life journey and reminds me to be mindful in my decision making, and in the words I choose to speak. It assists me in being honest with myself, to be a realist without losing hope for the future. It has brought magic into my life. I was finally able to stop taking medication recently, and to close a chapter in my therapy sessions as well. Things could take a dive for the worse at any moment, but I have a new found resilience to face these changes.

This may not be the most "spiritually enlightening," "come to Jesus" story regarding Moldavite. What it taught me was that these crystals are whatever we need them to be. It taught me that Moldavites are capable of bringing out the light inside us. In order to do that, we have to allow them, with zero expectations.

HEATHER IRWIN
AUGUST, 2022

Hello there Robert, my name is Luke . . .
I am not good at introductions (haha), but I saw your email and I have been meaning to write to you for a few months regarding Moldavite! (I hope I am not too late!)

I have been working with Moldavite and crystals for about thirteen years. My first crystal "experience" was actually with a nice piece of Tanzan Aura Quartz. When I held it, I felt an "electromagnetic internal wind buzz of both hot and cold" rush up in through my central nervous system and through my bone marrow and into the very crystalline matrix of my being (the only way to describe it, the marrow of my soul?). That led me to other crystals, such as Phenacite, Nuummite, Black Opals and of course the legendary Moldavite!

When I first held Moldavite I didn't get blasted as in the classical "Moldavite flush," but instead, I had a deeply calming and grounding sensation. It almost felt like I had somehow always had it, even before this lifetime. (And my favorite color has always been dark green, like forest evergreen.)

When I hold Moldavite now, I feel it as calm but I can also feel its intense heat blast, depending on the state of my consciousness. (haha) For example, if I drink or smoke, it is very powerful and I can literally hear it buzzing and singing. And I feel it "crawling in my skin" and "out of my eyes," and it's very powerful. (I am trying to answer all the questions in your email before I tell you about a couple of, uhh, jarring experiences . . .)

I seem to have increased synchronous events, especially when I am carrying Moldavite along with other crystals. My piece will find other Moldavite users (haha), as if it has a type of psychic sonar to manifest other crystal/Moldavite users.

I have never had it disappear or reappear, but it has occurred with a lot of Moldavite I have given away—those people had it disappear and reappear in strange ways that even blew my mind when they told me! I went through like a ten-year phase of hoarding as much Moldavite as possible and giving out little pieces for birthday gifts and other special events for friends and family, or even strangers . . . (gotta' love to get above). . . . Anyway, I shall try my best to describe a few events that happened when I had Moldavite on me . . . My heart's pounding outta' my chest typing this, like I'm violently shaking with (heh) the power of the Moldavite blasting my pockets right now as I type (hahaha). Love ya, man!

Ok so hmm. . . . Back in 2014, I was living in Washington State . . . beautiful Moldavite-green forests everywhere and majestic mountains and rivers and all that (haha). So I took a trip to the beach (won't say which beach and also something is going on along the coast, but I can't say) with a very close buddy of mine, who was also into Moldavite and crystals. We got to setting up camp and all that stuff when you go camping and build a fire. A few hours passed and the sun went down and our fire grew weak and flickery. I got the urge to go on a "midnight beach walk" and take my Moldavite with me, and my buddy, too. He had a fatty "mothership" piece of Moldavite. We shall name my friend "D," and that's all I can say because . . . well, yeah, shit's too weird. Ha, anyways we get ready to go and I'm like "Yo, let's listen to some music and walk!" So he's like "Haha, ok what should we listen to?" I'm like (artist and album) and he's like. "Oh shit, ok hahaha" . . . (intense metal music) . . . so we started the album at the exact second it turned 11:11 local time, (lol) just for shits and giggles. We started walking down the beach for, I dunno, a half hour and then we decided we wanted to go sit on the dune and watch the stars, 'cause they were looking superrrrr brilliant, and we saw some shooting stars . . . big ones . . .

We sat down and he got ready to roll up some tobacco to have a smoke, and out of NOWHERE I saw a light. (Cars can also drive on this beach, and such so I was like, "Oh, a car, heh.") That light was speeding down the beach, man, like the fuckin' dude was going mach five! I'm like, "YO, THAT GUY IS SPEEEEDING . . . HOLY . . . HOW'S HE NOT FLIPPED IN THE SAND, WHAT A MAD MAN!!!" And it's dark and a little hard to see 'cause there was ABSOLUTELY NO LIGHT ASIDE FROM THE HALF MOON. I told D to look and he's like (he taps me and points as he tells me) "Yo, dude, the beach goes that way!" And I look and I'm like, "Oh shit . . . that's not a car man, and that's waaaay out in the water, and wtffffff how is he going so fast??!!!" Like, it blew me away. I couldn't wrap my head around how a boat would even move that fast . . . like what? Lol, Star Wars shit, out of nowhere. My Moldavite in my pocket starts BUZZING LIKE AN ENGINE!!!! Like it was literally MELTING in my jeans, man, like wtf! And my eyes felt instantly dilated, and my consciousness altered drastically, and I was in shock and awe.

Something was happening, out of NOWHERE! Again!! Haha, this—what I can call a giant light—comes out of the fucking ocean, like a giant see-through spinal cord with a lotus flower light thing at the top, shimmering like Wab Wab Wab (((o))) type of thing. And I felt the most terrible amount of fear ever, that I have ever ever ever humanly felt. Man, like I was like, "Oh shit, yoooo, it's fuckin aliens, D! Wtf, yooo!" Like I could not compute it . . . energetic overload, man. Like, I looked over and his eyes was just like double zeroes, but calm as an ox, and I was like, "Oh man, this is it, or like wtf do I do?"

Well, now I know ETs exist, like my whole entire life flashed before my eyes man, like all in a few seconds. Then this thing starting emitting like a VIBRATION LIKE AN OMMMMM, and the entire beach was like as if I were sitting on an idling car, just vibrating, but intensely. This "lotus flower serpent/spinal cord thing" just started like moving around like it was trying to induce some type of trance on us. And my Moldavite was breaking that connection to keep me safe? Or was it attracting this thing? Entity? Craft integrated consciousness??!?

My buddy just sat there kind of rocking with anxiety, but curiosity, I couldn't stop looking at its physical structure. Robert, this shit was fuckin REAL, man, like 3D. I can touch its shit, but I didn't dare walk close to the edge of the water . . .

So what I can describe this thing to be is, well, obviously it's not human (and if it is, they were getting a laugh, but that's not the vibe that was projected at all). But it was like I said—a giant Lotus flower thing made of golden light, atop of what looked like a see-through spinal cord made of the clearest Quartz you have ever seen. And it had like neon lights and bright brilliant blues and hot pinks moving through it like lightning, and I could feel it. And after a few seconds of it doing that "dancing cobra" thing, it like got bigger and brighter.

I was sitting on the dune looking around to see if any other people/campers or anything were seeing this. Man, like wtf, the entire beach all the way to the forest edge was BRIGHT GOLDEN LIGHT, man, like a mini sun on that thing.

After the fear subsided, I felt an immense love, like I can't even describe. I still felt the power of the residual fear. But my Moldavite, I think, was sending some type of sonar to that thing, and it was like, "Yo, let's go check it out!!!"

Here's a funny thought I had: Like, you know how humans will mess with cats like with a laser pointer? And they go all crazy and chase it and get all cracked out over it? (Lol) I felt like the "ETs" were inside, like "Hehy bobbay, look at them Earthlings over there on that rock! Turn on the ol' spinny light for them and trip them out! Hahahahahah!" And the ETs are just laughing at us, 'cause we are like. "Awh shit, D, look it's mother fuckin aliens!!! And shit, omgggggg, aliens are real!" But it also felt like a giant cosmic joke and made me feel like I'm on a giant cosmic alien ant farm. Anyways, I am rambling about it . . .

The craft stayed there probably a solid fifteen minutes, and I wanted to get it on my phone, but I only had an Ipod at the time. But I somehow felt that if I had a recording device this event wouldn't have manifested in the first place. After staring at it in shock and awe for a few minutes, my buddy was like, "I'm leaving." And I was like, "Dude, we can't go anywhere. What are you doing? If it wants us it'll take us!" He's like, "Man, yeah that's true, what do we do!?" So I just walk halfway to the craft thing and I bowed humbly and said, "Thank you, you are beautiful, please don't hurt us. I mean well for this Earth and all her inhabitants!!!"

The thing made like a jolly mechanical sound . . . what I can describe as a HORSE NEIGH, and then the light went from gold to hot pink!! Flashed!!! The Quartz spinal cord body thing retracted! Then it went suuuper fast under the ocean shelf and it was like a BRIGHT LIGHTSABER BLUE AND BLACK effect under the entire ocean in front of us, I was absolutely smitten, man. Then it literally just shot out to the horizon as a bright blue and black smoldering orb. And then, dude, it shot out wayyyyy in the ocean, up to space, and all that you could see was a burnt blue green and black vertical smoke trail, made of some type of plasma. And it had a shimmering fizzle effect that gently dissipated. And yeah . . . I didn't sleep for three days . . . this shit still gets me shaking. . . . I don't know any message or point to all that, Robert. I just felt like it was the High saying hi to the Low, and just observing each other.

For some time after that event, I would see a series of UFOs around my house, and I felt like I was being studied, using Moldavite and Magick. And a lot of weird shit still goes on, man, like men in black stuff. . . . Moldavite is no joke, but its spirit is everywhere in the cosmos, I feel, not just Earth. It was also telling me they make Moldavite when other planets are being designed, so after a certain time on that planet's time matrix, the material will rise when needed, or that species can discover it. I have so much love for Moldavite and I wear my pieces almost every day. Sometimes they give me the spins and other times they ground me . . . maybe me having ADHD has something to do with it . . . but who knows? I guess we shall see. I hope you enjoyed this experience of mine and maybe you will tell the world. Sorry I curse like a sailor when telling my stories, man, cause it just flows out through these little 3D thumbs (haha).

And soooo much love to you and Kathy and everyone and everything at Heaven and Earth. You are a blessing to the world, man, and to me, so thank you for existing, I wish I could meet you one day before we leave this Earth. You are one of my heroes, whether you know it or not, along with Moldavite, and we shall be the heroes of this Earth!

Another thing real quick: (Sorry to write so much; this is like a once-in-a-lifetime opportunity to write to the legend himself!!!) Something I notice about Moldavite is that, well, especially when I wear it around "normies" or like the "average Joe," it like hacks their mind. And it either brings out like violent, demonic energy . . . Like, I'll be filling up at a gas station and the clerk will be normal, and then when I get into "range," they like get possessed or say some super-weird stuff to me. Like they somehow trust me or something? I notice this more with Nuummite than Moldavite, or when I wear it with Moldavite, but, yeah, the cosmos is a strange place, brother. And I'm keeping my Moldy close at all times! It's my little aetheric cell phone (haha).

My favorite piece of Moldavite is a 1.5 gram faceted pear/teardrop. It literally feels like psychedelics holding it. It's akin to a microdose, just holding this little sweetheart, and my faceted Burmese Phenacite together. They can summon literal thunderstorms, using focus and stuff, but that's a whole other topic—weather manipulation through Orgone and crystals (heheh).

Thank you vastly, Robert, for your time, energy, and existence, and your consideration of my Moldavite story. I wish I could include more details and stories, but I'd have enough to write a book! Have a wonderful day! Blessed be.

LUKE H.

JUNE 3, 2022

[AUTHOR'S NOTE: We received a second note from Luke H. on June 6, 2022, with a little more information about his Moldavite connection. It is presented below.]
As far as my connection with Moldavite goes, it feels like a piece of my soul externalized and crystallized into a third dimensional object, holding that vibrational pattern indefinitely. Helping me to remember my soul incarnation and my soul's purpose!!!

As far as physically, it feels like straight-up stimulants. Sometimes it's very grounding but more so the opposite. (Lol) Moldavite is like a cosmic drill sergeant!!! If you are slacking in the world, or Spirit it is like, "Hurry, get up, you have shit to do! GO, GO, GO!!! Fix this!!!! Fix that!!!!! Wtf is wrong with THAT??!!! Hahahahaa! So it can become overwhelming in the sense of "to do and fix things of people," but it also feels like an infernally hot cocoon of extremely high vibrational and protective light!

In my body it feels like my skin is emitting some type of diode, like light into the local environment, and it connects to plants, animals and humans (and other entities, haha). It makes my auric field feel expanded, like sometimes when I drive with it, I feel like I am the car, and traffic will like move and twist with my intention and very existence, haha. It's like a video game at times. It seems to fast-forward time itself (and just time dilation in general), and align the best events in that specific time matrix at that very moment of space, time, and experience—all at once converged into the present moment of immediate experience.

It gives me a feeling of "being at home," in the sense of being grounded properly in my body and my physical skin in the present moment of space and time, haha.

I found Moldavite actually through research of the Aethyr-net, and stumbling upon your book, *The Book of Stones!!!!* And it struck my curiosity (after my other Tanzan Aura Quartz experience), so I went to a place called the House of Raven Wood in Yellow Springs, Ohio, and I had my first Moldavite experience!!!!

I hope this helps! If you need more information I can try to give you more strange experiences with it!!! Thank you Robert!!! Blessings!

LUKE H.
JUNE 6, 2022

AUTHOR'S NOTE TO READERS: We hope you have benefitted from this variety of perspectives on the energies and uses of Moldavite. Upon reading these letters, Kathy and I were struck by the commonality of experiences and their similarity to many of our own, as well as their wide variety. We want to express our deep gratitude to all those who sent us information, for these personal stories have given this book a richness that could not have been achieved without them. We are still collecting Moldavite stories and other information on people's experiences with stones. If there is anything you wish to share, we would like to hear from you. Write to us at: heavenandearth@earthlink.net

Many Blessings,
Robert Simmons and Kathy Helen Warner

PS: For readers traveling to Czech Republic, I recommend a visit to the Moldavite Museum in Cesky Krumlov. Many world class Moldavites are on display there, along with a lot of great information about Moldavite's history, localities and mining. To find out more, turn the page!

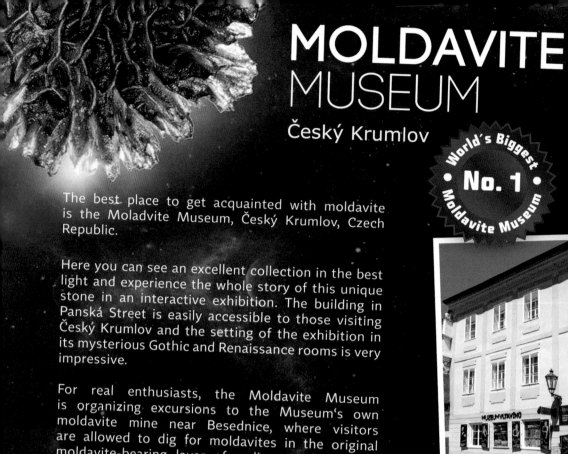

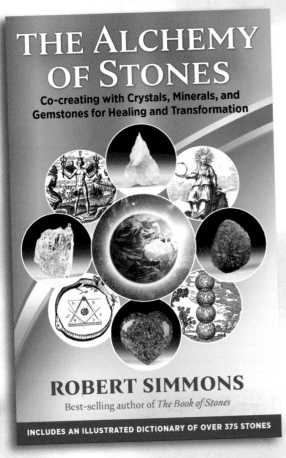

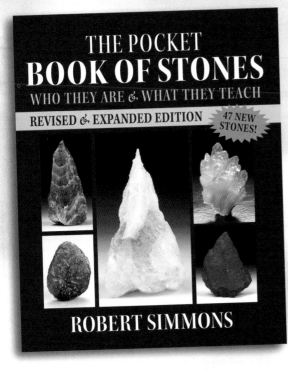

ABOUT THE AUTHOR

Robert Simmons has been a student and investigator of many spiritual paths since a spontaneous mystical experience during his first year at Yale changed the course of his life. Fifteen years later, an encounter with Moldavite activated his latent capacity for perceiving stone energies. This shifted and expanded his horizons yet again. In 1986, he married Kathy Helen Warner, and together they established their company, Heaven and Earth, which began as a crystal shop specializing in Moldavite, and expanded into a mail order company offering thousands of stone, gem and jewelry items to both individuals and store owners all over the world.

In 2013, Robert and Kathy moved to New Zealand's Coromandel Peninsula, and in 2016 they opened a Heaven and Earth crystal, stone and jewelry shop in Tairua, New Zealand. Both the USA and New Zealand companies continue to provide a huge array of minerals, gemstones and crystals for people who appreciate their energies and their beauty.

Robert has been writing and teaching about the metaphysical qualities of stones for over thirty-three years. In 2014, he began his exploration of spiritual alchemy. He soon realized that the work he and others had been doing with crystals and minerals had much in common with the ideas, aspirations and practices of the spiritual alchemists of past centuries. Further, he understood that the alchemical worldview has the capacity to greatly enrich and expand the experiences of healing and awakening that he and many others were seeking in their work with stones. He also recognized that envisioning the stones as Beings in their own right was a key to unlocking the spiritual secrets they offer. These insights led to the research that resulted in the writing of *The Alchemy of Stones*, published in 2020.

During the lockdowns of the Covid pandemic, Robert entered into daily meditation practices that greatly deepened his experience and understanding of the realms of consciousness accessible with the aid of high-vibration stones. This led to a re-invigoration of his relationship with Moldavite, and to the creation of this book.

Robert is the author of several other books, including *The Book of Stones*, *Stones of the New Consciousness*, *The Pocket Book of Stones*, and the award-winning visionary novel, *Earthfire: A Tale of Transformation*. He collects stories from people who have powerful experiences with Moldavite, as well as other crystals and minerals, or with no stones at all. He believes there is a great potential for worldwide transformation and enlightenment, and that engaging spiritually with the Stone Beings and the Soul of the World offers us a golden opportunity to actualize this possibility.

Robert sometimes offers teaching workshops in the USA, Japan, Australia and New Zealand. To receive notifications about Robert's upcoming teaching events and new publications, or to share your story of spiritual awakening, send an email request to heavenandearth@earthlink.net.